!Zhirinovsky!

!Zhirinovsky!

Vladimir Kartsev
WITH TODD BLUDEAU

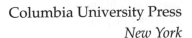

Columbia University Press
New York

Columbia University Press
New York   Chichester, West Sussex
Copyright © 1995 Columbia University Press
All rights reserved.

Columbia University Press thanks its friend David B. Hertz
for his gift toward the costs of publishing this book.

Library of Congress Cataloging-in-Publication Data

Kartsev, Vladimir Petrovich.
    !Zhirinovsky! / Vladimir Kartsev with Todd Bludeau.
       p.   cm.
    Includes bibliographical references and index.
    ISBN 0–231–10210–0 (alk. paper)
       1. Zhirinovskiĭ, Vladimir, 1946–   . 2. Politicians—Russia
(Federation)—Biography.   3. Russia (Federation)—Politics and
government—1991–   4. Liberal 'no-demokraticheskaiâ partiiâ Rossii.
I. Bludeau, Todd.   II. Title.
DK510.766.Z48K37   1995
947.086'092—dc20
    [B]   95–960

Printed in the United States of America

c 10 9 8 7 6 5 4 3 2 1

Contents

Preface

Despite its title *!Zhirinovsky!* this book is not simply a biography of the man nor a history of the party he leads: the Liberal Democratic Party of Russia, which won the December 1993 elections to the State Duma, the lower house of the Russian parliament. It is my view that Zhirinovsky's popularity and his electoral victory are due less to the demonic appeal of this undeniably exceptional political maverick than to the extremely explosive conditions that have arisen in present-day Russia. Russians today almost unanimously associate the present disastrous situation with the apparatchiks of the former Communist state who, under the assumed name of "democrats," have seized the commanding heights in post-Communist Russia and use them, in alliance with the so-called Russian mafia, to enrich themselves on an unheard-of scale. The current chaos has been given a name borrowed from the language of the Russian underworld, the slang term *bespredel*, which roughly translates as "anything goes." Without law, order, morality, or ideology, *bespredel* has inflicted unprecedented damage on Russia's political, economic, social, cultural, and moral existence. It has brought misery to a vast proportion of the population, whose circumstances many serious analysts regard as significantly worse even than under Communist rule. Curiously, the West, unaware of other alternatives, idealizes the present high command of the Russian "democrats," with whom it feels on familiar ground. Associating itself with the lame ducks of Russian politics responsible for the current situation and already rejected by the majority of the Russian population, the West is losing its former enormous appeal to Russians.

I believe that it is because of bespredel that the Western world has not found the calm and stability that seemed inevitable after the collapse of Communism. Sometimes I even think that the world is more dangerous and unpredictable than it was ten years ago. The triumph over the USSR could prove to be a Pyrrhic victory for all of us. It is precisely the conditions of bespredel that have produced such political figures as Zhirinovsky, who utilize previously unthinkable methods, ideas, and language—the methods of bespredel—to fight against the very bespredel that gave rise to them. Zhirinovsky's extravagance, which strikes the West as exceptional, is more than matched by the outlooks and behavior of other leaders of opposition parties and groups in Russia today, many of whom are objectively much more frightening and dangerous. The West knows nothing of them—the enemies of democratic reform, the real fascists, the racists, the anti-Semites, the revolutionaries who are already calling people to the barricades for a battle to the death. They are not as interesting to the Western press as Zhirinovsky, who cuts a more colorful figure and is so greedy for the media's attention.

It would be a colossal political error to dismiss Zhirinovsky as merely a clown, a demagogue, a madman, or a fool and to imagine that if only he went away, the ugly trends in Russia and the threat they pose to the rest of the world would disappear. On the other hand, it would be a dangerous oversimplification to concentrate only on Zhirinovsky, his personality, national origin, family life, past career, his real or imagined sins, and his actual words, or the journalists' distortions of them. When the more serious publications take up this question, in fact, the accent tends to shift from Zhirinovsky to the political atmosphere that produced him. In the same way, in this book, the social, political, and historical background to Zhirinovsky's biography is no less important than the biography itself.

Today, practically every mass publication in the United States has taken a solidly negative stand against Zhirinovsky, and in writing a book about Zhirinovsky in the specific context of Russian life today, I may arouse suspicion in some quarters. Critics may lambaste me for appearing to be too tolerant of a man who is so roundly disliked in the United States. If they read with open minds, however, they will see that my purpose is neither sympathy nor apology; I simply subscribe to the democratic ideal under which everyone is entitled to a fair hearing and all sides of a question are presented, allowing one to draw conclusions based on balanced information.

Just one day before the beginning of Zhirinovsky's visit to the United States in November 1994, his lecture at the Harriman Institute (which had been scheduled at my suggestion and was one of the reasons for his trip to the USA) was canceled. The academic community's lack of interest in hearing from the original source of a current controversy puts me on my guard. Do we really want to turn back into closed societies and live with ideological blinders on? Surely, the more we know, the less likely we will be to make disastrous mistakes?

I am grateful to my old friend John D. Moore, the director of Columbia University Press. He and I were part of a large group of Soviet and American publishers who, more than a decade ago, did what we could to break the ice of the Cold War between our two countries. I am especially grateful to him today for his understanding the necessity for the truth to be written about contemporary Russia, for his invaluable advice on reworking the manuscript of this book, for his endless patience in accepting my delays—acceding to my wish to include the latest events—for his courage in supporting the very controversial idea of a book about Russia and Zhirinovsky that is in a somewhat different key from other works on this subject in the United States. I am also grateful to Prof. Peter Reddaway, professor of political science at George Washington University, and Dr. Richard E. Ericson, professor of economics and director of the Harriman Institute at Columbia, for their criticism and advice. I would also like to thank the superb staff at Columbia University Press. My special thanks are also due to George Shriver of Tucson, Arizona, who did a great job of putting into English the very Russian notions in this book (working in particular on chapters 1, 2, 4, 5, and 10), and to Sarah St. Onge, who did a wonderful job of editing.

Translator's Note

On the Spelling of Russian Names and Titles of Publications

In regular text, the more familiar and readable method of transliterating Russian has been used: for example, Zhirinovsky (rather than Zhirinovskii); Novodvorskaya (not Novodvorskaia); and Zyuganov (not Zjuganov). However, in bibliographical material, titles and author's names have usually been spelled according to the Library of Congress method of transliteration, to assist readers wishing to look up references. In cases where an author in a bibliographical reference also figures in the general text, the more familiar spelling is used for his or her name—e.g., Yeltsin, not El'tsin.

In some cases the more familiar or preferred spelling of a Russian newspaper is used, instead of following the Library of Congress system. Thus *Novoye Russkoye Slovo* is the spelling used by this Russian émigré paper itself (the largest in the United States). Likewise, *Izvestia* has been used (not *Izvestiia*).

On Russian Administrative and Territorial Subdivisions

The term *region* has been used for the Russian *oblast*, which is roughly the equivalent of a province. Under the tsars the term for a province was *guberniya*, a term that also appears in the present text. The term *region* has also been used when there are references to *Stavropolskii krai* or *Krasnoyarskii krai* (the Stavropol region or the Krasnoyarsk region), although sometimes the translation "territory" is preferred for *krai*. Russian cities are divided into *raion*'s (as are the rural areas of *oblast*'s), and the preferred translation for *raion* is "district." Under the Communist system, each *oblast* or *raion* had its own Communist Party committee, which was the most influential power in the area. Hence the abbreviations *obkom* (for regional committee) and *raikom* (for district committee).

On References to the Communist Party of the Soviet Union

For many decades, of course, the Communist Party of the Soviet Union (CPSU) was the single ruling party and the only legally permitted political party. In the text, therefore, references to "the party" or "the party's Central Committee" are to the CPSU. My preference is not to capitalize such references, i.e., not to use the style "the Party."

Communist or *Communism* is capitalized when referring to the specific political organization or movement, or a government or society under the rule of such a political party. Thus capital C is used in such terms as "post-Communist era" or "anti-Communist witch-hunt." In references to the general ideas of this philosophy or the concept of a future society of material abundance without class divisions, small *c* is used.—G.S.

Vladimir Zhirinovsky at his dacha. In the course of four years this obscure lawyer has become a world political star. Is he dangerous?   *Courtesy of LDPR*

NOVEMBER 7, 1989
Lines of Soviet soldiers march in step in front of Lenin's mausoleum during
the traditional military parade commemorating the 1917 Bolshevik Revolution.
Dominique Dudouble. Reuters/Bettmann

FEBRUARY 1990
McDonald's opens in Moscow.
Fotokhronika TASS, Sovfoto

NOVEMBER 4, 1990
In search of ideology: demonstrators in Moscow carrying a Russian icon and placards of Czar Nicholas II and Lenin.
Gennady Galpern. Reuters/Bettmann

MARCH 28, 1991
Defying a Kremlin ban, thousands of radical democrats stage a rally in support of Boris Yeltsin and demand Gorbachev's resignation.

Gennady Galperin. Reuters/Bettmann

JUNE 1991
Vladimir Zhirinovsky at his polling station during the Russian presidential election in June 1991. Yeltsin came in first; Zhirinovsky, third.

O. Buldakov. TASS, Sovfoto

JULY 1, 1992
An elderly woman walks past the unidentified bodies of Russians killed in the cross fire between Moldovan government forces and ethnic Russians in the besieged city of Bendary.   *Reuters*

SEPTEMBER 25, 1992
During his visit to France, Zhirinovsky met with many important politicians, including Jean-Marie Le Pen.   *Courtesy of LDPR*

DECEMBER 3, 1992
A customer exchanges dollars for rubles at a mobile "bank" in Moscow. The unstable ruble has given rise to professional currency speculators.

Reuters/Bettmann

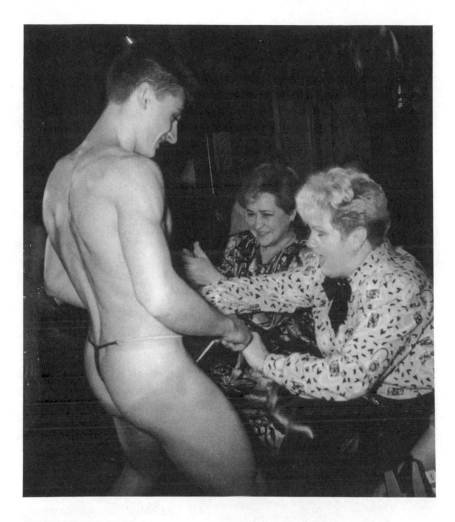

FEBRUARY 14, 1993

A spectator at Moscow's first women-only club exclaims after she is approached by a male stripper.   *Reuters/Bettmann*

New Year's and Christmas sale in the joint-stock company GUM, formerly the largest state-owned store in the Soviet Union.

R. Denisov. TASS, Sovfoto

An elderly Muscovite tries to exchange a used sweater for a fish at a flea market in Moscow.

Viktor Karatayev. Reuters/Bettmann

FEBRUARY 1993
Altay Territory. People search for food in a dump.

V. Sadchikov. ITAR-TASS/Sovfoto

Russia's biggest tractor works, in Vladimir, shut down at the end of 1993. It is now for sale for $5,000,000.   *A. Markovkin. TASS, Sovfoto*

OCTOBER 4, 1993
Tanks aim their guns at the burning building of the Supreme Soviet ("White House") during an all-out attack by pro-Yeltsin forces. Later, troops renewed their assault on the legally elected parliament.   *Reuters/Bettmann*

NOVEMBER 26, 1993
Russian president Boris Yeltsin (*right*) speaks to leaders of electoral blocs, while Zhirinovsky (*center, standing*) and the leader of the Russian Communists, Gennady Zyuganov (*left, standing*), look on. Yeltsin warned groups campaigning for parliamentary elections that he would rescind their access to free television broadcasts if they used them to attack his project for a new constitution.

Reuters/Bettmann

FEBRUARY 4, 1994
Vladimir Zhirinovsky *(left)* gives recommendations to his colleagues in the
State Duma, the lower chamber of the new Russian parliament. His party won
the parliamentary election in December 1993.   *Gennady Galperin. Reuters/Bettmann*

APRIL 4, 1994
Zhirinovsky listens to the hymn of his Liberal Democratic Party. The LDPR's
fifth congress granted him dictatorial powers in the party for ten years and
named him as its candidate in future presidential elections.

Reuters/Bettmann

AUGUST 1994
The remains of three beheaded Chechens who were political opponents of General Dudayev. They were executed and their heads put on display as punishment for cooperating with Russians. These atrocities are overshadowed by what happened during Russia's military involvement in Chechnya.

Photo of Argumenty i Fakty

AUGUST 1994
The corpse of the fifteen-year-old boy who had been at the controls of a Russian International Airlines airbus shortly before its crash, which resulted in seventy-five fatalities. Analysis of the plane's black box revealed that the boy piloted the plane just before the impact.

Panorama

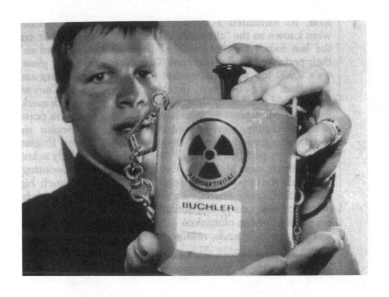

AUGUST 1994
A canister with Russian plutonium seized at a railway station in Bremen, Germany. *Michael Koch. AP*

Eight Soviet submarines sit on a barge in Rotterdam's harbor, waiting to be sold as scrap. In October 1994 a journalist investigating illegal sales of Russian military equipment was murdered. *Reuters/Bettmann*

Russian politicians showing "the right way to go" (collage by Andrei Doro-
faev). In front *(left to right)*: Zhirinovsky, Zyuganov, Gorbachev, Yeltsin,
Shakrai, Grachev, and Yavlinsky. Looming over them are Stalin, Lenin, and
Khrushchev.   *Argumenty i Fakty,* November 3, 1994

APRIL 25, 1994
Vladimir Zhirinovsky holds a globe presented to him at
the celebration of his forty-eighth birthday.

Reuters/Bettmann

!Zhirinovsky!

Prologue: Lost Wager

*Zhirinovsky must be seen as a symbol of something
very real, very powerful.*
—Yegor Gaidar, chairman of Russia's Choice Party

One evening in late December 1987 Vladimir Zhirinovsky stopped by my office at the Mir Publishing House in Moscow. A light snow was falling. The glow from the shrouded Kremlin-style table lamp on my desk dimly lit the room; through the window the oaks and maples that dominated the company's extensive grounds were still visible. The cheerful calls of children on their sleds echoed outside.

It was a Friday. All the employees had already left the office, full of plans for their weekends. The New Year was approaching, and after that Russian Orthodox Christmas, which falls thirteen days after the Catholic Christmas by the Julian calendar. Everyone was looking forward to the holidays, busily exchanging greetings and congratulations, buying presents for children, queueing for scarce goods, raiding the rare liquor shops (Gorbachev's anti-alcohol campaign was then in full swing) for champagne incredibly cheap by Western standards, and trying, with cunning, coercion, and sweet talk, to breach the system of hidden distribution that controlled the sale, at rock-bottom prices, of all manner of wonderful items—wines, fruits, caviar, sturgeon, chocolate, hams, cheeses—both domestic and imported for the party and government bigwigs. The preholiday hustle and bustle were proceeding normally, and the mild weather that had begun to set in toward the end of the month promised a beautiful white Christmas.

Zhirinovsky seemed to be in no hurry to get anywhere. As I understood it, he had been staying with his elderly mother until her death in 1985, his wife and son living elsewhere on their own. One-quarter of his small (though above average) salary was going toward child support. His failure with one of the company's beauties, a six-foot blonde graphic artist, was no secret to anyone in the publishing house. Her unequivocal rejection of his advances had left no room for misinterpretation: she had gone off with someone else to celebrate New Year's in the ancient city of Suzdal, leaving him once again—and there were many such occasions—to suffer alone. Clearly he had come by my office not on business but simply to chat. He wanted company, someone to listen to him, and despite the many battles we had waged during our general company meetings, he and I were adversaries in what Zhirinovsky termed "an honorable fight" and at the very least capable of hearing each other out. His late visit to my office, the building empty of secretaries and other personnel, was not remarkable. Such visits had occurred before.

Zhirinovsky was the publishing house's lawyer, a member of the company's top brass, and he had the unwritten right to walk into the office of the director—his immediate and only superior—without having to announce his intentions beforehand or respond to the demeaning questions of secretaries. But something was different this time. Perhaps the fuss of the impending holidays and the solitude he felt among people consumed by their own family concerns made him more candid than usual. It was as if he had made a crucial decision, private but vital to share with one important person. Whatever the reason, this Friday he spoke to me of feelings he had previously kept bottled up, thoughts no one would have expected to hear from him.

Zhirinovsky entered the room silent and preoccupied. Without uttering a word he crossed the soft rugs covering the floor and sank into the armchair. Engulfed in the soft leather chair, he began looking intently around the room, as if he were seeing everything for the first time.

"What is it, Volodya?" I asked, addressing him with the Russian nickname for Vladimir. "Are you here on business or simply to sit and rest a while?"

He took his time answering, continuing to scan the walls of the office, where a portrait of the late Communist Party boss Leonid Brezhnev had been replaced first by one of Andropov, then by Chernenko's, and finally by one of Mikhail Sergeyevich Gorbachev. But the portrait of Lenin with his sizable forehead still glistened in the most visible and honored spot in the room. Here and there were also hung several small engravings from Petrine times, lovingly set into frames by the company's own cabinetmaker.

Zhirinovsky's glance gradually came to a rest on my desk where, alongside piles of contracts, correspondence, and other business-related papers, lay a parcel of just-delivered books—ten free copies of my new biography of Isaac Newton and fifty more I had bought to hand out to colleagues. Zhirinovsky, unaware that I wrote books, was amazed by what he saw.

"May I have a look, Vladimir Petrovich?" he asked.

"Be my guest, Volodya," I replied.

While I busied myself with a stack of papers, Zhirinovsky dug into one of the copies, flipping through the entire book and paying special attention to the illustrations.

"So, what do you think? Would you like a copy with my autograph?"

"Wouldn't be such a bad idea."

Zhirinovsky took a long look at the signature and then suddenly said, "Newton, of course, was a genius. You're a director, a writer, a Ph.D., a big shot. I'm a nobody. The Communist Party and Soviet nomenklatura have ruined my life. I'm already past forty, with no decent apartment or dacha, a piece of junk for a car, and a salary of a hundred eighty rubles that I have to pay alimony out of. But, say, do you want to make a bet? One day you will write a book about Vladimir Zhirinovsky!"

I smiled, patted him on the shoulder, and said, "I will gladly write a book about you, Volodya. But first you have to become as famous as Newton. For example, you could become a celebrated lawyer like—"

"It's not in the cards for me to keep on being a lawyer," he interrupted. "The road to the Moscow Collegium of Lawyers is closed to me because I'm not a party member. And the KGB won't let me into the party. I don't want to join anyway. I guess since there aren't any other parties in the Soviet Union, I'll just have to create my own."

"Now there's an idea!"

"Wait, don't laugh! We need something in the spirit of European social democracy. Look how they live in Europe. In comfort and peace. True, I don't like the socialist allusions in the name 'social democratic party.' It's not that socialism is such a bad idea in itself; it's just that nobody realized at first how many strings are attached to it: isolation, the one-party system, and so on. We've had enough of socialism, even its so-called developed form. 'Democratic' can stay in the name, though. Democracy is the only acceptable way to make decisions, the only alternative to our totalitarian system. But the direction of the movement does not have to be so defined. Not socialism, but what? Capitalism? No. . . . Liberalism—that's the word for it! Free development of all the country's creative forces. A party of democratic liberals or liberal democrats. The first would be better, but it doesn't sound as good, even though the meaning is more precise. We need a new party. Right now, we have one ideology, which we're forbidden to criticize. We have to learn a lesson from science. When the editor of a scientific journal won't publish articles with alien viewpoints, would-be authors start a rival journal. It's the only way for them to become well known! It's just a lot more difficult to start a new party. Difficult, but not impossible. But what about the bet?"

Obviously, Zhirinovsky won this informal wager. He founded his party, the Liberal Democratic Party of Rusia (LDPR), and he could become the next president of Russia.

I hired Zhirinovsky in 1983 to be Mir's in-house lawyer and clashed with him innumerable times during staff meetings, when he would irresponsibly promise the employees—almost seven hundred people— free apartments, free food, free recreation, free transportation, and even free automobiles, raising expectations and riling them up, while I was compelled to play the role of spoilsport and demolish his beautiful illusions with the sober language of numbers. At the same time—and on several occasions at the risk of my own career—I came to his rescue when he fell victim to illegal persecutions by the local party and KGB organizations. He worked for me more than six years, until 1989, when I was appointed director of publications at the United Nations, after which he tried to get himself elected as my successor at Mir.

He and I met again in 1990, when, visiting New York in his new capacity as chairman of the Liberal Democratic Party of Russia (LDPR), he paid me a visit for old times' sake. That year I also met with Stanislav Zhebrovsky, the second in command of both his party and his brain trust, who also once worked at Mir, as the deputy head of the physics and astronomy division. In 1994, I saw Zhirinovsky in Moscow and New York in connection with his visit to the United States. To this day I am in touch with these men. Because of this connection, forged more than ten years ago at Mir, I possess unique, firsthand information, never before published, concerning the rise and present status of the Liberal Democratic Party, its leaders, and many of its members. Aside from its obvious interest, this information may also be extremely useful to a wide range of Western readers who have found it difficult at times to get a clear idea of the dramatic events occurring in Russia today, not to mention Vladimir Zhirinovsky's place in them. With its victory in December 1993's parliamentary elections, the Liberal Democratic Party's significance has reached beyond the borders of Russia. For this reason a book that examines Zhirinovsky's life, views, and his possible role in the current and future politics of Russia had to be written now. It is also necessary to explain the unusual popularity of this inexperienced politician, a phenomenon that I believe is attributable to a highly specific social aspect of contemporary Russia known as *bespredel*, a kind of laissez-faire gone mad that has arisen from the cynicism bred under totalitarian conditions and running rampant in today's democracy. It connotes total permissiveness—the abrogation of tradition, the rules of the game, the rules of conduct, and, at times, even fundamental decency and common sense.

After the shocking results of the parliamentary elections held on December 12, 1993, when the Liberal Democratic Party garnered almost 25 percent of the votes cast, crushing the already broken ranks of the democratic parties, Zhirinovsky became overnight one of the best-known individuals on the planet, a man of the year. Suddenly, just as he had predicted (though no one believed him then), he had become a figure in Russian politics much more interesting and quotable than President Boris Yeltsin himself, his name mentioned almost daily in newspapers and broadcasts. Zhirinovsky both welcomes and shamelessly promotes his new celebrity. He writes openly of his youthful sexual failures, of Russia's rights to Alaska (at one time he maintained—wrongly—that Alaska was not sold to America but merely leased for a hundred years, a term that expired in 1967), and of a new supersecret Russian weapon. He criticizes Yeltsin but plays checkers with him on Saturdays, advises Bill Clinton to stay home and practice playing his saxophone instead of coming to Russia for state visits, loudly announces his plan to send toward the Baltics a lethal radioactive cloud from Russia's dumping grounds after he is elected president, and promises to exile to the frozen north or punish by other means all those who have made his blacklist of betrayers of Russia and Russia's cause—a list that numbers a hundred thousand people. He unabashedly dreams of the day when Russian soldiers will wash their boots in the warm waters of the Indian Ocean and only announcers with fair hair and blue eyes will grace the nation's television screens. He is not afraid of being compared to Hitler and openly meets with the leaders of Europe's profascist organizations. When abroad, he criticizes the government of each country he visits and almost always appeals to the citizenry to toss out their current leaders and elect new ones.

All this, of course, is utter nonsense, a tweaking of the civilized world's nose intended to arouse controversy and make everyone talk about him. Helping Zhirinovsky in this effort are his advising psychologists, including the notorious hypnotist Anatoly Kashpirovsky, who once conducted a live mass healing of millions of Soviet television viewers. Without doubt, Kashpirovsky's lessons helped Zhirinovsky attain unprecedented popularity during his energetic preelection interviews when, eschewing the long-winded, stultifying approaches favored by his opponents, he peppered his remarks with extremist statements and promises of comfort, peace, and the resurrection of Russia's past greatness and, using vibrant, emotional images, sharply rebuked the government and deplored its odious reforms. It is no surprise that the Russian people, having lost in just a few years the basic comforts of the welfare state and their belief in the future, not to mention all feeling of pride in their centuries-old empire, came out in convincing numbers for Zhirinovsky.

A whole team of young politicians from the former Soviet Ministry of Foreign Affairs advises Zhirinovsky on geopolitical issues. The number of his followers among Russian diplomats and United Nations employees, who supply him with valuable topical information, is also growing. The eccentric Russian writer Eduard Limonov, at one time the minister of security in Zhirinovsky's shadow cabinet, taught him the practical use of exhibitionism. A philosopher, Professor Irina Kulikova, edits the articles in his party's publications, and poets and rock musicians (there is even a rock magazine called *At Zhirinovsky's*) provide him with imagery for his speeches. All his emotions are carefully calculated, and all his apparently impromptu behavior is painstakingly orchestrated. Zhirinovsky is by no means a fool; nor is he a madman, even though at times during his fulminations he foams at the mouth. On the contrary, he deserves the most serious attention. Some of his views, however intolerable they seem to the West, have a broad appeal among Russians and reflect the dominant mood in that society today. It is impossible—and, moreover, unwise—to ignore him. And who is he really? Is he really the West's number one enemy? He is not. Russia's bespredel is.

PART ONE

Perestroika, Zhirinovsky, and Mir

1
Mir Publishing House from Stalin to Gorbachev

Recently the American press and television—giants such as the *Washington Post*, ABC's *Nightline*, and *Vanity Fair*—have taken a heightened interest in me. When the calls first began to come in, I didn't understand what was going on. Naively I wondered if perhaps *Regotmas*, my favorite of the books I've written, had at last become a best-seller, catching the attention of the press. Maybe my book on Newton was getting favorable notices. Or maybe I had just won ten million dollars from the Publishers' Clearing House. My new celebrity had nothing to do with me or my books, however. People had simply discovered that I was a good source of information about the most newsworthy subject of the moment.

Several years ago I was pondering whom to include in *Regotmas*, a book of reminiscences about prominent contemporaries of mine. Who would my readers be most interested in meeting—Andrei Sakharov, Pyotr Kapitsa, Oleg Tselkov, Vladimir Vysotsky, Mikhail Shemyakin, Jülo Sooster, Jackie O., Gerard Piel, the two secretaries general of the United Nations, the movie actress Lyudmila Gurchenko, the writer Yuri Nagibin, or the cosmonaut Aleksei Leonov? I had no inkling that another of my acquaintances should have been in the running, a man I didn't take into consideration when I began to write my memoirs, although even then I felt a premonition of his impending fame. Yet today probably every mass publication in the world has mentioned, at least once, the name of this man. It is Vladimir Volfovich Zhirinovsky.

I hired him to work as the general counsel for Mir Publishing House. Afterward I could have torn off my own arms and legs for having done so. I spent too many sleepless nights because of him, and sometimes I wonder if he hasn't taken years off my life. During our professional relationship, I fought against his views, though not all of them. And I won, as he himself admitted to me not so long ago in New York City. I won in public debate, followed by secret ballot, his favorite instrument for building democracy and the only one he recognizes. I defeated him honestly, without stirring up elemental forces among our publishing colleagues and drawing them into dangerous confrontations.

Maybe this is why my years of dealing with Zhirinovsky are of such interest today. People want to defeat him, and perhaps they think I know what should (and shouldn't) be done to achieve this. I welcome this honest approach, and, in my capacity as a specialist of sorts on Zhirinovsky, I call on those who have in mind more clever or more direct means of combating the man—for example, by a sniper's bullet to the head, or through an arranged automobile accident, or by cooking up a court case against him, ridiculing him as a clown, branding him a fascist, spreading doubts about his sanity, or persuading the world that he is a simpleton—to let all these ingenious plans wither unrealized. All such attempts would lead, and already have led, to the opposite result: more and more people voting for Zhirinovsky's party. The Russian people have too much sympathy for those who have fallen or are being made to fall. Such people too easily become martyrs. Before his coronation, even Tsar Boris (Yeltsin) himself more than once made use of his future subjects' sentimental feelings about those who were being hounded and persecuted by Gorbachev. The world doesn't need a Saint Vladimir.

In 1983, when the story of my relationship with Vladimir Volfovich begins, the Soviet system was still functioning. The population as a whole was still assured the basic necessities, not just the honorable poverty of China but a moderate minimum standard of living—an apartment with refrigerator and television, free education and health care, long leaves from work for pregnancy and childbirth, guaranteed employment and pension, and the other achievements of mature socialism, as Brezhnev called it (also known as actually existing socialism), or the universal welfare society. Yet rust was eating away at the system's central mechanisms, which had long since become obsolete, at times totally irrational, operating in defiance of all laws and not subject to quick change or drastic modification. To try to fix it while it was in operation was dangerous and incredibly difficult. It was falling apart before one's very eyes, unmistakably, from one day to the next.

On one occasion, during an overnight trip from Tallinn to Moscow, a young member of the Soviet Academy of Sciences and I figured out an effective way to gauge the system's disintegration: the disappearance of various goods and services, not all at once, but gradually, a few at a time, with temporary remissions, and then completely and definitively. On this train carrying us through a winter's night in 1987, we counted hundreds of name brands of food products and other items that had been available in the 1960s but were now completely gone—cheeses, sausages, French hard rolls, sweet curds, Georgian wines, American cigarettes, nuts, fish, and so on. Even milk, bread, and meat had begun to disappear.

Life demanded change without delay. Far-reaching and fundamental decisions were needed, but the party and the government thought that everything could be fixed by a series of decrees with titles that always began with such symptomatic phrases as "On the Improvement of . . . ," or "On the Perfecting of . . . ," or "On the Alteration of. . . ."

One such decision, I now know, was to strengthen the cadres in Soviet publishing houses by adding professional personnel from various sectors of the economy, science, and culture. The Mir Publishing House published scientific and technical literature in translation. When its director, Sergei Sosnovsky, a well-known legal expert who had taken part in the Nuremberg Trials, died in 1980, the Central Committee of the Communist Party decided to ask the State Committee on Science and Technology to recommend a young scientist or scholar with a publishing background to fill the post. After almost a year and a half of searching, the position was finally offered to me. At the time, I was working as a professor of new technology, economics, and management at the All-Union Institute for Advanced Studies and as assistant chief editor of an academic journal. I had already presented my second doctoral dissertation and published several translations of my books through Mir—in English, German, and Spanish editions.

The academic work into which I had been drawn was not financially rewarding: my salary was three hundred rubles a month (about five hundred dollars at the official exchange rate, but only one hundred dollars on the black market). It also carried none of the special perquisites enjoyed by the nomenklatura (those in particularly important positions filled exclusively by the elite of the ruling party, the Communist Party of the Soviet Union, or CPSU, then the only legal political party in the nation). On the other hand, it had one enormous advantage: it provided me with the free time necessary to write my books and to engage in research—in a word, to live the life I pleased. Therefore, despite its greater prestige (and salary), I at first took a skeptical attitude toward the Mir job offer, knowing how many more demands it would make on my time.

But Boris Ivanovich Stukalin—then the president of the State Committee on Printing, Publishing, and the Book Trade (Goskomizdat), later the Soviet ambassador to Hungary (where he took a benign attitude toward the velvet revolution going on there), and until recently the president of the Sytinsky Book Publishing Foundation of Russia—kept coming up with new facts and arguments, skillfully uncovering aspects of my current job situation that were unsatisfactory to me. Finally, he dispelled my last doubt:

"As for writing, you can always do that, if you still feel you have to. All your evenings and Sundays will be yours. Also sick days. Not to mention vacations."

I was persuaded. General Secretary Brezhnev, the thick-browed one himself, approved the appointment papers, and it fell to me—at once a difficult and happy turn of fate—to be the director of Mir from 1982 to 1989.

At the age of forty-two, I was unusually young to have been made director of a major Soviet publishing house, and I was closely watched by the staff members of Goskomizdat and the party mandarins of the Central Committee departments for propaganda, science, and international affairs. Also vigilant were the stalwarts of the Moscow municipal administration and, most important, the apparatchiks of the party committee of the Dzerzhinsky district (the part of Moscow where Mir was located)—the real day-to-day masters of destiny in the district entrusted to their care. The Dzerzhinsky district was located in the center of Moscow, and even secretaries of the Central Committee were under the district party committee's jurisdiction and paid them party dues. The apparatchiks of the district party committee were fully capable of subjecting even Central Committee members to official party reprimands or placing them or others on notice in some way—an indelible blot on one's record for the rest of one's life.

The apparatchiks diligently followed every step I took, waiting for me to make my first mistake so that they could replace me with someone more appropriate, some activist from the apparatus of party education, a graduate of the Higher Party School or the Central Committee's Academy of Social Sciences. The publishing house and I were also watched closely by another committee with headquarters on Lubyanka Square: the KGB. The KGB district representative, our handler (*curator*), appeared at the publishing house every week. First he would visit

his friends—the undercover informers, who were known only to him—
and then the men who served as informers because of their official
positions: his good buddy Alexander Aleshkin, secretary of the party
bureau at the publishing house, and Nadezhda Nikishina, the inspector of the special department. Afterward, he would visit me.

On the day before I officially began my work as director of Mir, I
entered the grounds with trepidation. Incognito for the moment—my
appointment hadn't yet been announced—I strolled through the big
shady park that spreads over more than ten acres and stopped in at the
buildings housing editorial offices that stood here and there. Making
way for passing trucks loaded with books and rolls of paper, I smiled
anonymously—or so I thought—at my future staff people. To my surprise, I received smiles in return. The on-the-job intelligence service
had been working with its usual precision: from the very first moment
I appeared on the grounds I had been under surveillance. ("The subject
is heading toward the editorial office for Spanish," went the report over
the phone, and the "Spaniards," as though by accident, poured out into
the hallway, suddenly confronting me with dozens of welcoming
faces.) I thought to myself, "I'll be coming here tomorrow to take
charge of this enormous organism. How will I be able to establish
smooth working relations with seven hundred people, all of them anything but ordinary? And what about my superiors, direct and indi-
rect?" I couldn't have dreamt of even a thousandth part of all the com-
plications connected with managing this publishing house, a major
state-owned operation.

After a sleepless night, I arrived at Mir—at nine o'clock on the dot
for the first time in my life, and riding in an official, chauffeur-driven
car, also for the first time in my life. The first discoveries were awaiting
me in my office, a huge room (about six hundred square feet) with windows all along the wall facing the park and filled with massive governmental furniture of Constructivist design dating from the 1940s,
upholstered in green wool, Kremlin-style. In the corner of the office
was a huge safe, colored to match the ocher paneling. Its keys had been
ceremoniously handed to me by the chairman of the Goskomizdat, a
minister of the Soviet government.

When I sorted through the papers in the safe, I came across the very
first documents associated with the founding of the publishing house
in 1945: the official order with Stalin's signature, together with numerous documents signed by Chairman of the Council of Ministers
Lavrenty Beria, all kept in a tattered and beribboned old green folder.
The purpose of the Publishing House for Foreign Literature—Mir's

parent company—was to translate books from foreign languages into Russian and to publish Russian books in foreign tongues. During the Iron Curtain era, when the concept of foreign countries was not quite acceptable to the ordinary Soviet citizen, such a publishing house could truly have been a window onto Europe. Whether that was the intention of its founders is hard to say.

The publishing house was directly subordinated to the Council of Ministers and to its chairman, Beria. Its first publication, in 1946, was a booklet entitled *When Will Russia Have the Atomic Bomb?* The American author's answer was optimistic: in twenty years at the earliest (Professor Igor Kurchatov and Colonel Pavel Sudoplatov's activities were well-kept Soviet secrets at that time). The translation featured a Russian preface, whose message essentially was, "You're wrong, my friend. It could be much sooner." The preface was not signed, but Mir's chief accountant, Grigory Oles, who had been working for the company at the time and was still employed there when I arrived, informed me that his account books contained a note acknowledging receipt of payment by the author, and the signature was a very familiar one: it was printed on the leather cover of every volume of the complete collected works of the late Joseph Stalin. Whoever he was, the author of the preface was correct: the Russians exploded their first atomic bomb in 1949, just four years after the Americans, and their first hydrogen bomb (as opposed to device) in 1953, one year before the Americans. It may even be that the urge to tell the world about the Soviet Union's work on atomic weapons was one of the main reasons for setting up the publishing house. This would also explain why the company was under Beria's direct control: he was responsible for both Russia's atomic program and for the country's espionage.

The safe revealed other secrets to me. Huge honoraria had been paid to foreign writers who "correctly" reflected the balance of forces in the world. Some staff members' indifferent appearances concealed extraordinary biographies: moles whose missions had failed and foreign spies who had fled to the Soviet Union, not to mention female comrades-in-arms of the insatiable Beria—all had had jobs at Mir. One confidential document signed by Stalin established the amount paid to heads of editorial departments at five thousand rubles—a ministerial salary at that time. The document also authorized an official automobile with a chauffeur for each department head and, on top of that, assigned to particular individuals the overcoats and galoshes that had been sent to the publishing house. At the time, the members of Mir's staff truly needed those items: the publishing house was located in a hospital town on the edge of Moscow, sunk in impassable tracts of mud in a neglected park bordering the former Sokolniki forest, where Ivan the Terrible used to hunt with his boyars and *sokolnichy* (special servants in charge of falconry).[1] Once, the entire settlement within the park—old-fashioned buildings, a small hospital, a church, storehouses, even a morgue—had been part of a Moscow retreat, a place of refuge founded by a well-known patron of the arts and fanatic of the theater, Nikolai Bakhrushin. Now, far from the din of the city, it housed the new Publishing House for Foreign Literature.

With the passage of time, the publishing house grew stronger and expanded. Being a privileged operation from the outset, it naturally gathered under its wings, in addition to former spies, wives, lovers, and children of the powerful, a first-rate assortment of editors and translators. In 1964 the Central Committee decided to divide the company into three parts, one dealing with imaginative literature, another with social and political literature, and the third with scientific and technical literature. Each unit was named to reflect its purpose: Raduga (rainbow) for belles lettres, Mir (peace or world) for social and political works, and Progress for scientific and technical material. During the many retypings of the documents relating to these decisions, a typist mixed up two of the names, assigning Mir to the unit that was supposed to serve scientific and technical progress and Progress to the one that was supposed to fight for peace. By the time the error was discovered, the documents had already been sent to the party's Central Committee, so it was decided to leave things as they were.

Mir's ties with foreign partners were substantially strengthened during the 1980s. We began to translate *Scientific American* from cover to cover. (You can have no idea how monstrously difficult it was to convince our superiors in the party and in the government ministries to allow us, for the first time in Soviet history, to translate into Russian from cover to cover a popular American magazine in which compliments directed toward the Soviet Union and Soviet science were by no means common.) Mir embarked on collaborative programs with other publishers as well, mostly American. New contracts with foreign part-

1. Incidentally, Sokolniki Park, where Zhirinovsky lives now and where he has his monthly rallies, furnished the name for his young followers: Sokoly Zhirinovskogo (Zhirinovsky falcons); one can see a falcon on the party's emblem, too. The Liberal Democratic Party evidently has a special feeling for falcons: it pays all their expenses at the Moscow Zoo. See the Moscow evening paper *Vechernyaya Moskva*, May 30, 1994, article entitled "Liberal'no-demokraticheskaia partiia poshla na dopolnitel'nye raskhody" (Liberal democrats decide on additional spending).

ners came across my desk literally every day. The legal department, consisting of only one department head—Georgy A. Kvelidze, a handsome Georgian heartbreaker ready to fight over anything, including trifles entirely unworthy of his attention—was utterly unable to cope with the flood of contracts. Kvelidze was kept busy with the ongoing legal affairs of the publishing house and devoted very little time to foreign contracts, not knowing any languages other than Russian and Georgian. To pick up this slack, in 1983 we finally decided to fill a position that had been open for several years: we would hire one more person for the legal department, a senior legal counsel who would specialize in handling foreign contracts and receive a salary of 150 rubles per month.

It proved no easy matter to fill this slot. Nikolai Kirillovich Barkov, the head of the personnel department and a retired general, knocked himself out trying to ensnare, using only 150 rubles a month as bait, a person with high qualifications and an unblemished record—this was 1983, when the various committees (Central, State Security, and others) would not approve just anybody for a job in so ideologically sensitive a spot as a publishing house—as well as a knowledge of foreign languages and experience in dealing with foreign contracts and international law. I couldn't understand why General Barkov didn't simply lure someone away from VAAP, the All-Union Association for Author's Rights, which at the time had monopoly authority over copyright matters affecting Soviet authors. Later I understood: some people at VAAP were involved in machinations that on occasion earned them ten times as much as their official salaries, which made our 150 rubles a month a poor temptation. Others, with backgrounds in international law, were drawn to the Foreign Ministry or were making careers for themselves in the UN or other international organizations.

Finally, after three or four months of searching, Kvelidze and the general burst into my office shouting, "We've found him!" His name was Vladimir Volfovich Zhirinovsky.

Kvelidze had found Zhirinovsky through his old connections at the Inyurkollegiya (the Collegium for Foreign Legal Matters), a highly specialized Moscow organization whose personnel were engaged, among other things, in handling legal details related to inheritances from relatives of Soviet citizens who had died abroad. To work in the organization, one had to know both international law and foreign languages. Our thinking was that, for a candidate with such assets to offer, the subtleties of copyright law could be learned on the job.

"But will the Collegium let him go?" I asked.

"Yes, although it's hard for them," answered Barkov. "He's a good worker. I spoke with the head of personnel and with Sarantsev, the director. They envy us."

General Barkov, an exceptionally thorough man, had a long interview with Zhirinovsky and personally checked all the information on his job application, seeking to reconstruct the prospective employee's history. He wanted to clarify for himself why a man of thirty-five with a double university education (from the Turkic Division of the Institute of Oriental Languages and from the Law School at Moscow State University) would agree to take a modest position—with an even more modest salary—as a publisher's legal counsel. Usually the graduates of these two prestigious institutions made brilliant careers for themselves at embassies or diplomatic missions or at the bar.

The explanation seemed to be that the fellow had had bad luck. On graduating from the Institute of Oriental Languages he had been sent to Turkey to gain practical experience with the language. There he had given out Soviet badges to some Turks he was trying to befriend, and this had landed him in a Turkish prison. Such evidence of frivolity and lack of circumspection had barred him from party membership, without which it was impossible to make a career in the diplomatic services. Forced to switch careers, he had decided to study law. But he was about five years too late: the lads who had graduated earlier had taken all the available openings; he couldn't make his way onto the bar. Now he was floundering around, at loose ends. Maybe at Mir he would find himself.

Everyone accepted this account of Zhirinovsky's background. His application was reported to Goskomizdat, which gave its approval in principle. And Zhirinovsky came to my office for the final interview. He was tall and thin, with light blue eyes and tightly curled reddish-brown hair. He was wearing a reddish-brown jacket that didn't go with his gray trousers. His tie was knotted a little more carelessly than I would have allowed myself if I were having an interview with my future director, and his shirt had evidently been worn once or twice before.

I very much wanted to learn more about Zhirinovsky and tried to get him to open up. The conversation proved to be lively and very revealing indeed. He showed himself to be a sharp-witted homespun philosopher who considered every step he took and had a clear aim in life. Unfortunately, however, he viewed himself as a failure and constantly compared himself with others. "For me, everything has gone not as it should, and for a long time. I'll soon be forty. I'm paying alimony. And what are one hundred fifty rubles today? It can bring you to tears! Taxes, deductions, alimony—what's left? I'm still young, though.

I need to go out with women. Ask them out to the theater or the movies or just dinner at a restaurant. You need a lot of money for that. Not a hundred fifty rubles. But I may still defend my dissertation. I have savings. I'll get a candidate's degree [something between a master's degree and a doctorate in the United States]. I'll make it onto the bar. I'll take big cases. I'll get recognition yet!"

Such candor, I must say, disturbed me a little. But I blamed myself. I was the one who had encouraged him to talk about himself. Someone else might have declined the invitation, but this man had tried to respond to my suggestion. What right had I to be displeased now?

Under the direction of his boss, Kvelidze, a man with a lot of experience in legal work and a candidate's degree in juridical science, Vladimir Volfovich grew quite sophisticated in his handling of the legal subtleties of his job. And he came to know his way around the publishing house. He would drop in on the other departments and editorial offices, spend a long time talking with people, and try to involve himself in their problems—not only work-related and legal but personal ones as well. To some extent this was part of his job, but I caught myself thinking more and more that I'd prefer it if he'd stay in his own office.

I was also afraid that Kvelidze, who acted as a constant and insistent mentor, would transmit to Zhirinovsky his own too-fiery passion as a fighter for justice and the law. I'm not against justice and the law, but my duty was to keep the whole of Mir's workforce in a state of productive equilibrium. When Kvelidze discovered a problem, however, even one that might be solved without fuss and bother (say, by adjusting the controls, if the radiators in some rooms were too cold in the winter or too hot in the summer), he never missed the chance to use it to strike out against his political opponents (of whom there were many). He would take to the speaker's stand at party or trade union meetings and inform everyone of the problem, hurling verbal thunderbolts at his enemies, transfixing them with his fiery gaze, and demolishing them with his bitter, angry perorations. Before his time at Mir, Kvelidze had worked as a prosecutor, and the style and manner of the prosecutor stayed with him. His speeches upset his colleagues, threw them off balance, made them furious. He exposed and denounced; his was the voice of state authority. This handsome Georgian was a proud man who put all his passion into denunciation, exposure, and speechifying on behalf of justice and the law. He invested not only his passion but his personal health in these efforts.

Zhirinovsky became fast friends with his new boss, and the two often had lunch together. Unfortunately, the newcomer acquired from the older man his prosecutorial zeal, aggressive tactics, extreme opinions, and refusal to tolerate disagreement. Gradually, though, he also learned certain skills in using loopholes in the law to serve the general good (of course, without forgetting his own interests). For example, up to that point, only editors at publishing houses had had the right to a bonus because of knowledge of foreign languages, but Zhirinovsky figured out a way to reinterpret the law to include legal consultants and other employees. (By winning this point, he increased his salary first to 180 rubles a month and then to 200.) On another occasion, he found a loophole in the law that made it possible for the management of the publishing house to arrange for virtually free lunches for all the staff. I supported him fully. This set a precedent that was appreciated in the rest of the publishing community, but my superiors on various committees—in particular, the new government minister Mikhail Nenashev, who later became the head of Soviet television in the perestroika period—began to view everything I did with increasing suspicion.

My superiors' suspicions intensified when the trade union committee at Mir, on Zhirinovsky's recommendation, arranged for staff members to have free consultations with medical specialists at those top-notch polyclinics where normally one was supposed to pay. He also arranged for Mir employees to receive substantial subsidies for the purchase of cooperative apartments (up to the full price of the apartment), vacation passes to health resorts at privileged rates, and bonuses of previously unheard-of proportions. All this was very unusual in Soviet publishing. Mir's experience has been studied by trade union experts, ministry officials, and other publishing enterprises. For Mir those years were ones of enthusiasm for work, a new generation of books, and the first naive democratic experience.

2

Zhirinovsky's Early Life

By the time I arrived in 1982, Mir's original staff members—selected right after the company's founding, in the late 1940s and early 1950s—had reached the age of retirement. I replaced many heads of departments and editorial offices, as well as managing editors. In place of these retirees—many of whom had been KGB "residents"—came young professionals with good educations, many with candidate's degrees. The main criteria for hiring personnel were ability to do the job, knowledge of foreign languages, youth, and, of course, membership in the CPSU. (Such were the qualifications, for instance, of one young man hired to head the editorial group concerned with physics. He had a candidate's degree in physical and mathematical sciences and an excellent command of French. His name was Stanislav Zhebrovsky, and today he is the number two man in Zhirinovsky's party.) It was when we were hiring this team of about twenty new young leaders that Zhirinovsky came our way.

In Soviet institutions, the hiring process was quite lengthy and fraught with grave responsibility, especially if an organization had anything to do with foreigners and foreign countries, or with state secrets. Mir unquestionably fell into the first category, and interestingly enough, it belonged to the second category as well, because through it certain confidential transfers of foreign currency were carried out to subsidize Communist and workers' parties throughout the world. This practice was common in all the publishing houses controlled by the Chief Administration for Publication of Literature for Foreign Readers, a body subordinate to Goskomizdat. A special department of the CPSU Central Committee saw to the uninterrupted covert subsidizing of foreign Communist parties through their party publishing operations. These publishing houses, usually run by a small number of people without reported last names, received books free of charge or at very low prices from Mezhdunarodnaya Kniga, the International Book organization, a subdivision of the Soviet Ministry of Foreign Trade. They then sold these books, mainly in English, Spanish, and German, through their party bookstores at standard world market prices or in some cases at prices far below the competition. The amounts earned went into the party treasuries.

For decades, then, the hiring of new staff members at publishing houses had been an extremely arduous business. Not until the early 1980s, when CPSU personnel policy relaxed somewhat, did it become possible to carry out large-scale replacements of aged publishing house cadres by relatively younger people.

Zhirinovsky's candidacy had been approved by the chief legal adviser to Goskomizdat, a man named Yuri Klimov, and General Barkov had checked with all higher bodies for approval of Zhirinovsky's candidacy, with the exception of one—the KGB. He didn't consider it necessary to consult them, apparently because the job of legal consultant in a publishing house was not considered a key position—after all, it wasn't half as important as head of the legal department. Subsequently, officials of the Dzerzhinsky district division of the Moscow KGB indicated to General Barkov that he had committed a serious error and displayed a great lack of caution in allowing an inveterate troublemaker and dissident into such an ideologically important government institution.

The general had been trained in the old party personnel traditions. He had cross-examined Zhirinovsky at great length, unobtrusively acquiring information about Zhirinovsky's parents, his childhood, his studies at the institute and university, and his subsequent work life. He did this unaggressively but persistently, spending several hours on the questioning, as I recall. Barkov was helped in his investigation by the fact that at one time Zhirinovsky had served in army units in Transcaucasia, where Barkov himself had headed the Political Directorate (a special agency of the Soviet armed forces that among other tasks checked on the political reliability of all military personnel). This gave the two something to talk about, and as they reminisced about the people with whom they had served, the general was able to draw out details about the candidate's life—for example, that Zhirinovsky had been born on April 25, 1946, in

Alma-Ata, capital of the Kazakh Soviet Socialist Republic, which, as Zhirinovsky put it time and again, had been "created by Stalin in the name of his misguided multinational Soviet state." At the time of the interview Barkov did not pay much attention to this comment, which turns out, in retrospect, to have been quite significant. It is still a frequent bugbear in Zhirinovsky's speeches, writings, and programs.

Although Zhirinovsky was not a party member, he regularly attended party meetings at Mir—for two reasons: first, he always wanted to be up on the latest events at the company, and all significant, strategic questions of life at the publishing house were decided at the party meetings; second, he wanted a platform to speak from. I don't recall a single instance when he failed to take the floor at a meeting, no matter what the subject under discussion.[1] Nationality policy, in particular, was a favorite theme in his speeches: "[Alma-Ata] began as a Russian fort named Verny. . . . It was only later that Stalin's decrees created a Kazakh autonomous republic and then a Kazakh Soviet Republic, with Alma-Ata as its capital. But that capital is really the city of Verny, founded by Russians, and I was born there among Russians," Zhirinovsky would say. "There was no state there of any kind when the Russians arrived and established the city. It was a city of Russian Cossacks, a *stanitsa* [Cossack settlement] on the bank of the river Alma-Atinka. There wasn't a single *aul* [native settlement] or yurt in the vicinity. Yet they turned this city into the capital of the Kazakhs, instead of letting it remain the city of Cossacks that it had always been. And the Russians were made into some sort of fertilizer for the soil on which this newly fabricated Kazakh state was supposed to grow and flourish." (These and similar statements made by Zhirinovsky have prompted modern Kazakh nationalists to sentence him to death.)

The problem of the national republics of the Soviet Union frequently came up in my private conversations with Zhirinovsky. He seemed to take my interest in the subject for granted, because I, too, had been born in Asia, in Samarkand in the Central Asian republic of Uzbekistan, which remained firmly Asiatic even though it was a Soviet Socialist Republic. I could hardly claim, though, that the Russians had founded Samarkand; its history goes back to the time of Alexander the Great,

1. Zhirinovsky is not being straightforward when he sometimes complains that he was excluded from party meetings. At Mir, the only time nonmembers could not attend party meetings was when elections (by secret ballot) were being held for the party bureau, the leading party body at the publishing house. According to the party rules, nonmembers could not be present at such elections, in order to prevent influences from being exerted from the outside.

who conquered it when it was called Marakanda, at a time when even the dream of a Russian state did not exist. And in the nineteenth century it had been devastated by the Russian army. This didn't stop Zhirinovsky, however. "No country called Uzbekistan ever existed," he would insist. "There were petty khanates—Bokhara, Khiva—and there were nationalities, such as the Uzbeks, the Tajiks, and the Afghan Pushtu. But they were not organized; they lived a medieval existence. They were highway robbers. Russia brought culture and modern civilization there—the railroad, European goods, brick buildings. And coal instead of dried dung for fuel. Not until then did they start to live like human beings."

He would say all this as though these "artificial states," where Russians, he felt, ought to be able to live well but in fact had hard lives, were a personal affront, an insult to both his nation and his own person. And in a sense he was right. The Communist Party, in its desire to create the appearance of national entities on the territory of the USSR, had, in fact, created some Potemkin states that later turned their backs on the very people who had organized them. These were set up with puppet governments, puppet academies of sciences, puppet leaders of ministries and enterprises, each unfailingly selected from among the non-Russian national cadres and each invariably supported by a Russian serving as chief assistant who really ran the show. In many cases, new states were even endowed with puppet cultures, "national in form, but socialist in essence" (as Stalin used to say), sometimes revived from ancient, half-forgotten traditions but often simply created anew, by analogy with the cultures of neighboring nationalities.

The Russians in the so-called Russian colonies, especially where the native cultures were primitive, were in an ambivalent position. On the one hand, they were privileged in that they came from a more educated nation—the mother country. On the other, because of the nationalities policy of the USSR, Russians could not hope for any kind of meaningful career in a non-Russian national republic. All such titles and positions as "people's artist" or "honored artist" of the republic, member of its academy of sciences, professor, government minister, enterprise director, or party leader were reserved for *natsmeny* (the Russian abbreviation for *natsionalnye menshinstva*—"national minorities"). From the beginning, the Russians in the non-Russian national republics felt themselves to be second-class citizens.

I remember telling Zhirinovsky why my family, which, like his, had been affiliated with the Turkestan-Siberia Railroad, was forced to leave Uzbekistan in the late 1950s and early 1960s. Our family had been linked

with the region for many decades. My great-grandfather, Professor Fyo-
dor Lebedev, an entomologist, organized the battle against locusts in
Turkestan (the region's name before it was reorganized into the six Soviet republics of Central Asia). My grandfather Alexey Pogodin went
there as an employee of the Turkestan-Siberia Railroad. My grandmother, Valentina Lebedeva, had been a teacher there. And my mother,
Sofia Kartseva, was born at the station of Chelkar on that railroad,
around which a new and modern life was gradually crystallizing. My
father, Pyotr Kartsev (he was really my stepfather; I never knew my real
father) had been evacuated to Tashkent during World War II as a valued
specialist. He worked in the department of electrical engineering at the
Central Asian Polytechnic Institute, defended his dissertation, and
expected to become head of the department. That never happened,
however, because the dogma of Soviet nationalities policy required that
the head of the department be an Uzbek. An Uzbek docent by the name
of Ikram Akhmedov, who had just defended his dissertation, was
appointed head of the department instead. The Russian candidates,
among them my father, were given places as his advisers. My mother's
career at the Tashkent Theatrical Institute was similarly restricted
because of her Russian nationality, as were those of my uncle, an engineer, my aunt, a physician, and a friend of our family, a professor. That
was the reason for our emigration from the sunny regions of Uzbekistan
to the cold and foggy but completely Russian city of Leningrad.

Despite all the difficulties their Russian nationality had caused my
family, the experience did not depress and embitter me to the degree
that much milder events had affected Zhirinovsky. He took it much
more deeply to heart. Here is what he wrote on the subject in his recent
autobiography:

> National oppression is something I experienced from my earliest
> childhood. I asked my mama: "Why do we live in such bad housing?
> Why can't we get an apartment of our own?" Mama would answer:
> "We're not Kazakhs. It's hard for us to get an apartment here. They
> give them first of all to the Kazakhs." Mama worked in a dining hall
> at an institute, and the instructors often told her about the entrance
> exams, about how sorry they felt for the Russian lads. A Russian
> answers a question [in oral examination], and they give him a two [a
> D], but a Kazakh gives the same answer and gets a four [a B]. The rea-
> son was that national cadres were needed. But the Russian fellows
> were left with their pain outside the walls of higher education. While
> Kazakhs who didn't have sufficient knowledge were enrolled. Tell
> me, isn't this national discrimination, isn't this really national oppres-

sion? Don't you think all this wounded my soul, affected my consciousness?[2]

I am not at all surprised that this resentment became the foundation of his political thinking about the countries of the "near abroad," the former non-Russian Soviet republics. He seems to have an inferiority complex about growing up as a Russian in a non-Russian national republic. The theme of the torments Russians have undergone in the national republics of the USSR is never missing from his reminiscences:

> My mother died in 1985. Looking back over her life, I felt such pain: she really never saw or experienced anything joyful. Throughout her life there were insults and injuries. It seems this was the fate of all our people. My mother and father were born in the Russian empire, my father in 1907, my mother in 1912. And throughout this century they suffered. First the tsar and the Russian empire, then the revolution and the civil war, then the Great Patriotic War [the Soviet Russian term for the war with Nazi Germany, 1941–45], and the constant moving from place to place, always with some kind of bureaucratic formality—internal passports, residence permits, this is forbidden, this is permitted—being relocated from one end of the country to the other, from Europe to Asia. They died before their time. And their whole lives were taken up with this constant moving from place to place. How many cities, how many different apartments they lived in. . . . Our entire nation was put on wheels. The entire Russian people—on a peasant cart, bouncing over the back roads, over the potholes. Throughout the twentieth century. We whipped the Germans and went into outer space. But the family was destroyed, and all the stable foundations. Archives were lost, and so were family ties. How many people were moved around and lost."[3]

A recent article quoted Dyusenbek Nakipov, a Kazakh and neighbor of the young Zhirinovsky, as saying about his old acquaintance, "We considered him such a small fry, we didn't think he was fit for wiping our feet on. We sent him to buy cigarettes, and he would ask, 'May I join you guys?' The usual answer was, 'Get the f— out of here,' or just a kick in the butt."[4] The author then goes on to interpret this statement as evi-

2. Zhirinovsky, *Poslednii brosok na iug* (The last dash to the south), 7. All shortened references in the notes can be found fully cited in the bibliography.

3. Ibid., 5. Zhirinovsky's talent for self-serving exaggeration is evident in this quotation. In fact, his mother lived to turn seventy-three—quite an average life span for women of her generation.

4. Fedarko, "Rising Czar?" 41.

dence of what a terrible, miserable person Zhirinovsky was as a child. Zhirinovsky, however, could cite the same quotation as an example of how Russians are mistreated by non-Russians in the national republics, and a lot of people who know the problem would agree with him. Certainly, in my own opinion, the quotation reveals less about Zhirinovsky than it does about Dyusenbek Nakipov and does indeed illustrate to a certain extent the very nationalities problem that Zhirinovsky talked and talks so much about.

Still, while the inherent injustice of the situation for Russians in Central Asia may have forced many of them to leave the places where they had been born in order to seek their fortunes in the purely Russian cities of the mother country, it is unquestionably true that during World War II and for some time after it, the trend was reversed. Many Russians tried to get to Central Asia. Many were evacuated eastward, away from the theater of operations during the war, and later many sought refuge there from the hunger and cold that marched across the Russian plains after the war.

From Zhirinovsky, I learned that he grew up in a very poor family. In 1994 some authors have tried to disprove this claim. "A *Time* investigation of his past has revealed that much of Zhirinovsky's up-from-poverty life history has been embellished or distorted," wrote Kevin Fedarko in *Time*.[5] His efforts to discredit Zhirinovsky this way are laughable to me. Judging from her photograph, Zhirinovsky's mother, Aleksandra Pavlovna, was a very beautiful woman, but she was also poorly educated and worked as a cleaning woman in a dining hall. She had five children before Vladimir Volfovich, all of them living in one room. What could be poorer than life in a single room with six other people, eating the scraps one's mother brings home from the cafeteria where she works as a cleaning woman? Kevin Fedarko tries to convince us that the fact the house where the family lived had a toilet is proof that Zhirinovsky was well provided for in his childhood. I recently visited the slave houses preserved on a plantation near Charleston, South Carolina, and as far as housing conditions go, those slaves lived better than the Zhirinovsky family did.

Arguments are raging today over who Zhirinovsky's father was, especially over whether he was Jewish. And all the participants in these squabbles are trying shamelessly to make political hay for themselves. Some argue that *ebre* (people who are half-Jewish) are even worse than

5. Ibid.

goys as far their attitudes toward Jews are concerned and that if such a person came to power, pogroms against the Jews would start. Then there are the ultranationalist Russian leaders of the type represented by the political adventurist Eduard Limonov, who recently wrote:

> The Jew who masquerades as a Russian nationalist is an extremely unhealthy, downright pathological phenomenon. How we will find our way out of this pathological business (we the voters, Russia, Vladimir Volfovich himself) is something I cannot imagine. . . . Today, when the West itself is preoccupied with the question of Zhirinovsky's nationality, no one can reproach me for racism . . . and it is possible to reflect unhindered upon the shameful story of Vladimir Volfovich, shameful for Russia and the Russians. Whereas Gaidar's nationality is a matter of indifference to me—he is nonetheless the bearer of non-national, "mondialist" ideas—the question of the nationality of Vladimir Volfovich, and of his father, Volf, is important. A Jew masquerading as a Russian nationalist is a sickness, a pathology. IT IS MUCH TOO MUCH.[6]

In fact, there is some confusion concerning Zhirinovsky's father. Zhirinovsky has said all sorts of things about him, and it is also difficult to know what he has actually said and what has been ascribed to him. I am guided by personal recollections, some of which have been confirmed by Zhirinovsky in his autobiographical book *Poslednii brosok na iug* (The last dash to the south). To me, for example, he once said that his father, whom he claimed was named Volf Andreyevich, was an ordinary legal consultant who worked for the administration of the Turkestan-Siberian Railroad and died in an automobile accident the year Zhirinovsky was born. Elsewhere, however, he presents his father in other guises. Often, instead of an ordinary legal consultant, he describes his father as a jurist or even as a graduate of the Sorbonne. Publications also have quoted Zhirinovsky as giving his father various nationalities (his mother's differs, too—sometimes she's described as a Ukrainian, sometimes as a Russian). Sometimes his father is a Pole, sometimes he is said to have come from the Western Ukraine, sometimes he is a Jew, and sometimes even a German. This last variant, if I recall correctly, was the one General Barkov adhered to. "His patronymic [Volfovich] sounds strange to the Russian ear. But for Germans it's a familiar name. The German name Wolf is short for Wolfgang, as with Mozart," General Barkov used to say.

6. Limonov, *Limonov protiv Zhirinovskogo* (Limonov versus Zhirinovsky), 88.

The problem of identification is complicated by the fact that Zhirinovsky's mother was married more than once. Five months before he was born, she married Volf Isakovich Edelshtein, a thirty-eight-year-old planner who worked for a cooperative producing clothing and footwear. According to Maureen Orth, he was "officially listed as Jewish."[7] Aleksandra Pavlovna's previous husband, Andrei Vasilyevich Zhirinovsky, had worked for the NKVD (the predecessor to the KGB) but was arrested and purged from that organization after he lost some files considered to be confidential. He ended his life on the Turkestan-Siberian Railroad, serving as head of the railroad's construction-machinery supply unit. Maureen Orth states that he died nineteen months before Vladimir was born, so there is no way he could have been Vladimir's father.[8] His younger brother, Aron Isakovich Edelshtein, thirty-four, was a senior engineer of the forestry division of the railroad. He had been born in Ukraine, right next to the Polish border, and had graduated from Lvov University in law and economics. According to police records, both Volf and Aron had residence permits for and lived at the same address where Aleksandra Pavlovna had lived after the death of Andrei Zhirinovsky and where Vladimir Zhirinovsky was born.

Zhirinovsky himself rejects those "discoveries" as KGB fabrications and blasts them as unlawful intrusions into his personal life. But for all the discrepancies in his oral accounts of his provenance, in his autobiography Zhirinovsky writes about the subject of nationality with feeling:

> I was born in a building where only Russians lived, and throughout the city the people for the most part were Russian. To this very day 90 percent of the population there is Russian. Therefore I always considered myself a Russian, born to a Russian woman, Aleksandra Pavlovna Zhirinovskaya, maiden name, Makarova, whose mother, my grandmother, was Fiona Nikiforovna Makarova, maiden name, Serguicheva.[9]

He simply applies the Soviet principle for determining nationality, whereby citizens having parents of differing nationality could, on reaching the age of majority, choose either nationality for their own.

Zhirinovsky himself is indignant at the fuss the mass media have made over his name and origin. Vladimir Kozlovsky, a journalist con-

---

7. Orth, "Nightmare on Red Square," 84. Aleksandra Pavlovna's passport listed her as Russian.

8. Orth, "Nightmare on Red Square," 84.

9. Zhirinovsky, *Poslednii brosok na iug* (The last dash to the south), 4.

cerned with international affairs who was a classmate of Zhirinovsky's at the Institute of Oriental Languages, describes the way Zhirinovsky has reacted to the press campaign dealing with his nationality.

It never bothered me much whether or not a classmate of mine was Jewish (although at our institute he [Zhirinovsky] did not particularly spend time among Jewish students), but people all around seemed to bring up the subject, and my reporter's sense of duty prompted me to ask the fatal question: "There are suspicions about you in regard to Jewishness, do you know why?" I asked; "Because when they ask you who your parents were, you say: 'Mama was Russian, and papa was a lawyer.' This makes people suspect that you're hiding something."

To this Zhirinovsky replied:

No, wait a minute, I was recounting my biography in general, my mother was the subject of discussion, and I told everything about my mother. Then the subject changed to my father. I told where he had studied, that he was a lawyer, everything. Then further questions were asked about my nationality, and I told them about my nationality. But I can't start with the same thing about my parents every time: that my father was this, he was that, what his nationality was. What are you bugging me for!? For forty-five years no one asked me about my nationality, forty-five years! No one asked me anything about it. And now for three months it's been, 'Tell everyone: who was your grandfather, who, who!' . . .

My grandfather was Pavel Ivanovich Makarov! My grandfather was pure Russian, a soldier in the tsarist army, Pavel Ivanovich Makarov! My grandmother was Fiona Nikiforovna Makarova! But what exactly is all this anyhow?! Why is it that I have to come up to everyone and start in from the beginning about what's my nationality, last name, first name, middle name, where and when I was born? After all, this is my personal life! Why should I go up to everyone and tell them about it? And what if there might be some Jews in my family tree? How would I know? That wouldn't bother me or trouble me one bit! But no, I can't find any. Here they all are hanging on the wall [photos of his family]. And there aren't any others! Here's my grandfather, my grandmother. Here's my mother. That's all. . . . And here's my father, he studied in Paris.

What can I do? On my father's side there's nothing more. If I had a complete genealogy on my father's side, I would tell about it, but what can I do if he's from the Western Ukraine, where the Germans plowed everything under? They burned everything, shot everyone! What can I do? He alone survived, got to know my mother in 1945, they got married, I was born in 1946. He died soon after, and then what? Then my mother died. That's all! What am I supposed to do? Make up a new biography?[10]

Zhirinovsky has often proposed: "Take a sample and analyze my blood. If you find even five percent Jewish blood there, I will be proud of it. But it isn't there." This statement, however far it is from science, seems sincere.

And yet there is a simpler way of noticing that a man is not Jewish. We used the same washroom at Mir, and I can say that Zhirinovsky could never pass for Jewish because he has not been circumcised.

I see nothing suspicious in the fact that Zhirinovsky considers himself Russian, the son of Volf Andreyevich Zhirinovsky, a legal consultant, even one who studied in Paris. I believe that, as a typical semi-orphan child of the postwar Soviet years, Zhirinovsky did not know who his real father was. His mother never talked about this with him, and so, I think, he fashioned for himself an ideal father, drawing on fantasy and borrowing favorite features from three real men, taking his last name and his nationality from one man, his middle name from another, and the profession he attributed to his father from a third. He even had a formal basis for the details of his claim: at school and at the Institute of Oriental Languages he was listed as a Russian and his patronymic was on the records as Volfovich. Everyone around him, his teachers and fellow pupils, knew him as Zhirinovsky, Volodya, the son of Volf, and a Russian.

Zhirinovsky was conceived at a chaotic time in Russian history. The war with Germany had just ended; the war with Japan was not quite over. Russian armies were being concentrated in the eastern part of the Soviet Union, because Stalin had promised Roosevelt that the USSR would enter the war against Japan three months after the defeat of Germany. An army of many millions had not yet begun to demobilize, millions had died, and there were millions of invalids—all young men of child-producing age. Millions of women on the home front had no men in their lives. Only a very few had husbands who could stay constantly by their sides. I, too, did not know my real father. I spent my school years under the name Pogodin, the last name of my grandfather. Not until the age of sixteen did I receive documents officially made out in the name Kartsev, my stepfather's name.

10. Kozlovsky, "Zhirinoviana: Genealogicheskoe drevo" (Zhirinovsky's family tree), 9.

When Zhirinovsky was born on April 25, 1946, World War II was over, but the Soviet Union was having difficulty catching its breath. It was a time of hunger; the stores were hardly functioning at all, and everything was rationed. Each worker was allotted a certain number of ration cards (those who did not work received none) that gave one the possibility of purchasing bread, sugar, flour. Without them, one could not buy anything in the stores, even with money. With ration cards, whose quantity varied depending on which category of worker one belonged to (some being more equal than others), one could in theory buy a maximum of two loaves of bread, a kilogram of flour, and a kilogram of meat each month. One could buy shoes once a year and an overcoat or a suit every two years. One could also trade ration cards, which served as a kind of foreign currency. Without them, at the Alaysky bazaar in Tashkent in 1946, a loaf of white bread cost one hundred rubles, while a loaf of black bread cost sixty rubles. A cleaning woman was paid three hundred rubles a month.

Zhirinovsky's mother was a cleaning woman, and she had six children to feed. No wonder she snitched a little food from the dining hall where she worked. In fact, petty thievery was universal in the Soviet Union. There was even a special term for those who pilfered from the plants or factories where they worked: *nesuny* (takers). In theory, the crime was punishable by law (before the war, such laws had been strictly enforced, and simply scavenging a little spilled grain could lead to a lengthy prison term), but after the war everyone understood that such petty theft was unavoidable, and it was overlooked. A new saying began making the rounds among Soviet humorists: "What's yours to guard is yours to have." This has proved to be an unusually long-lived slogan, whose accuracy was illustrated with particular vividness during the privatization in Russia in 1992–93.

The mother of six could also turn to the universal welfare system, under which the government provided everything except food and clothing, including medical care for mothers giving birth. Such medical care was, to put it mildly, imperfect. On the day of Vladimir's birth, the ambulance was late arriving. A retired midwife was summoned, but she, too, was late. The only person available to help Vladimir's mother as she gave birth was an uncle by marriage, who cut the umbilical cord with a kitchen knife.

As a working mother, toiling six days a week (as did all working people in the USSR back then), Aleksandra Pavlovna could not devote any substantial amount of time to the infant. He was immediately placed in a twenty-four-hour crèche that also cared for twenty other children. (On Sundays, the mother would bring her son home for the day.) Later, when Vladimir reached the age of three, he switched to a six-day-a-week kindergarten. On Sundays at home, he was left on his own: "At our house, I didn't even have my own corner of the room; there were no toys, and no children's books. I took books for grown-ups and read them—for example, Theodore Dreiser's *American Tragedy*," Zhirinovsky has recounted to me. Even on his first day of school, no one went with him or welcomed him home afterward. Understandably, he felt abandoned.

> From the time I was born I went everywhere alone, all by myself, to put it bluntly. And I always had a certain dissatisfied, angry, bitter feeling, because I never experienced any happiness, no happiness at all. No one ever welcomed me or greeted me; no one hugged or caressed me. Mama never had time; she had to work. I was still asleep when she left for work and had gone to bed by the time she came home; sometimes I didn't see her for a week. Even on Sunday, her only day off—when Saturday was made a holiday I had already left home—on Sunday she was also busy with various things: the laundry, the dishes, the housecleaning; they had to be done, especially because it was a communal apartment.[11]

He had no warm shoes or boots for the cold Asiatic winter, and no nice clothes (though this was true for all children at that time; I well remember walking to school in Tashkent in 1952 wearing women's boots that had belonged to my aunt, an army doctor, and a refashioned overcoat of my grandfather's). His clothes were bought at the *barakholka*, a kind of chaotic, illegal flea market, where people sold just about anything, including old clothes of suspicious origin, possibly even taken from the dead. The mother bought whatever was cheapest and patched it up.

There is nothing particularly noteworthy about Zhirinovsky's school years. He studied at a school where Russian was the language of instruction, and his fellow pupils included Russians, Jews, Germans, Koreans, Uigurs, Dungans, Kirghiz, Greeks, and Kazakhs. His schoolwork was fairly average, although by nature he was undoubtedly quite capable. He devoted much of his time to civic activity as a member of the Komsomol (the Young Communist League, known as the "true helper of the Communist Party," to which virtually all young people in the USSR belonged); he was often elected as one of the class officers and served as chairman of the council of his class's Komsomol detachment. He was even a Komsomol organizer, although that brief experience

11. Zhirinovsky, *Poslednii brosok na iug* (The last dash to the south), 7.

ended badly: never one to knuckle under to those in charge, he was deemed "unreliable" and reduced to the ranks by the class leader, the English teacher Esterna Blinder. He also took part in the people's courts that were very much in fashion at the time and that partially—in the case of petty crimes or minor violations—replaced the regular judicial system. In one civic trial organized at his school, a case against two pupils who had stolen spare parts from an auto repair shop, Zhirinovsky took the role of prosecutor and gave a notably impassioned speech. Such early practice honing his talents has borne fruit: now, when Zhirinovsky accuses someone or criticizes something, he does it with unsurpassed mastery and with an eloquence that is sometimes sincere, sometimes artful, and worthy of any professional prosecutor.

Zhirinovsky's decision to attend the Institute of Oriental Languages seems to have been virtually programmed into him as a result of being born and raised in an Asian republic. As Zhirinovsky confided to me in 1984–85, after finishing eleven grades at the best Russian high school in Alma-Ata, where he was photographed on the last day of classes with his schoolmates, his first friends (fleeting), and his first loves (unrequited), he arrived at Moscow's Vnukovo—the airport for domestic flights—on an IL-18, the pride of Soviet aviation, on July 3, 1964. He carried a worn suitcase containing underwear, darned socks, second-hand clothing, books with which to prepare for the entrance examinations (documents and money were pinned to a secret pocket of his trousers), and a basket filled with the gifts of Asia—real tomatoes, the taste of which was prized throughout the USSR, and young sweet strawberries. The basket was to serve as grease for his first visit to the institute's selection commission.

For fifty kopecks a bus took him from the airport to the center of Moscow, to Revolution Square, across the street from the building housing the USSR Council of Ministers (and subsequently the State Duma, where he would one day struggle for a "New Russia"). From there, he had to find his way to the Institute of Oriental Languages. At that time it was impossible to buy tourist guides to Moscow, not because it was feared they would reveal secrets to the enemy, as in the past, but because publishing houses' first duty was to publish politically correct and propagandistic literature. Yet in Moscow were institutions little known to the rest of the world: public information bureaus where, for fifty kopecks, one could receive the address—complete with directions—and telephone number of any citizen or institution in the whole Soviet Union. This achievement of the Communist system was made possible by the system of registration. No privacy was allowed, and since no one under any circumstances could lawfully have two residences, keeping track of people's addresses was a simple process. The information kiosks stood near all metro and train stations. From one of them Volodya learned that the Institute of Oriental Languages (formerly the Oriental Faculty of Moscow State University and later given the more politically correct name Institute for the Countries of Asia and Africa) was nearby—housed in one of the lovely buildings of the old university on Mokhovaya Street, just across Marx Prospect and Gorky Street and behind the National Hotel.

The selection committee, composed of young assistant professors and language laboratory assistants, gave the seventeen-year-old a rather frosty reception. They were clearly unimpressed by his documents and records, including a report card that showed more fours (Bs) than fives (As) and even a few threes. Moreover, as an out-of-towner, he would need accommodations arranged for him. But his greatest flaw was that he lacked a recommendation from the Komsomol *raikom* (district committee).

This may have been the young Zhirinovsky's first experience with the Communist Party's disregard of law, with assumed party omnipotence, an experience sooner or later inevitable for everyone living in the Soviet Union. A recommendation from the Komsomol and its *raikom* was not formally required for enrollment in any institute at all. Why then should Zhirinovsky need one? The answer is simple: Future graduates of the institute would work with foreigners as translators, diplomats, representatives abroad, and bureaucrats of Soviet institutions dealing with foreigners. A recommendation from the Komsomol guaranteed the primordial ideological reliability of a candidate and his or her adherence to party criteria. Most important, it guaranteed eventual party control over the individual.[12]

Dismissed until he could present the proper credentials, Volodya didn't know where to go. Hotels were cheap then—one or two rubles per day—but to get a room one had to pay a bribe or bring authorization from Moscow's Department of Hotel Services, impossible for anyone with no contacts. Volodya had neither money nor connections, so he took a commuter train to the home of his older brother outside the city.

12. The secretary of the Komsomol district committee belonged to the bureau of the corresponding party district committee and usually sat alongside the other mandatory member of the bureau—the chairman of the district KGB, whose chief function was to ensure unanimity of opinion and root out dissidence and heresy at its base. The Komsomol and KGB were bosom partners; indeed, many KGB leaders were former Komsomol secretaries.

From his brother's place, Volodya telegraphed his mother that he needed a recommendation from the Komsomol. She rushed to the high school to see what she could do, but it was summer vacation—no one was there. She then went to the Komsomol regional committee and finagled the recommendation.[13] The achievement was quite remarkable. If the committee had known there was a possibility that Zhirinovsky had a Jewish parent, it could, if necessary, quickly have found a reason not to issue the recommendation. For that matter, Zhirinovsky's far-from-brilliant academic record would have given the committee a perfect reason to refuse him.

After he received the long-awaited registered letter from Alma-Ata, Volodya brought his papers to the selection committee and was allowed to take the entrance examinations. He was also given temporary lodging in the student dormitories where some rooms had emptied for the summer. There, Volodya prepared for the five examinations in composition, spoken Russian, written Russian, the history of the USSR, and spoken and written English. He needed a total of eighteen points to pass—only one less than was required for acceptance into the elite Moscow State Institute of Foreign Relations, which turned out diplomats. He was certain of five points in history, a subject he knew and loved. His Russian was somewhat doubtful, however, and his English was a disaster. Where was one supposed to find in Alma-Ata—and in Russian schools in general—good teachers of English? The students had never even seen an English person or an American. The English then taught in Russian schools bore little resemblance to that spoken by natives. He had to do something about it.

Fortunately, the selection committee took pity on the Alma-Ata native and recommended a tutor for the English examination. Back then, tutoring was a flourishing business largely monopolized by teachers from the higher educational institutions, many of whom were connected with the selection committee and capable of influencing its decisions. Such influence did not come cheap, however. Judging by the small fee Zhirinovsky's tutor charged—one hundred rubles, or ten rubles per session—he was in no position to sway the committee but instead honestly tried to fill in the more egregious gaps in Zhirinovsky's knowledge. For Zhirinovsky, though, this was a fortune, and once again he sent a telegram home, this time with the standard student text: "Love you, kiss you, send money."

13. Maureen Orth maintains that the name on his passport was changed from Edelshtein to Zhirinovsky at about this time. See Orth, "Nightmare on Red Square," 82.

Why should a healthy seventeen-year-old have to ask his mommy, with her miserable pay, for money? The answer is simple: the Communist system. All earnings were strictly regulated. The goal of maintaining full employment meant that part-time jobs were practically forbidden. Nor did Zhirinovsky have the option of making products since that required a license not given to students. Paying for babysitting was considered disgraceful, so that means of earning was also out of the question. In general, the party viewed supplemental income as shameful—any desire to have more was a sign of immodesty. Consequently, the only cash young people had, if not the fruit of thievery, came out of their parents' pockets.

Not many Asian provincials made it into the capital's prestigious higher institutions without connections or bribes. An education received anywhere other than Moscow was considered inferior, and provincials confronted the natural arrogance of Muscovites in general and especially of their fellows in the institutes. But the results of Zhirinovsky's entrance examinations testified to his abilities and preparation. His being from Kazakhstan might even have worked in his favor: all institutes in Russia were required to enroll a certain number of provincials, and their examination results were evaluated somewhat more leniently when quotas still had to be met. Even so, this was an incontestable success for the young man, who had demonstrated a capacity to set ambitious goals for himself and to achieve them.[14]

14. Zhirinovsky did not tell me much about his university years and his work before Mir. Those who are interested may find relevant information in his *Poslednii brosok na iug* (The last dash to the south), an English translation of which will soon be published in the USA by Barricade.

3

Zhirinovsky, the KGB, and Me

One of the most widespread and persistent allegations lodged against Vladimir Zhirinovsky is that he is connected to the KGB. His accusers maintain that the Communist Party of the Soviet Union and the KGB, in the course of ostensibly withdrawing from the political scene forever, devised a plan by which Zhirinovsky's party would first become a legal puppet opposition to replace the real opposition represented by Yeltsin and eventually the possible ideological heir of both the CPSU and the KGB. According to this scenario, the LDPR inherited these two organizations' money, which it subsequently used to buy itself votes in the 1991 and 1993 elections. So Saint Petersburg's mayor, Anatoly Sobchak, stated to me during a conversation I had with him at the United Nations in 1993. This view was also supported by KGB general Oleg Kalugin, 1959 graduate of the Columbia University School of Journalism, spy, and head of Soviet counterintelligence, who has maintained in numerous interviews that although there is no evidence, he knows that Zhirinovsky infiltrated the system early on. General Kalugin's statements should be taken with a grain of salt, however, especially as his sensational revelations about American POWs and MIAs in Korea and Vietnam allegedly interrogated and detained by the KGB appear to have been bald-faced lies designed to revitalize declining media interest in him as a quotable source after Gorbachev's expulsion of him from the security organs.

Maureen Orth told me that one of the Russians she had interviewed for her *Vanity Fair* article on Zhirinovsky, former KGB colonel Aleksan-

dr Kichikhin—expelled from the organization for whistle-blowing—
claimed that he personally had no doubt that Zhirinovsky was being
used. "Look at it in terms of the kinds of jobs he got . . . ," he told her.
"Probably all the time from college on he was in contact with the KGB.
It's impossible to break off with this organization; they never leave you
alone."[1] Of course, the KGB, like the CIA, is a very mysterious entity
that holds its secrets close to the vest, and trying to get complete information on any matter involving either is tricky at best. Nevertheless, it
should be possible for someone like Kichikhin, who had access to *all*
Communist Party and KGB top secret files (he worked on President
Yeltsin's commission investigating the 1991 coup d'état), to be more
specific, instead of merely citing a number of interesting but not necessarily relevant documents.

Zhirinovsky himself, as well as top-level LDPR officials such as
Andrei Zavidia, who stood shoulder to shoulder with Zhirinovsky
when he struggled for the presidency of Russia in 1991, and Viktor
Kobelev, Zhirinovsky's 1993 campaign manager (both he and Zavidia
have since left the party), as well as Mikhail Gorbachev and former KGB
chief Vladimir Kryuchkov (whose frank confessions would be the ulti-
mate proof), consistently reject suggestions that there has been participation on the part of either the Communist Party or the KGB in creating
and financing the Liberal Democratic Party of Russia. Lately, however,
Zhirinovsky has not been reacting so heatedly to such rumors. Instead,
his response has been more along the lines of "I would really like to have
such a powerful sponsor and ally, but unfortunately that's not the case."

Still, as a result of the allegations, practically everyone who has written on the Zhirinovsky phenomenon depicts him as a dangerous KGB
creation run amok who, in the event he wins the next Russian presidential election, will immediately be replaced by someone even more
dangerous and more fanatical.[2] According to Tankred Golenpolsky,
currently editor in chief of the Moscow newspaper *Yevreisky Mir* (Jewish world) and a former colleague of mine at Sovaminco, a Soviet-
American joint-venture publishing company, "The moment he soars to
a top post, his Jewish origins will be remembered and he will be dis-
carded and replaced with a real Fascist."[3]

1. See also Orth, "Nightmare on Red Square," 97–99, and Menzheritsky,
"Vladimir Volfovich protiv Vladimira Volfovicha" (Vladimir Volfovich versus
Vladimir Volfovich), 5.
2. For dissenting voices, see Hockstader's analysis in the section titled "KGB
Ties? Accusers Lack Proof," in "How Russia's Zhirinovsky Rose" and Specter, "Why
Russia Loves This Man."
3. Orth, "Nightmare on Red Square," 100.

The question remains, is Zhirinovsky linked to the KGB and the Communist Party? If yes, then for how long? Does the connection date from his student days, as Kalugin maintains; from his Mir years, as Viktor Dashevsky says; or, as Sobchak avers, from 1990, the year Zhirinovsky's party was founded? Answering this question—finding out, once and for all, who has backed and is backing Zhirinovsky and might assume power in the event of his victory—is extremely important for the well-being of people and their governments the world over. Are Zhirinovsky's true masters KGB orphans, such as the Russian Federative Security Service, or one or more of the contemporary Russian parties that have inherited some of the baggage of the former Communist Party of Russia, such as the Communist Party headed by Gennady Zyuganov and Nina Andreyeva's All-Union Communist Party (of Bolsheviks)? Do they, their views, programs, intentions, and methods represent a real force and real danger for today's world? To begin to respond to these concerns, I will tackle the following two-part question: (1) beginning in the mid-1960s, did the KGB use Zhirinovsky as its agent, and (2) since the mid-1980s, has the KGB thought of him as its hope and a future heir to the Communist Party?

I can shed a little light on this question. The KGB was a common topic of my conversations with Zhirinovsky from 1983 to 1989, a period when I was also in constant contact with the KGB in the Dzerzhinsky district, where Mir was located. Moreover, being practically of the same generation as Zhirinovsky—I am eight years older—and traveling in approximately the same social circles, I can use my experience as a model for what could have happened to Zhirinovsky. Comparison will allow me to bridge some of the gaps in information about KGB involvement in Zhirinovsky's life. In addition, travel beyond the Soviet Union's borders is a splendid indicator both of an individual's relationship to the authorities, especially the party and the KGB—and the depth of their trust or mistrust.[4]

One of those striving to find a Zhirinovsky-KGB affiliation is the very influential Russian journalist Yevgeniya Albats, whose experience working on various presidential and Supreme Soviet committees and access to the KGB's most secret files has undeniably made her one of the leading experts on the KGB.[5] Even Russian superspy Yevgeny Pri-

4. A recommendation for travel to a fraternal socialist country, for instance, demanded the consent of party organs, but a trip to hostile capitalist countries required the direct approval of the KGB.

5. Albats's good opinion is so valued that the American ambassador to Russia, Thomas Pickering, apologized to her after she accused American consulate officers in Moscow of acting rudely toward Russians applying for visas.

makov, the academician who heads the Federal Service of Counterintelligence , one of the branches of the new KGB, granted her a lengthy interview during which he spoke candidly about his organization. She has also written a book about the KGB for Farrar, Straus, and Giroux. However, in my own long conversation with her at the beginning of 1994, she could not provide me with any concrete evidence of Zhirinovsky's KGB connections. Instead, she tried to get information from me. I think she had met with me in the secret hope that I was the missing link that would finally and resoundingly prove her theory. Aware that I had been director of Mir Publishing House and Zhirinovsky's direct superior, she quite likely considers me to be the very individual who recruited or recommended Zhirinovsky for the KGB.

She is not alone in this opinion. Not long ago, someone anonymously sent me an article quoting a certain Viktor Dashevsky:

> In 1987–1988 Zhirinovsky sharply criticized Gorbachev and condemned the war in Afghanistan. The director [of Mir], Kartsev, scared to death, phoned the KGB, after which the authorized KGB agent for Moscow's Dzerzhinsky district called Zhirinovsky in for a talk. That is most likely when his contact with that organization began. Apparently, it is also when he began receiving money from them and they, in turn, began counting on him—especially when in 1991 Politizdat [Political Publishing House] published the program of his Liberal-Democratic Party, even though there was no such party and Gorbachev was still running the country. Incidentally, the sources of Zhirinovsky's financing to this day remain unknown.[6]

Vladimir Solovyov and Elena Klepikova, the husband-wife team of emigré journalists who have written extensively on modern Russian politics, borrowed from Dashevsky, quoting him without attribution in their own forthcoming book on Zhirinovsky, excerpts of which appeared in the leading Russian-language daily in America, *Novoye Russkoye Slovo*. And so the snowball continues to grow. The situation reminds me of an article I once approved for publication, following a fierce battle with the editorial board, in the journal *Historical Problems of Natural Science and Technology*. The piece described the mechanism used to create the myth in the USSR that the bicycle was invented by a serf named Artamonov. The author skillfully traced the path by which a vague mention in a newspaper one hundred fifty years ago of someone showing up at a tsar's coronation riding a two-wheeled carriage grad-

6. Kontsevaya, "Borot'sa s fashizmom v Rossii" (To struggle against fascism in Russia), 1.

ually evolved into a story featuring a "real" person complete with name, patronymic, and surname, followed by the alleged discovery in some forgotten archive of a description of the carriage's actual construction, which, incredibly, looked just like a contemporary bicycle. Presto! The Russians had once again rubbed the foreigners' noses in the dirt, having invented the bicycle a half century before the French!

Since Dashevsky has already introduced my name and since Solovyov and Klepikova have already added to the legend, which the next generation of journalists will inevitably embellish further, I feel compelled now to give a frank report of my relationship with the KGB and Zhirinovsky. After all, it is hardly a sensational revelation: very few people with successful state careers in the former Soviet Union managed to avoid contact with the KGB, and anyone who says otherwise is either disingenuous or blessed with a faulty memory.

At the beginning of the 1960s, when I was a postgraduate student at the Moscow Power Institute preparing to defend my first doctoral dissertation on superconductivity, I taught evening classes at the All-Union Polytechnic Institute. I would go there at around six in the evening and sometimes stay until midnight with students who wanted to improve their education without having to abandon their daytime jobs. As a rule, these were people already on a career track—engineers and shop, divisional, and even departmental managers and specialists—who lacked formal higher education or sufficient knowledge in their particular fields, which could have limited their chances of advancement. To avert such potential disaster, people already busy with families, children, and professions would devote practically all their free evenings and weekends to earning their engineering diplomas over a six-year period.

In early 1965 I became friendly with one of my students, Nikolai Vakhromychev, my senior by about five years, who was deputy director at a secret plant. After having brilliantly defended his diploma, he took me aside following a ceremonial banquet and said, "Volodya, I am very grateful to you for what you've done for me. I want to do something for you. I have some party ties. If you want, I'll help you get an apartment, a dacha, a car, a garage, and a pass to get into special shops. What do you want?"

"Nikolai, I don't want any of that. The only thing I would really like to do is travel abroad and see a bit of the world. But you can't help me with that."

"You're right, that's a tough one. Where would you go?"

"To England. I'd like to see a real queen," I said jocularly.

"Forget about it. I could understand Bulgaria, maybe."[7]

Naturally, I would have liked to go to America. Since the time of the World Festival of Youth and Students held in Moscow in 1957 and especially since 1959, when I shook the hand of Vice President Richard Nixon who was standing near the entrance to the first American exhibition in our capital, I had been openly Americanized (while remaining a Russian patriot, of course), a kind of Russian dandy known back then as a *stilyaga*. I wore skintight pants, thick-soled shoes, and an Elvis Presley–style haircut. I loved American literature and had a collection of popular American music, including records by Ella Fitzgerald and Dinah Washington. I was enamored of American cars and read *Scientific American* in the library. (Comparison of the two societies and their achievements had led me to the unambiguous conclusion that something was not quite right with mine—seditious thinking in the fifties and sixties.) But mainly I was in awe of American scientists with their discoveries and laboratories. Their successes in the field of superconductivity, the field in which I worked, were simply incredible.

So why did I choose England instead of the United States? Because I didn't take Vakhromychev's question all that seriously. Even though the border had opened slightly following the World Festival of Youth and Students, travel outside the country was still virtually inaccessible, a prospect both mysterious and seductive for the overwhelming majority of the population. Those who had been abroad took on a new status and were invited to clubs to talk about what they had seen. A popular television show of the period was *The Club of Movie Travelers*, in which anyone who had made an amateur film while traveling abroad could count on the rapt attention of all Soviet viewers. Names like India, Thailand, Holland, and Brazil confounded the senses. I remember a tantalizing report my friend Zhenya Petrov published in a local newspaper. Under the heading "Prague-Brno-Bratislava," he described small cafes—unheard-of in the Soviet Union—where one could sit all evening long listening to music while sipping a single cup of coffee, shops with forty different kinds of sausage, and other amazing things. Our youthful eyes dimmed with lust when we read a serial epic on Czechoslovak automobile enthusiasts who had crossed half the globe in their Skodas, stopping to tune up their vehicles in full view of Mount Kilimanjaro.

The obsessive desire to travel was yet another anomaly of Soviet life,

7. At that time, Bulgaria was not considered beyond the border—Soviet citizens used to joke in the 1960s, "Kuritsa—nie ptitsa, Bolgaria—nie zagranitsa" (A hen is not a bird, Bulgaria is not abroad)—but even traveling there was not easy.

perhaps without analogy anywhere else in the world. If the border had been more permeable, this yearning to change places might not have become such a fixation. Yet this desire has long existed in Russia. Only the tsar personally could grant permission for travel outside the country. Pushkin, who was never allowed to leave, died with an unsatisfied yearning to see the world. In the Soviet Union, as in tsarist Russia, travel abroad just for the hell of it, without the blessing of the authorities, was impossible at any price. The official tourist agency, Intourist, almost exclusively served the families of party and government functionaries.

"I can't promise you anything yet, but I'll speak to some of my friends and contact you," Vakhromychev said when we parted. A week later he called to explain that making arrangements was going to be complicated, but he nevertheless asked whether I was married and a member of the Komsomol [the Russian acronym for the Young Communist League]. At twenty-seven, I was both. By this age, true Communists had already handed in their applications to join the party, and at age twenty-eight, when their tenure with the Young Communists officially ended, they were expected to make the smooth transition to their next incarnation as full-fledged members of the Communist Party. Skeptical of party slogans, I was not intending to join the party, a decision made easier because I was seriously involved in scientific work, where neither party affiliation nor nationality played such a critical role in one's career. The sciences were filled with nonparty Russians and Jews, among them my first mentors, professors P. Kapitsa, E. Kasharsky, and E. Kazovsky. Still, for now anyway, I belonged to the correct—and only—political club.

"Well then, if you're married and a Komsomolets [a Young Communist League member], that's good. Then there's hope. You'll have to make yourself more visible, get involved in some community work. I've already arranged with the Moscow City Committee of the Komsomol for you to be a freelance instructor in their department of propaganda. Go there today to see Yuri Lunkov. He needs people like you."

At the Moscow City Committee of the Komsomol, then occupying offices on the second floor of a luxurious prerevolutionary home on Kolpachny Lane, I encountered a group of truly capable individuals. The committee's first secretary, Boris Nikolayevich Pastukhov—whom everyone called Pastukh (shepherd)—was a man of outstanding talents, indisputably progressive for those times. (He is currently deputy minister of Russia's Ministry of Foreign Affairs, responsible for the "near abroad," primarily Georgia; Yuri Gavrilovich Lunkov, too, is now

a prominent diplomat in the Ministry of Foreign Affairs.) Pastukhov
was passionate about all kinds of Young Communist innovations. He
founded the first Institute of Public Opinion to study the true views
and interests of youth. Aware from the institute's research that the concept of the Young Communist in its dogmatic form was becoming unattractive and obsolete, he was searching for a new ideology and fresh
ideas. Unfortunately, there being no strong intellectual tradition in the
party and the Komsomol, Pastukhov's search for ideological alternatives led mainly to the rise of homegrown patriotic movements, some
of which acquired openly reactionary traits over time. For example,
Molodaya Gvardiya (Young Guard), the publishing house of the Young
Communist League's Central Committee, filled with graduates from
the committee, acquired the regrettable reputation of being openly
anti-Semitic. (I remember bringing my outline for a biography of Newton there. For a long time the editor shuffled the pages in her hands
until finally she spotted my subject's first name, Isaac. "You're coming
to us with *this*?" she asked incredulously.) Valery Skurlatov, who had
worked as an instructor in the propaganda department of the Moscow
City Committee of the Komsomol, organized an openly racist under-
ground group with its own code of morals, which was clandestinely
copied and widely distributed as samizdat. The code championed the
cult of race, alluding to the "voices of Russian blood" and "the cosmic
role of the Russian people"; invoking "duty toward one's ancestors," it
advocated the sterilization of women who consorted with foreigners
and other such programs. Yuri Zhivlyuk, the secretary of one of the
Komsomol organizations at the Physics Institute of the USSR Academy
of Sciences, sent this document to the Central Committee of the Young
Communist League, where it came as a complete surprise. Both parties
were punished, Skurlatov for committing ideological mistakes, and
Zhivlyuk for airing dirty linen in public. The rebuke had little effect on
Skurlatov, however; time has not softened his views, and in the 1990s
he founded a new party that borders on the fascistic.

In the search for a new national and ideological identity, some forgotten Russian authors were unearthed. In addition to the "Russian
idea," young people in the 1960s could find in the works of Vladimir
Solovyov, Nikolai Berdyaev, and Sergei Bulgakov the formulations of
genuine freedom and democracy and read for the first time about universal love and compassion. These works feature the long-suffering
Russian, full of empathy for all suffering and fallen creatures; the "Russian dream" and the Russian people's capacity for self-restraint and
self-sacrifice in the cause of peace; Russian messianism; the possibility

of replacing government and bureaucratic interference in people's lives with national discussion; the priority of spirituality and creativity, heroism, and asceticism. The negative features of Russians were also delineated at length: sloth, sloppiness on the job, expectation of manna from heaven, the inclination to act by intuition or leave things to chance rather than plan anything in advance. The "Russian idea" was often contrasted with Westernism, with its notions of personal liberty and the primacy of the individual over society.

It would be unfair, however, to dismiss all patriotic and national Russian movements as reactionary. Patriotic movements, from the time of their inception in the Komsomol depths in 1964–65, came in many forms. They arose in reaction to the October 1964 plenum of the party's Central Committee, which removed Nikita Khrushchev and hinted at the possible restoration of Stalinism. In Soviet society an obvious and not-so-obvious struggle for ideological influence took hold—a struggle between the Communist regime, gravitating toward ever more conservative political and ideological positions, and social forces, both inside and outside the party, opposing the conservatives. A widespread sentiment for change had developed inside the party and its apparatus (the party and the Komsomol then had members numbering in the tens of millions). Faced with the double impossibility of following the example of Western democratic values, which were taboo by definition, and that of the Eastern cultures, which were held in low regard, patriotism seemed like the only option. Only later did some of its variations take on extreme, misshapen forms.

There is very little information in the West about ideological struggle within the party.[8] Generally speaking, more or less peripheral ideological movements in Soviet society (dissidence, samizdat) were widely known and studied outside the USSR, while mainstream opposition within the party, which eventually brought Gorbachev to power, has not been considered. The highly publicized dissident trials, the dramatic personal lives of Sakharov and Bonner, and the infamous *psikhushki* were more newsworthy than ideological struggles at countless party meetings.[9] Consider, for example, that only six or seven Sovi-

8. See Medvedev. *Lichnost' i epokha* (The individual and the era).

9. See Reddaway and Bloch, *Soviet Psychiatric Abuse*; Reddaway, *Uncensored Russia*. This last reprints in English translation the first several issues of *Khronika tekushchikh sobytii* (Chronicle of Current Events), reorganized thematically with extensive commentary and annotation. *Khronika tekushchikh sobytii* was an uncensored samizdat publication that appeared regularly in the USSR from 1968 through the mid-1970s.

et dissidents openly protested in Red Square the invasion of Czechoslovakia in 1968, whereas millions of party members participated in hot discussions on the subject and a great many were against the invasion, wrote letters, protested, and so on. In fact, after the trial of Andrei Sinyavsky and Yuli Daniel, who were arrested in 1965, not a single dissident trial passed unnoticed within the Soviet Union: aside from the usual contingent of judge, lawyers, participants, and witnesses, the audience would include samizdat writers and BBC and Voice of America commentators. Of course, the outcomes of these trials had already been more or less decided by the party; courtroom procedure was a formality. Public information about the trials, though biased, nevertheless existed—something unthinkable during Stalin's time and even during Khrushchev's.

So far, little is known about the really massive intraparty struggle in the arena of ideology. However, a liberal and highly progressive (for its day) current of party ideology did begin making itself known in the beginning of 1965—albeit in the usual veiled, allusive form—in a *Pravda* article by its then editor in chief, A. M. Rumyantsev, behind whom stood the international departments of the Central Committee, headed by Boris Ponomaryov and Yuri Andropov. Rumyantsev advocated that the party stand by the decisions made at the Twentieth and Twenty-first Party Congresses espousing intraparty democracy and opposing the rehabilitation of Stalin. The liberal line was also touted in the journal *Novy Mir* (New world), whose editor, Aleksandr Tvardovsky, published an article promoting criticism, debate, and "discussion, no matter how sharp they might be."[10]

The conservative, pro-Stalin line was led by the party's point man on ideology and certainly one of the grayest of all the gray Soviet gerontocrats, Mikhail Suslov, abetted by Sergei Trapeznikov, head of the party's department of science and higher educational institutions. A complicated situation arose in the Moscow City Committee of the Komsomol. Though directly subordinate to the conservative Suslov, the committee sympathized with the liberal trend. The patriotic movement, a concept acceptable to the party bosses, became in essence a cover for liberal viewpoints. The few engaged critics only saw the reactionary groups of nationalists and patriots and had no inkling of the whole spectrum of Komsomol free thinking. The Komsomols included virtually all young Soviets: moderate nationalists who had raised the question of the factual nonexistence and dilution of Russia in the USSR

10. See Medvedev, *Lichnost' i epokha* (The individual and the era), 139–49.

(for just one example, every republic had its own academy of sciences and the state had its USSR Academy of Sciences, but there was no Russian academy); radical patriots; racist patriots; monarchist patriots; adherents of "ethical socialism"; Christian socialists, who drew parallels between an ideal communist society and a society based on the teachings of Jesus Christ, as set forth in a book by Hewlett Johnson called *Christianity and Communism*. There were also the proponents of a democratic Communist Party later defined as "socialism with a human face."

At the Moscow City Committee of the Komsomol, Boris Pastukhov and Yuri Lunkov welcomed nonconformism and a broad range of free thinking. After all, they themselves had called for change, the right of free discussion and disagreement with the official line, in direct opposition to the orthodox thinking of the country's main ideologue. I remember stormy meetings when we expostulated aloud, though rather circumspectly, on the need for new ideas in the Komsomol. "Argument," Lunkov would say. "That's the word, that's the secret. Everybody is afraid to say anything that is meaningful and unorthodox. We have to organize debates and discussions. Discussions at Komsomol meetings and congresses, discussions in the newspapers, on the radio and television. Down with all the approved views! We don't have to agree with everything! Give us new ideas!"

With the help of his instructors, Lunkov selected the first groups to participate in a new discussion club, which he was determined would be shown on central television. Locating several freethinking students from Moscow State University and the Institute of Oriental Languages, where Komsomol members had organized their own discussion club, he proposed that they discuss the idea of democracy as it was understood both at home and abroad. His goal was simply to challenge some of the Komsomol's petrified views.

Two of the participants in one of these discussions, the first held in the summer of 1965 and the last in December 1967, were Komsomol leaders at the Institute of Oriental Languages, Vladimir Kozlovsky and Vladimir Zhirinovsky. Without inhibition, they said things that could have landed them in jail just ten years earlier. Their televised debates became the talk of the town. Though I do not remember their words exactly, they left the impression that they were openly advocating dramatic changes in the Soviet system and praising Western democratic institutions. There was a joyous outburst in the Moscow City Committee of the Komsomol—these were exactly the kinds of individuals capable of provoking argument, the standard-bearers of new ideas. The

Moscow City Committee of the party thought otherwise. Not only did it not support the Moscow Komsomol, but it issued a warning as well. Kozlovsky and Zhirinovsky were branded as suspicious types.

"There you have it, Volodya," said Lunkov, "We'll do another televised debate now. We'll invite the well-bred, the famous and authoritative. Let them duke it out. What is not permissible for the lads from the Komsomol is okay for our national artists and scientists. You go on, too, but don't raise such a ruckus." On his own, he decided to invite artists and scientists to tackle the issue of *podvizhnichestvo*, a typically Russian attitude toward creative activity and creative freedom that favors asceticism and subordination of the self to society. The program lasted one hour and was broadcast throughout the Soviet Union. Its freewheeling tone amazed everyone. But, even though the only topics under discussion were creative freedom and *asceticism*, the idea of creating without concern for possible repercussions, the plug was eventually pulled on this program as well.

My job as a freelance instructor for the Moscow City Committee of the Komsomol allowed me to add to my request for travel abroad a recommendation that included the decisive and absolutely necessary statements: "His political consciousness is highly developed, he is of irreproachable morality, and he lives modestly in his personal life. He can be recommended for the trip." Not only did I get to travel to England as part of a youth package arranged by the newly created youth tourist bureau Sputnik, but the itinerary was set out in such a way as to satisfy the wishes of each member of the group. My dream to see the queen was realized with the help of Hewlett Johnson, the "red dean" of Canterbury, a long-time friend of the Soviet Union and proponent of Christian socialism. Mikhail Suslov's daughter wanted to see the Beatles and spend a week with her husband, who was then on a work-study program with a computer firm in England. The wish of Irina Mitrofanova, researcher at the Pushkin Museum, was to visit certain divisions of the British Museum. Dzhondo Natradze, a surgeon, wanted to see a hospital where neurosurgical operations were performed.

Practically the entire group was connected with the KGB in one way or another. This thought first struck me during the flight to Heathrow Airport in London. We traveled in a TU-104, the first jet-propelled passenger airplane in the world. During the descent into London the landing gear of the plane failed to function, and we had to ascend once more and circle over Europe. Panic reigned in the cabin. Suslov's daughter, sitting next to me, had had an unlucky premonition about the trip; she became extremely agitated and called to a few people in the back rows—also "tourists"—who marched resolutely toward the cockpit. There was no doubt as to their affiliation with state security. I have no idea what they said or did, but the landing gear came out right away, and we landed without further incident.

Everyone in the group knew that the meeting with the queen had been arranged on my behalf, and, as a result, I was a hot shot for a while. On the eve of our Easter procession in the court of the Canterbury Cathedral, I awoke to a quiet knocking on my door in the Canterbury guest house. It was long past midnight. I opened the door to find an engineer from Siberia, one of the two non-Muscovites in the group. Without speaking, he indicated that I was to follow him out to the courtyard because it was not safe to speak where we were. Half-asleep and uncomprehending, I nevertheless agreed. My companion, Yevgeny B. (some names in this text have been changed, for obvious reasons), led me under the canopy of hundred-year-old elms surrounding the square in front of our quarters. He quietly turned on a transistor radio and began to whisper in my ear: "Volodya, I've been watching you all this time, and I see that you are a reliable and decent person. I can be frank with you. I'm a captain in state security. Tomorrow we are meeting the queen. There will be a big crowd. I'm not worried about you, but I have my suspicions about Mitrofanova and Natradze. They might try to leave."

"Leave? To go where?"

"Run away. Betray the motherland." His eyes sparkled in the darkness. "I have an assignment for you. Make sure they don't leave. Otherwise . . ."

"Where would they go? They have families, interesting jobs, apartments, children."

"I've told you everything I can. If you see something, let me know. I'll be standing near the tower. But if they leave, watch out . . ."

Naturally, I couldn't fall asleep again after that.

In the cool and overcast morning, we all set out for Canterbury Cathedral. There was indeed a crush of people, and Yevgeny B. pushed me closer to Mitrofanova and Natradze. But I was totally absorbed by the spectacle of the queen, the duke of Edinburgh, the Queen Mother, and the royal children. If Mitrofanova and Natradze had decided to duck out of the crowd, they could easily have done so. They made no attempt to leave, however, and B., evidently occupied with matters of greater importance, disappeared right before the meeting with the queen, only turning up again at the end of the day, soaked, tired, and in a foul mood.

In the evening some local girls invited me and another guy from the group to a dance. In accordance with our instructions, I informed our group leader. Later, in the bar, while casually looking out the window, I spotted B. outdoors, absorbed in tying his shoelaces—this time he was keeping an eye on us.

The girls were unsuccessful in recruiting us as agents, not that they even bothered to try. My innocent behavior apparently led B. to recommend me to the resident agents in London. On our arrival there, I was invited to the Soviet Embassy, where a gloomy character bluntly proposed that I collaborate with the KGB. I hedged, citing my poor athletic abilities, shortsightedness, absentmindedness, and bad memory. Neither surprised nor even the slightest bit disappointed, he asked me in passing if I would snap some photos of B. in various locales around London. I subsequently realized—unfortunately, after the embassy driver had, with utmost caution, relieved me of my film—that it was not B. but the backdrops that were important: I had probably (and unwittingly) carried out my first assignment for the KGB.

Later, after talking with many of my friends, I concluded that almost every more or less prominent Soviet citizen traveling abroad, regardless of his or her future ties to the organization, passed through a similar trial as a kind of loyalty test. I also know that several refused, but the omnipotence of the KGB was such that refusal was very difficult. For someone with a career, it was even more damaging than not being a party member was, for the latter shortcoming could always be attributed to political and ideological immaturity, whereas refusing to cooperate for the good of the motherland could only be viewed as pernicious behavior.

When I finally did join the party in 1969 (the implication having been made that if I remained unaffiliated, I would not be made dean of the faculty of Advanced Studies), I still did not realize how close the ties were among the party, the KGB, and my routine life and work. Immediately after joining I was surprised by an invitation from a Major V., head of the newly established Babushkinsky district department of the KGB, to visit him at a private apartment on Galushkina Street. He said he had a thick dossier on me, knew practically everything about my life, and was pleased that I had joined the party. He also informed me that, despite my objections in London to cooperating directly with the KGB, I was now obligated as a party member to report to the KGB anything that could threaten the security and well-being of the Soviet state.

"We don't demand anything of you, but we do expect you to take your new party responsibilities seriously," the major told me.

Because I had not exactly been a fount of information for an extended period of time, at eleven o'clock one evening I was again summoned. This time, however, the conversation took place out on the street, to the accompaniment of a miniature transistor radio intended to guard against the possibility of eavesdropping.

For a long time, we walked along the quiet Moscow streets—back then completely safe at any time of the day or night. The major began on a curious note, almost paraphrasing the discussion that Kozlovsky and Zhirinovsky had participated in, lauding the merits of American democracy and the American electoral system. Fearing a provocation, I answered him with the orthodox criticism that clearly distinguished the freethinker from the dissident. The major frowned.

"All right, we'll leave you alone. But we hope you'll help us."

"Help you with what?"

"We know a lot. We know that you are meeting with Academician Sakharov. We would like to know more about him."

I found the courage to refuse, claiming that Sakharov and I were not such great friends, that he was much higher than I on the social ladder and did not particularly trust me. I also resolved never to call Sakharov again, even though we had earlier agreed that I should.

In 1968 I had indeed become acquainted with Andrei Sakharov and had seen him on several occasions. He had showed me his only copy of *Reflections on Progress, Peaceful Coexistence, and Intellectual Freedom*. I was shaken. Here were the answers to the questions that had long been tormenting me and my colleagues: convergence, borrowing the best elements both societies had to offer, socialism with a truly human face. Sakharov had also written a very nice foreword to my book *A Treatise on Attraction*. In my signed copy to him I had written "Success in *all* your beginnings," meaning the beginning of his new political activism. But like an idiot, I had sent the book through the regular mail instead of giving it to him personally, as a result of which the KGB had direct evidence of our meetings. No doubt my visits to his large, beautiful, airy apartment near the Kurchatov Institute for Atomic Energy, filled with many voices and the sounds of classical music, were under constant observation: as the creator of the Soviet hydrogen bomb, he knew a considerable number of the government's most important secrets; as an outstanding physicist, he was a target of interest for many intelligence agencies; and as a beginning dissident, he was of interest to the KGB.

From the time of my refusal to spy on Sakharov, I became untravelworthy, a condition further exacerbated by my divorce. In spite of my entreaties and complaints, directed as high as the party's Moscow City Committee and its secretary for ideology, the KGB put me in quarantine for travel to capitalist countries. I learned of the quarantine by chance. One day out of the blue, Znanie (Knowledge), which had published my book *Superconductors in Physics and Technology*, received a letter from the publisher Mondadori in Bologna asking for permission to translate the book into Italian. The publisher also wanted to know what kind of advance and royalties I would like to receive. During those days of minimal contact, a proposal to translate a book in the West—with money involved, to boot—was highly exotic, not only for me personally but for my editor as well. We exchanged shocked glances. Finally, my editor said, "Listen, Volodya, no matter what happens, you're not going to get any money. VAAP isn't going to do anything on your behalf, and even if it does, it will take eighty percent. I guarantee you that you won't see a single Italian lira. Where's the letter from, Bologna? Then let them send us each a raincoat. It won't cost them anything, but it would be nice for us." A raincoat—known as a Bologna in Russian—was truly a major rarity back then. One could fetch as much as three hundred rubles, which at the official exchange rate translated to about five hundred dollars, or fifty to sixty dollars on the black market.

Naturally, we were denied permission to respond at all, but to our amazement we received copies of the Italian translation only three months later. Even more extraordinary was the accompanying invitation to me to give a series of lectures, at Mondadori's expense, at the University of Milan and in other cities. They also offered to pay my airfare. No one had remotely expected such a turn of events. From that time forward, I became Znanie's favorite author.

Clutching the letter in my hand, I walked down the long corridors of the All-Union Polytechnic Institute, where I was now working as an assistant professor and dean of the faculty.[11] To take advantage of

11. I had been forced to abandon hard science in 1967, after I had written a letter to the vice president of the USSR Academy of Sciences, academician Mikhail Millionshchikov, and the party's chief of science Sergei Trapeznikov, about the irrational spending of millions of rubles for research on the MGD generator, which I considered to be a dead end. (In fact, the research seems to have been intentionally encouraged by the CIA, via American scientists, to divert money and talented people from other more promising scientific tasks and to drain the Academy of Sciences' finances.) Academician Vladimir Kirillin, Trapeznikov's predecessor and my boss, was leading the research. My letter was forwarded from the party's Central Committee directly to Kirillin, my immediate forced resignation being the result. I believe Zhirinovsky's letter to the Central Committee, dated April 15, 1967, on improving Soviet agriculture, education, and industry, met with a similar fate: the letter was never answered but further damaged his reputation with the party.

Mondadori's offer, I would need a recommendation for permission to travel, in which all my professional and moral qualities would be described, signed by the "triangle"—the rector of the institute, the secretary of the party committee, and the chair of the local trade union committee. In particular, I was looking for an encore appearance of that magic phrase: "His political consciousness is highly developed, he is of irreproachable morality, and he lives modestly in his personal life."

The first step was to convince my party group—the party organization of the faculty where I worked—to give me a recommendation. The group consisted of about eight Communists, who spent a few hours grilling me on the details of my professional and personal life, as well as the reasons for my wanting to take this trip, my foreign acquaintances, England, and even the queen. I got the recommendation, but not unanimously. One elderly professor, who had taken an instant dislike to me, said that there were worthier candidates for such a trip, apparently alluding to himself.

The next step was the party bureau of the department, of which the faculty was part. The secretary of the party bureau, an extremely unpleasant type with a thin, pockmarked, and wrinkled face, foamed at the mouth about how the KGB had first to determine what kind of people had sent the invitation, whether they were acquainted with the people I had met in England, and whether they were spies trying to seduce a young specialist. In plain Russian, he said that I, having carried out espionage in the past, was hoping to return to my foreign masters, this time forever. Many of the bureau's members agreed with his understanding of the situation. The vote was four to three in my favor, another victory, but the trend was dispiriting. So many rungs of the ladder remained to be scaled: the party meeting of the faculty, the professional bureau, the party committee of the institute, the rector, and the Foreign Travel Commission, headed by a bunch of old Bolsheviks of the district committee of the party. Only the secretary of the bureau of the district committee could sign the recommendation for travel, but that didn't mean that he was the one responsible for the decision. The recommendation and my personal case also had to follow a circuitous secret path from the personnel department of the institute to the so-called special department, then to the district KGB, and then to the city KGB. The final decision was made at the level of the Central Committee, in the Department of Science and Higher Institutes of Learning and the International Department, as well as the Foreign Travel Commission, where the comments of the district and city KGB were examined and appended to the information and opinions received through their own channels.[12]

A few months passed as the recommendation made the rounds. Finally, I stood before Comrade Professor Aleksander Bubennikov, the secretary of the party committee of the institute.

"Oh, it's the guy who likes to take trips. Here's what I have to say to you, Volodya. It's still too soon for you to go abroad. Stay here a while."

"You're refusing me the right to a hearing on my recommendation with the party committee," I snarled.

"Okay, if you insist, we'll discuss it," replied Bubennikov, calmly but menacingly.

It came as no surprise that I was not approved at the meeting of the institute's party committee. The vote was four yeas to eleven nays. Ciao, Italia!

One month later I was unexpectedly called down to the Ministry of Higher and Special Education to see the deputy minister for foreign relations, who inexplicably proposed I go to Italy after all. "But not for a month to give lectures. Why squander your talents on trivialities? We'll send you for one year on a work-study program. We'll get the approval of the party committee."

I was supposed to suggest a logical site for the program, as well as a professor who could serve as my adviser. It would have been immeasurably more interesting and useful to go to the United States, where large-scale experiments were being carried out on a level much more exciting than anything Italy had to offer, but the desire to travel, so acutely felt by every Soviet person, was impervious to reason. Rummaging through some old articles, I managed to find the name of Professor Adriano Sacerdoti of the University of Rome. I wrote him and almost immediately received his positive reply. The ministry put me through a grueling examination in my specialty and in English. It also provided me with an Italian language teacher for one year.

She was tall, slender, energetic, fluent in English, French, and Italian, about thirty-five years old. She had bright red hair and unusually penetrating eyes of blue. She came to the institute three times a week to spend three hours per session working with me on Italian. This was her only job, which in a country that boasted full employment was rather unusual—nine hours a week instead of the normal forty. But this did not put me on my guard.

For every session she prepared texts specially attuned to my future

12. See Voslensky, *Nomenklatura*.

conversations with Professor Sacerdoti. To the usual phrases for addressing the stewardesses on Alitalia, hailing taxis, and introducing myself, she added dialogue for the laboratory and a few new Soviet jokes to loosen things up. She also drilled me on dozens of painstakingly prepared speeches about my family life and life in general in the USSR.

About a half year after our lessons began, three months before I was to take the Italian examination, she announced that it was no longer convenient for her to visit me at the institute and proposed instead that we continue the lessons at her apartment. She lived alone, in a small but well-appointed apartment furnished with expensive foreign items and a beautiful piano. The lessons quickly began to evolve into something more than a simple transfer of knowledge from teacher to student. We began speaking to each other more freely, and on one occasion she opened up.

"I've lived my whole life abroad thanks to one person. I can't tell you his name because he occupies too high a position in our government. Once, it was almost twenty years ago, I was crying while walking in the rain from the Kremlin along the Kamenny Bridge. Someone approached from the other direction, from the House of Government. He comforted me and began helping me out with my life. I became his lover. He couldn't marry me because of his age and position. A divorce would have created an international scandal. I wanted travel, so he found me husbands, with whom I lived abroad. I've spent the last ten years in France. When we came back here, I split up with my husband. There wasn't anything between us—it was strictly a marriage of convenience. I was his pass to the outside world—unmarried people can't travel—as he was mine. We had different interests."

Her eyes began welling up with tears. She professed her love for me and proposed we leave for Italy together. She looked at me searchingly, and suddenly I saw that the shock of fiery red hair had slid to one side—it was a wig. And one of her eyes was not bright blue but dark brown. Her face, despite the ersatz tears, turned hard and resolute. I realized that, at the very least, she was a lieutenant colonel, maybe even a colonel in the KGB like Rosa in *From Russia with Love*. I saw that it was *she* who was supposed to go to Italy. I suddenly understood everything, and I ran. Ignoring the phone calls from both the institute's rector and the new chief of the Babushkinsky district KGB, I ran from the KGB's embrace, a flight that has cost me a good deal. My travel quarantine stayed in place: for more than ten years I was prohibited from traveling to capitalist countries. Strange things began happening.

Once, while negotiating a turn at normal speed, the left front wheel of my car came off on its own; it was sheer luck that I escaped death. On another occasion, I was dragged into court on the absurd charge of raping "Citizeness M," whom I hardly knew. The events of my stay in England were dredged up anew: had I slept with any of the girls with whom I'd gone dancing? I was pressured to move out of the co-op apartment I lived in and to change my job.

It became clear that I had to flee for real—if not to another country or city, then at least to another part of the city, where I would be unknown to the district division of the KGB. I found work elsewhere. The KGB agent from the Babushkinsky district came to say good-bye to me. He wasn't pleased, though he seemed to understand my situation. That didn't stop him from asking one last time, "So, did you sleep with that girl in England or not?"

Many years went by. During that time I defended my dissertation, became a writer, professor, and editor, and settled down and remarried. After fourteen years, I was once again allowed to travel to capitalist countries. In 1982 I was appointed director of Mir Publishing House, where I became one side of the triangle signing recommendations for travel abroad. Naturally, this assumed interaction with the KGB.

The Soviet Union used to have a KGB "servicing system" for its firms. Each state enterprise (there were no other kinds) had a KGB "handler" who would visit it on certain days. He (or she) would let the director of the firm know what kind of information the KGB had on certain employees. With the director of an international publishing house such as Mir, which employed up to twenty foreign translators and editors at a time, all of them constantly under KGB scrutiny, as well as almost seven hundred employees traditionally skeptical of Soviet power, the KGB handler had plenty to talk about. A new handler was appointed from time to time, but all who filled the role were none too bright. Traditionally the handler was a lower-ranking officer, usually a lieutenant, dressed in civilian clothing and going by a double false name—Nikolai Nikolayevich, Valeria Valerievna, Sergei Sergeyevich, or the like.

Mir's handler usually visited on Tuesday mornings, stopping to talk to various people—many of whom had long since figured out his or her true identity—and spending an especially long time with the secretary of the party organization or the chief of the special department, who I assume were informants. At the end of the day, the handler would come to my office and initiate an apparently casual conversation. It usually began with an overview of the lives of Mir's foreign employees, who were automatically taken to be spies, anti-Soviet rabble-rousers, and enemies of the regime. Each handler usually demanded that I dismiss them; my job was to keep them on board.

The KGB was categorically opposed to Zhirinovsky's presence at the publishing house, considering him unworthy of employment at such an ideologically important organization. They wanted me to terminate him immediately. The handler used the information provided by the secretary of the party organization, who despised Zhirinovsky, to turn the whole district committee of the party and the district KGB against him. He had more than enough material at his disposal. Zhirinovsky had criticized the Communists, Gorbachev, the war in Afghanistan, the district leaders, me, national cadres in the union republics, and so on. Convincing anyone of his unsuitability was not particularly difficult. Following every meeting at Mir, after one of Zhirinovsky's inevitable speeches, someone would phone the KGB to report on his latest escapades. The meeting hall was located literally two minutes from my office, but even before I had sat in my chair, the KGB line of my phone would already be lit up. Nikolai Nikolayevich or Sergei Sergeyevich would be demanding yet again that I fire Zhirinovsky for his inadmissible utterances.

From the very beginning, neither I nor the head of personnel took any stock of the KGB's opinion of Zhirinovsky, although such indifference was a breach of etiquette. (Regard for the KGB's views was not mandated by law but was considered bon ton in the relationship between any plant and the regional KGB.) But, to be honest, if I had fired Zhirinovsky, things would have been a lot quieter around Mir. The man was a pain in the ass. What he achieved through his demagoguery could have been managed more easily on the sly, with the same or even better results, but he was an opponent of the entire repellent system and uninterested in being subtle about his hatred. With his sharp and at times convincing speeches, he sought to awaken the company's employees from their Communist slumber. Mir was a pioneer of perestroika. It was the first in its industry to allow employees to purchase their apartments and household appliances like refrigerators and television sets at its expense. It also had a very strong workers' council. During that period, the publishing house needed Zhirinovsky, but it was more in need of someone capable of steering it in a more peaceful course.

Yet after Kvelidze left, Zhirinovsky was the only lawyer we had. There were absolutely no legal grounds for sacking him, and I did not see any reason to invent any: he came and left on time, did not disrupt the daily routine, and took care of his assignments. (Dashevsky maintains that Zhirinovsky lost every case he handled. This is not true. Zhirinovsky fully satisfied the needs of the publishing house, although he did lose a few cases.) On top of this, Zhirinovsky knew his rights under the Soviet Labor Code inside and out. He was completely (and justifiably) convinced that, if he were fired, the first court that heard his case would reinstate him. Whenever he felt the ground beginning to rumble under his feet, he would imply that any actions "undoubtedly dictated by political motivation" would immediately be "interpreted by the international community as just the latest violation of an individual's basic rights in the USSR."

The authors of the book *Absolute Zhirinovsky*, writing under the pen names Graham Frazer and George Lancelle, mistrust my reasons for keeping Zhirinovsky on: "Mr. Kartsev, despite being a Communist himself, refused [to fire Zhirinovsky] on the grounds that the law did not allow dismissal for political reasons. Again, there is probably more to this than meets the eye. As Mr. Kartsev would well know, dismissals (and rather worse) for political reasons were very common in the Soviet Union."[13] With this statement, Frazer and Lancelle betray their ignorance of the realities of Soviet life under perestroika. From 1985 forward, no Soviet citizen had been dismissed from work or had "rather worse" done to him or her without a formal trial inevitably covered by the international media. Moreover, few workers lost their suits. The press closely monitored party pressure on the judiciary.[14]

My refusal to fire Zhirinovsky placed me squarely between the hammer and the anvil—my conscience, on the one hand, and the KGB and the district committee of the party categorically demanding my cooperation, on the other. "It's either him or you, Vladimir Petrovich," I was told by both the head of the propaganda department of the district committee and the secretary for ideology. "You can be dismissed from your position for failing to meet your obligations, and you will

13. Frazer and Lancelle, *Absolute Zhirinovsky*, 124–25.

14. Everything was changing then in Russia—even travel abroad became possible. I remember how several times, before perestroika, Zhirinovsky tried to obtain permission to visit a Young Pioneers' camp in Czechoslovakia with children of Mir employees or to travel to East Germany on an exchange basis. Each time the recommendations—signed by me—were barred by the party's district committee and the KGB. Zhirinovsky was not simply undesirable—he was hated. They began letting him out only when the party organizations started disintegrating in 1988–89. By then, the system of issuing permission for travel outside the country had been fundamentally simplified.

not go to the United Nations. [I had been recommended for the post of director of the UN Publishing Division at that time.] Don't forget that we're the ones who sign your recommendation for travel abroad."

The threat was real. I turned for protection to one of my friends, who in turn contacted a general in the central KGB who reluctantly promised to help. I hung on to my job, and my recommendation for going to New York to work at the United Nations was signed. About Zhirinovsky, however, the general was adamant: "You have to get rid of him. And the sooner the better."

In my view, the party and the KGB would never have agreed to let Zhirinovsky represent their interests: I repeat, they hated him. To me, then, any talk about Zhirinovsky as their creature is devoid of sense. Still, speculation demands an examination of the man's potential ties to the KGB.

The very first contact can be traced to the time when Zhirinovsky was a student at the Alma-Ata (now Almaty) High School. This was a privileged Russian school, the best in the city. In those years, owing to the poverty of the city and district departments of public education, a portion of the expenses for maintaining the schools was borne by a so-called *shefy,* usually a large factory, military unit, or state institution. Every institution's financial plan earmarked an amount of money to be allocated toward social needs, and patronage was the best way to dispose of the large sums that built up. Assigning a thousand or two rubles to a sponsored school or sending the school chairs and tables, lathes, gym equipment, or even potted plants was considered the proper thing to do. Although such donations were not officially considered to be tax write-offs, the institutional sponsor reaped benefits in the form of favorable press and mentions in the annual reports of the city and district committees and perhaps even in the reports of the regional executive and city executive committees.

The patron for Zhirinovsky's school was the Alma-Ata KGB, which helps explain the relatively good equipment with which the school was outfitted, as well as Zhirinovsky's acceptance to the Institute of Oriental Languages, a typical KGB spy's nest. The sponsorship did not mean that every student at the school or the institute was a KGB employee, informer, or confidant, but, as everywhere, the KGB kept an eye on the students, and a high achiever like Zhirinovsky (his marks had improved dramatically at university), lonely and withdrawn but active nonetheless in academic life and even a group leader, was undoubtedly among those singled out for future cooperation with the KGB.

That changed, however, after the memorable televised discussion on democracy in December 1967 and the letter of criticism Zhirinovsky sent to the Central Committee of the Communist Party. In 1984 Zhirinovsky told me approximately the following: "As you know, I took part in a debate announced as 'Democracy for Them and Democracy for Us.' I honestly spoke my mind, which raised the hackles of the university officials who were obliged by the party to attend such gatherings. A black mark was struck against my name, and retribution was sure to follow. The following year everything was remembered when it came to endorsing a recommendation for me to work for a month as a translator for a sports delegation to Turkey. The recommendation was shelved by the party branch on the pretext that I was politically unreliable.[15] By then we had real dissidents, trials, Daniel, Sinyavsky, Solzhenitsyn. Some were prohibited, others allowed. But I had nothing to do with that; I only said what everyone already knew but was not bold enough to say aloud. But that was enough for them to consider me unreliable." The KGB never again considered Zhirinovsky as a potential *seksot*, a secret employee who can be trusted to work abroad with some innocuous job such as interpreter, journalist, or trade mission employee as a cover.

"So how was it, Volodya, they let you go to Turkey later?" I asked him sometime in 1983.

"Only thanks to my obstinacy. I wanted to go to Turkey on a work-study program in my specialization and to polish my language skills. But it was impossible—no one but the institute's bosses traveled. But then I found out that there was the possibility of travel through the committee for foreign economic relations. The leadership of the committee sorely needed me—Turkish translators were worth their weight in gold—and they were able to overcome the KGB's opposition. When the group of engineers was formed, it included me as well."

When it came to prioritizing students for its own ends, the KGB had definitely placed Zhirinovsky on the back burner. Aside from not receiving the recommendation for travel to Turkey with the sports delegation, when the time came to name the potential candidates to be sent abroad for foreign language practice, Zhirinovsky did not figure on the list. Still, whereas Kozlovsky, as a Jewish human rights activist,

15. The timing supports Zhirinovsky's assertion that he was not allowed out because of the debate: earlier, in 1966, Zhirinovsky had been permitted to go to Hungary for voluntary work with a students' building brigade during summer vacation.

was repeatedly denied permission to travel to Israel, the signature on Zhirinovsky's recommendation to go to Turkey as a translator for the State Committee for Foreign Economic Relations testifies to the fact that the KGB did not then consider him outright anti-Soviet.

In Turkey, Zhirinovsky experienced what he called a "minor incident": he ended up in prison for handing out badges.[16]

After the 1957 World Festival of Youth and Students in Moscow, badges had become a mania in the Soviet Union. In some houses, the walls were festooned with badge-covered cloths, while many people made a small fortune from the hobby. When leaving for Turkey Zhirinovsky discovered that he had more currency than was allowed to be taken abroad. He bought badges at the airport which bore images of Tolstoy and Pushkin. Zhirinovsky distributed these badges as presents to Turkish youth. When the Turkish police, who were evidently watching every move made by the Soviet specialists, took an interest in what Zhirinovsky had been freely dispensing, it turned out that Soviet imagery fell under a very strict article in the Turkish criminal codes on propaganda, making Zhirinovsky susceptible to a protracted Turkish prison term. Somebody mistook Tolstoy and Pushkin for Marxist leaders! Zhirinovsky was arrested. The Soviet consul was called in. To avoid an international incident, it was decided that Zhirinovsky should be sent back to the Soviet Union. On the day of his expulsion, he had not been charged with anything specific, although the Turkish prime minister and the Turkish ambassador to the United States, Nuzhed Kandemir, claim that he was arrested, spent several days in prison, and was expelled from Turkey as "a KGB agent."[17]

This incident, I think, forever put an end to KGB attempts to use Zhirinovsky. They realized that he didn't just stand out (as evidenced, for example, by his letter to the Central Committee), he behaved like a bull in a china shop and was totally unsuitable for quiet intelligence work. The episode with the badges also undoubtedly put an end to any international career he might have forged as a graduate of the Institute of Oriental Languages. From being a free-thinker, he became untrustworthy. I do not believe that this opinion is likely to have changed over time, though it is possible that Zhirinovsky had some sporadic contacts with the KGB. However, following all his subsequent irrational behavior, the KGB would hardly have thought of using him in any of its intrigues.

When someone accuses him of being thick with the KGB—and this happens often—Zhirinovsky immediately counters with "Show me the

16. Zhirinovsky, *Poslednii brosok na iug* (The last dash to the south), 15.
17. ITAR-TASS, March 25, 1994.

documents." And he's always ready with a document of his own, issued on August 28, 1991, in a court case against one of his many accusers and bearing the signature of a deputy director of the KGB, V. Lebedev: "The KGB of the USSR has no materials of any kind testifying to the cooperation of the chairman of the Liberal Democratic Party, V. V. Zhirinovsky, with the organs of state security." I wonder if I could get a similar document from the KGB. I doubt it.

PART TWO

Zhirinovsky: The Man and the Party

4

Zhirinovsky's Runs for Power

It was in 1987 that the name Zhirinovsky first appeared in the Soviet central press, in the official Moscow party newspaper with the darkest, most obscurantist leanings—*Moskovskaya Pravda*, then edited by Mikhail Poltoranin, who is today a confidant of Boris Yeltsin—and then in *Vechernyaya Moskva* and on the television program *Good Evening, Moscow*. Each reference occurred for a different reason, and all at once Zhirinovsky's fame (or notoriety) extended to all of Moscow.

In the late 1980s Zhirinovsky's sphere of activity broadened. Mir was a very important publishing house with international business, but its framework had become too limiting for him, his duties as legal counsel too burdensome. Beginning in 1987 he sought to break out and become one of the leaders of Moscow's Dzerzhinsky district. This expansion into a new, broader field of activity, the level of a Moscow city district, was extraordinarily important to Zhirinovsky. Not everyone understood this back then, in 1987, when the Dzerzhinsky District Executive Committee of the Soviet of Workers' Deputies of the City of Moscow (or more concisely, the Dzerzhinsky Ispolkom) granted Mir the opportunity of proposing from its midst a candidate for the soviet of the Dzerzhinsky district.

A district soviet was usually made up of deputies "chosen by the people." The candidates for deputy were discussed in advance at the bureau of the party committee, and the subsequent choices coordinated with the party's citywide committee. Summaries of the discussions went from the city committee to the party's Central Committee, where the final decisions were made. The ballots would then be printed, and the elections held, with all the candidates usually receiving 99 percent of the vote.[1] The corps of deputies was suppose to include a certain percentage of nonparty people, representing such categories as women, blue-collar workers, young people up to age twenty-eight, scientists and scholars, officers, Jews, representatives of native peoples, ballerinas, directors, and so on. Many prominent figures in the Soviet Union and post-Soviet Russia first made careers for themselves by happening to be in the right place at the right time, when the nonparty quota in a certain category had not yet been filled. I remember, for example, that at one point in the 1970s there appeared among the members of the Ispolkom (Executive Committee) of a Moscow district soviet a model rather notorious in the city as an airhead and a tramp. In her district, it turned out, there had been a shortage of candidates for the soviet in the category of "nonparty women of the younger generation working in the sphere of culture." Subsequently she made a successful administrative career for herself in the soviets, obtaining a direct phone line to the Kremlin, an excellent rent-free apartment, a car, a dacha, and a colonel for a husband—all the earmarks of success in the Soviet Union.

The decision to entrust Mir with the responsibility of nominating a candidate for the soviet was made somewhere in the inner recesses of the Dzerzhinsky district committee of the Moscow Communist Party organization and the Dzerzhinsky district division of the KGB. The district soviet of course operated under the careful supervision of those two bodies; in fact, its office was in the same building as the party district committee's, though one floor down. The chairman of the district soviet was usually also a member of the bureau of the party's district committee, as was the chairman of the district KGB. The bureau was the most important body of the party district organization, and as part of that body the head of the district soviet and the head of the district KGB met regularly with the most important leadership—the party leadership—of the district, gave their reports, and received their assignments. The structure was essentially military, and it operated with surprising precision. Every lower-ranking body trem-

1. The authorities did try to make sure that candidates were not known personally to the voters at a given polling station. When this rule was disregarded, awkward incidents could occur. The workers at a certain factory might easily vote down their director, for example, or the voters from a building where theatrical personalities lived might do the same to some well-known actress.

bled before every higher-ranking one. Every higher-ranking body glo-
ried in its power over the lower levels of the hierarchy. The power of
any and every higher rung was absolute and unchallengeable. Everybody had a dozen bosses, at every rung of the administrative ladder.
The only place to seek protection was at the very top. A successful
administrative or governmental career could go only one way—up.
Zhirinovsky, too, having already chosen for himself the career of a
politician, could go in only one direction: he had to move outward and
upward, from the publishing house to a role on the district level and
then beyond.

Zhirinovsky's moment arrived when Mir was assigned a place in the
district soviet to be filled by a deputy representing the "work collective
of the enterprise." According to the rules, a candidate for the slot had
to be nominated at a general meeting open to all the members of the
work collective. The law also defined a very complicated nomination
procedure. Everyone sought to simplify this procedure as much as possible, however, well aware that elections to the local soviet had very little effect on actual life in the district. The only deputies with any influence on decisions in the district—what would be built and where, how
many buses to put on any given bus line, how many polyclinics and
hospitals to have, what shows and performances to grant permission
for, and most important of all, who would get the free government
apartments and dachas in the district—were the functionaries of the
Ispolkom, who were usually elected at particularly reliable military or
industrial plants. The others had only one responsibility: to vote correctly so as not to interfere with the Ispolkom's work. In return for this
support, they received a small stipend and any number of perks that
considerably brightened their everyday lives.

Nobody took elections to the local soviets seriously. Attempting to
cast a secret ballot drew unwelcome attention to oneself, so most people simply voted in the open for the candidate they knew was supposed to win. Yet even though elections were strictly pro forma, they
required time, money, resources, and attention, even though the results
were known beforehand. I remember sitting at a polling station once,
waiting for 10 P.M. when the report could be sent off to the *ispolkom* and
raikom attesting to yet another great victory by the officially sanctioned
bloc of Communists and nonparty people. All the eligible inhabitants
of the district had voted—the members of the election commission having voted on behalf of those absent—and all the voters' lists had been
put away. At 9:50 P.M., an old woman came in. She had just gotten back
from her cottage outside the city, she said, and she wanted to vote.

Without batting an eyelash, the chairman of the election commission handed her a leftover ballot. She filled it out under the stern gaze of our commission.

"Now where does the ballot go?" she asked.

"Toss it right in the urn there!" said the secretary of the party bureau, half-joking, half-insulting, as he pointed to the spittoon behind her back. (In Russian, the word *urna* means both "ballot box" and "waste receptacle.") Such was the value of a vote in a Soviet election.

By granting Mir permission to put forward a candidate for the position of deputy to this puppet body called the district soviet, the party district committee had made a great show of its confidence in the organization. The former secretary of Mir's party bureau nobly offered to spare the rest of us by agreeing to be the candidate. All that remained was to hold a pro forma meeting, vote for him, type up the minutes, and send them to the Ispolkom. That's how it had always been done. But this time, things were different; this time, there was Zhirinovsky to deal with.

On Friday evening, February 21, 1987, at the end of the working day, a meeting of the entire work collective—actually consisting of a few rank-and-file individuals who were anxious to hurry home, a number of party and trade union activists who invariably attended meetings, and the various managers and heads of departments and offices who had to be there by virtue of their positions—was held in Mir's assembly hall. The candidate the meeting was going to select was well known. The price he would pay for the honor—the loss of his free time—was also well known, as were the perks he would inevitably receive: access to the special store for soviet deputies where imported goods could be purchased cheaply; entry into the Ispolkom canteen, where high-quality but inexpensive meals were served; free travel on public transport; and direct access to tickets at movie houses, theaters, airports, and railroad stations without having to wait in line. Also present at the meeting was Vladimir Zhirinovsky, Mir's senior counselor on legal matters.

There were no warnings of a coming storm. The atmosphere was dull: an ordinary meeting, the usual formalities. Soon all the speeches had been made, the candidate "discussed," with glowing recommendations for him all around, and a motion made to proceed to the vote. Some people were already gathering up their bags and briefcases. The meeting was coming to a close.

Then Vladimir Zhirinovsky asked for the floor.

Everyone looked around. They couldn't imagine what there was left to discuss, but they knew that Zhirinovsky wouldn't ascend to the speaker's stand unless he had something to make a fuss about. This would be worth hearing.

Zhirinovsky took his place at the rostrum and loudly asked the chairman of the meeting, a member of the party bureau at Mir: "How many people are present at this meeting?"

"Well, probably about sixty," the chairman answered.

"No, I've counted, and you can count, too. There are forty-six."

"Yes, but the day is over . . ."

"That is of no significance. I have in my pocket a small book—*The Law on Elections.* According to this law, which we must abide by, when a candidate for deputy to a soviet is proposed, no less than three-fourths of the whole staff of an enterprise must be present. Six hundred and forty people work here at Mir. That means there should be four hundred and eighty in this hall. Otherwise any decision at this meeting will be invalid under the law.

"We don't have a hall that would hold that many!"

"If we don't have a hall with that many seats, we can't propose a candidate. That's what the law says. Furthermore, the law says that not one candidate, but several, must be nominated and that we must choose among them. But we have only one! Moreover, the law says that candidates must be discussed from all sides, and we have discussed only the positive qualities of our candidate—whom I have nothing against, by the way—he is a good editor. But what does he know about the law? Does he have an inclination and a desire to concern himself with all the economic problems of our district? Will he fight for us? Will he see to it that all of us have good apartments, that the party bureaucrats don't snap up all the good buildings in the district? What I think is, let him keep doing his work as an editor. And I propose that the candidate you choose for deputy to the soviet be me. I am a lawyer. I have demonstrated in numerous court cases that I can defend the interests of the publishing house and its employees. Who better than I to represent our publishing house at the district soviet?"

No one knew what to say. That's how unusual this speech was, in both form and content. Also unusual was the experiment in self-nomination, a thing unheard-of in the annals of Soviet democracy. Another puzzle was Zhirinovsky's motive. No one was eager to obtain the rather petty privileges of a district deputy at the expense of the demeaning mechanical procedure of voting at district soviet sessions, at the expense of all that lost time and the insult of participating in an activity that in all aspects was prearranged. Everyone viewed the local soviet elections as a necessary evil, one of the rules of the game that one had to go along with despite the senselessness of the whole procedure. And the candidate was generally regarded as a sacrificial lamb who usually went along grudgingly, for only one term, and then only after lengthy persuasion. At the next election a new offering had to be found. Yet here was someone volunteering for the slaughter! It was cause for wonder and dismay, as were so many of Zhirinovsky's speeches and actions.

I think this was the first instance in Moscow when an employee at a state-owned enterprise, taking advantage of the election law (which no one else had on hand) was able to demand, solely on the basis of formalities, that a meeting to propose a candidate for deputy to the district soviet be canceled. Zhirinovsky was aided by the fact that even then Mir was a very liberal, freedom-loving organization, in which much that was out of the way was overlooked or forgiven. Matters not directly related to one's duties as an employee were one's own business. I tried not to pressure my staff members, despite the wishes of several devotees of the firm hand. In every way I could I attempted to instill free thinking and encourage mutual understanding, cooperation, and culling the best from the two competing systems of socialism and capitalism. It is no accident that at the very height of the cold war Mir was the pioneer among the Goskomizdat enterprises in establishing good relations with American publishers. As I have mentioned, Mir was the first to translate *Scientific American* into Russian; Mir also arranged for members of the staff to participate in work-study exchange programs in America, where, for example, they were among the first to attend the publishing courses offered at Stanford University. Our collaborations with U.S. publishers reached their apotheosis with a book we copublished with Addison-Wesley, *Home Planet* (in Russian, *Nash Dom-Zemlya*), which featured photographs taken from space by the cosmonauts and astronauts of many countries. More than a million copies of this book were sold in twelve countries, and it played an enormous part in the movement to save the environment and promote not only ecological thinking but a new way of political thinking, at the base of which is the recognition of our place on this planet. Ray Bradbury reviewed the book for the *New York Times* in the fall of 1988 and, if I remember correctly, called it the "Bible for the third millenium." *Life* magazine (October 1988, 189–97) excerpted it.

Such free-thinking positions were not at all typical for enterprises under Goskomizdat, which was generally quite conservative. Mir held a similarly radical stance with regard to party education, which at that time was still compulsory. Once a week we were supposed to refresh our knowledge of Marxism and Communist Party history by reviewing the works of Lenin and the reports of the latest party congresses, but as a doctor of sciences and a professor, I was able to extract permission from the Dzerzhinsky district committee of the party to do something different. Our alternative was a methodology seminar for the Mir leadership, conducted under my direction and with the participation of all the leading members of the Mir staff—the heads of departments and editorial boards, undoubtedly including Zhirinovsky. Once a week we would discuss burning issues of the day—perhaps the concept of nuclear winter or the Star Wars program.[2]

Mir was in the vanguard in another respect. Its employees were among the first to obtain the most varied types of benefits from the enterprise's fund for social and cultural improvements and its material incentives fund. Two members of Mir's trade union committee, its chairman Stanislav Zhebrovsky and Vladimir Zhirinovsky, displayed extraordinary virtuosity in finding uses for these funds. Under the conditions of steadily worsening shortages during the perestroika years, the funds were used to purchase first-rate imported goods for staff members. It turned out, for example, that the Vietnamese currency that the publishing house possessed in copious amounts, which we had thought perfectly useless, could be profitably exchanged for a large shipment of imported television sets, one of which virtually every Mir employee was then able to purchase for a pittance. Many

2. Using material from these seminars, we published several excellent books, among them, *The Night After*, on the consequences of a nuclear war, and *Weaponry in Space*, an anti-SDI book, which proposed, among other things, countering the staggering costs of Star Wars technology by using small metallic bits, or beads. I sent several copies of these two books to an old acquaintance of mine, Professor Ivan Timofeyevich Frolov, a historian and philosopher of science who was then an assistant to Gorbachev. In turn, he must have given them to Gorbachev, to whose "new thinking" they undoubtedly contributed. Gorbachev then presented the books to Reagan at the Geneva and Reykjavik summit meetings. Everyone at Mir who was connected with the books was officially thanked for them, and the Goskomizdat leadership gave each of us a bonus of approximately fifty rubles. The question immediately arose: Should Zhirinovsky receive a bonus? After all, he had had no direct part in the production of the books. He was able to prove, however, that he had been involved in legal arrangements related to them, and so, having shown once again that truth was on his side, he received his bonus.

apartments also were purchased for staff members at the trade union's expense.

Mir was unusually receptive to everything new. We were the first Soviet publisher to prepare camera-ready copy of our books, using some excellent Compugraphic equipment we had purchased, as well as the first to begin using computerized typesetting, desktop publishing, and electronic mail. Nor did we allow orthodox views to limit our choices of translation projects, sometimes going directly against the wishes of our superiors. In light of all this, it is not surprising that Mir was an early supporter of perestroika. Everyone at the publishing house applauded Gorbachev's initiatives (although Zhirinovsky criticized him as a thick-headed Communist), and ours was the first publishing house to adopt the mechanisms Gorbachev introduced for self-financing, by which enterprises could operate on the basis of their own earnings, without relying on state funds or subsidies.[3]

Perhaps the benevolent atmosphere that reigned at Mir is best exemplified by our amateur theatrical performances. On every major holiday—New Year's, May Day, November 7 (the anniversary of the Bolshevik revolution)—the employees organized an evening of performances, under the perennial direction of Valentina Samsonova, a member of the physics editorial office. These smorgasbord offerings were called *kapustniki* (literally, "cabbage soups") and included music, dancing, choral singing, and skits about life in the publishing house, in which I was invariably depicted—quite aptly—by someone sporting a mop simulating fair hair, big glasses, and a copy of *Home Planet* under his arm. Zhirinovsky was always portrayed by one of the staff members singing a well-known Soviet song, the first line of which was "Choose me! Choose me, the bird of tomorrow's happiness." The concert included an obligatory can-can, performed by the good-looking, long-legged women editors of the foreign language departments. In the finale the entire audience would hold hands and join the choir on stage in singing the company song—"We hold up Mir gigantic / Upon our hands of stone"—accompanied by an amateur orchestra under the directorship of Sergei Stalnov, a member of the English-language editorial department and a fairly good pianist in his own right. I can't

3. We did not, however, approve of Gorbachev's unwise antialcohol campaign, during which the finest Soviet vineyards, located in the Caucasus and Crimea, were cut down and the number of liquor licenses granted was drastically reduced. We had an especially big fight over a Mitchell Beasley encyclopedia that we were publishing in Russian at the time. Under pressure from the censors we were forced to cut the article on viticulture and the wine industry.

recall those evenings without a touch of nostalgia, as I'm sure is true for all the Mir-ites of those days.

It proved to be no simple matter to abide by the letter of the election law that Zhirinovsky invoked to make his first challenge to the system of party bureaucracy. Party and trade union meetings were usually held in the assembly hall at the publishing house, furnished with antique carved easy chairs and a massive table for the presiding body. Here, too, we held seminars and sessions of the editorial councils and presented lectures by leading scholars and scientists and visiting foreign guests, including the Nobel laureates Linus Pauling and Konrad Lorenz. However, the hall had a seating capacity of only 150. To meet the requirements of the election law, we needed a hall that would hold at least five hundred people.

Thus it was that all of Mir's employees went over to a rented hall after work one day in order to attempt, once again, to put forward a candidate for the position of deputy to the district Soviet. When everyone had taken a seat, and the records committee had made a count of those present, it turned out that although there were more than 420 people seated in the hall, a quorum was lacking. The temptation was great to go ahead with the meeting anyway, but Zhirinovsky and Zhebrovsky insisted on sticking to the rules. They got their way. Another day was set for the meeting, and Mir was obliged to rent the hall again.

The second time, the hall was not only full but overflowing, and for some reason radio and television reporters also showed up. As a member of the presiding committee, I sat on a high stage, together with Lev Glotov, head of the German-language editorial department, who was chairing the meeting, and Zhebrovsky, head of the trade union committee.

We began to discuss the candidates—all fourteen of them. At Zhirinovsky's insistence, each one was discussed in detail from the most varied angles, with appraisals of their fighting qualities as well as their practical, workaday abilities. Since all this was taking place after a day of work—the meeting began at 6 P.M.—people began to get tired. A decision was made to finish discussing the candidates and then to hold the election during one last meeting. The number of candidates began to dwindle—some were rejected and others withdrew on their own. And despite our intentions, the most interesting and controversial one was left for the next meeting.

Finally, at around 9 P.M. during the fourth meeting, the time came to discuss the candidacy of Zhirinovsky. The room fell silent. Just then, a special postal service messenger, all dressed in leather, sidled up to me on the stage with a large envelope.

"Express special delivery. Confidential. Please sign," he said.

I signed, broke the official wax seal, and opened the envelope, keeping the contents out of view of the other members of the presiding committee. Although delivered to me, it appeared that it was addressed to the secretary of the party bureau at Mir. In the upper right-hand corner, stamped in large purple letters, were the words TOP SECRET.

The letter was from the chairman of the Inyurkollegia, where Zhirinovsky had worked before Mir. I don't remember the exact wording, but the drift of the letter was that Zhirinovsky should not be proposed as a candidate for the district soviet because he was politically unreliable. There was something to the effect that he had made demagogic speeches at party meetings. (Well, that was certainly no surprise to us.) More importantly, the letter alleged that Zhirinovsky had not left the Inyurkollegiy of his own free will but had been driven out for improper behavior, specifically, bribe taking. (I was also familiar with this incident—Zhirinovsky had told me about it himself.) The letter concluded with the recommendation that its contents be read aloud to those assembled at the meeting in order to prevent a vote in favor of Zhirinovsky's candidacy.

I was outraged. First of all, why was I being asked to read aloud a letter stamped TOP SECRET? Second, why had a letter addressed to the party bureau secretary been delivered to me? Third, I remembered perfectly well that the entire leadership at the Inyurkollegia—the chairman, the party bureau secretary, and the head of personnel—had given Zhirinovsky glowing recommendations when he was transferred to Mir. (Note, too, that he had been *transferred*, precisely—as we all understood—so that he would retain seniority by keeping his record of continuous employment intact. Of course, there is always a temptation to give a good recommendation to get rid of a trouble-maker or a poor worker, but among the nomenklatura, it was considered poor form to stoop to that.) Fourth, this letter was not a cry from the heart from some honest official who had decided (after four years) to warn a colleague about a former employee; it had been written especially for the circumstances and had been delivered not only to the appropriate meeting but at exactly the moment when it would have the greatest shock value—just before the discussion of Zhirinovsky's candidacy.

Deciding not to say anything to the assembled crowd, I gave the letter to the new secretary of our party bureau—the same General Barkov who had investigated Zhirinovsky before his transfer to Mir. He, too, was offended by the hypocrisy of the Inyurkollegia chairman and decided to hold his tongue. Zhirinovsky was elected by an overwhelming majority.

The next morning the newspaper *Moskovskaya Pravda* featured an article headlined "Why Did the Party Bureau Secretary Remain Silent?" The piece criticized the publishing house for opening the way to a seat on the executive committee of the soviet to a man with a tarnished reputation. For others, however, Zhirinovsky became the hero of the day; media reports loudly attacked the party apparatus for suppressing the free expression of the will of the Mir work collective. But that didn't make things any easier for me. I was summoned to the party district committee for a session with the secretary for ideology and the head of the propaganda department, who, without mincing words, warned me that if I didn't restrain Zhirinovsky, they would raise the question of removing me as director of Mir. I was also warned by the head of Goskomizdat—though not in a very obvious way. It was evident that the party wasn't sure how to proceed in the face of strong opposition from an entire work collective and consistent media support for Zhirinovsky.

The story of the bribe Zhirinovsky allegedly accepted isn't worth a cracked eggshell. As I have explained earlier, the entire Soviet system, which in general did not have a high crime rate, was universally infected with the petty ailment of small-time bribery. Bribe taking took place on a big scale, too, of course. For example, some relatives of Brezhnev, government ministers, and heads of major government agencies received thousands and millions of rubles in bribes paid for apartments, dachas, cars, and jobs as directors and ministers. Brezhnev's son-in-law, Yuri Churbanov, a deputy chief of the Ministry of Internal Affairs, was jailed by Andropov for taking bribes amounting to hundreds of thousands of rubles. A man named Ivan Tregubov, chairman of the Moscow Department of Commerce, was shot on bribery charges, as was Yuri Sokolov, the director of the Yeliseyev food store on Moscow's Gorky Street. Bribes from Uzbekistan—millions of rubles paid for fictitious reports of cotton deliveries to textile plants in Russia—led to the infamous Fergana and Uzbek cases, which abounded in instances of murder and illegal incarceration.

For ordinary mortals, however, that was life in an altogether different world, incomprehensible and, fortunately, inaccessible. But small gifts were another story—a toy brought in from abroad, stockings, cosmetics, facial powder, rouge, packs of American cigarettes. Without this kind of grease, for all practical purposes the Soviet system would not have worked at all. Art books and other books of high quality were especially valuable. There was an unheard-of shortage of such books in the USSR, and they served as liquid currency in transactions with doctors, hair dressers, and the like. When I was accepted into the USSR Union of Writers, I valued most the right it gave me to enter the Writers Bookstore, presided over by K. V., known among writers as a truly hardened bribe taker. In that store one could, after paying suitable (that is, tangible) homage to K. V., purchase books that were in short supply elsewhere. I remember talking about this with the well-known Leningrad writer Daniil Granin, who said: "I make wide use of this opportunity. So does my daughter. I give her books from the Writers Bookstore. We just serviced the meat dealer down at the corner of the block, and now even the meat problem has been solved." Thus butchers and auto mechanics regularly received fine books and tickets to popular shows. Among the intelligentsia there was even a joke that at theatrical premieres you could hardly breathe because of the smell of grease from all the service station personnel. (It's not true. If they smelled, it was of the finest and most expensive men's cologne, supplied to them by wealthy foreign clients and an item inaccessible to the well-read intelligentsia, who were not of much use to anyone.)

I, too, took full advantage of this system. Whenever I prepared for a visit to the ministry, to the Moscow soviet, even to the CPSU Central Committee, I stuffed my briefcase full of books published by Mir. Among the top brass there were many lovers of science fiction, of Ray Bradbury and Robert Sheckley; there were also lovers of animal books, who particularly valued our premium products *The Joy of Knowledge* (translated from the Mitchell Beasley original) and *My Dog*, published by Salamander. The problem was not that these books were expensive—they were relatively cheap—they were simply hard to get (a standard condition in the Soviet Union). I didn't have to give the books away; I just had to make them available. The big bosses from the Central Committee or the ministry usually paid for them; top KGB personnel, to whom I also brought them, unfailingly did so.[4]

4. The KGB men were unusually firm in that respect; in fact, they appeared to me as paragons of virtue in a domain of universal petty vice. Westerners usually associate the KGB with its departments, which (undoubtedly on orders from party institutions) engaged in the detection and persecution of dissidents and in spying. There were other sections of the KGB, however, concerned with such tasks as fighting

Regarding the bribe he allegedly took, Zhirinovsky told me that it happened when he had helped an Armenian Soviet citizen obtain an inheritance from abroad consisting of a fairly decent sum in foreign currency. When a Soviet citizen received such an inheritance, rather than being paid in foreign currency, he was issued ruble certificates (whose value on the black market varied from one-and-a-half to five Soviet rubles) and offered the opportunity to spend them in the Beryozka hard currency stores. With such certificates, one could buy an apartment, a dacha, or a car fairly cheaply, as well as smaller items such as the kinds of books I've talked about or other hard-to-get Soviet products. Soviet citizens often bought ruble certificates at black market prices in order to get around the constant shortages and avoid standing in endless lines. (Zhirinovsky, incidentally, used the certificates he had earned while working in Turkey to buy himself a Zaporozhets, a rather poor make of Soviet car, from which one may conclude that his earnings in Turkey were not very substantial.) Using such certificates, one could also make a trip to a Soviet resort, for which ordinary vacation passes were very hard to come by. Zhirinovsky's client, grateful for his help, made it possible for Zhirinovsky to purchase one of these hard-to-get vacation passes. That was the bribe: Zhirinovsky bought some ruble certificates to obtain a pass to a resort. Of course, it would have been more honest for him not to have accepted the offer, but, as I have said, such exchanges of services were virtually universal in the Soviet Union. Perhaps everything wasn't on the up and up from the point of view of ideal morality—or even Western morality—but I could hunt a long time before finding a Soviet citizen justified in casting the first stone for this sin.

The party committee decided not to accept Mir's gift of the candidate Zhirinovsky gracefully. The electoral commission, under its control, refused to confirm the candidacy, and in the end the frustrated party chiefs canceled the election. The publishing house protested. For the first time within its ancient walls there could be heard uncensored criticism of both the district committee as a whole and specific members of it. Every day at the publishing house there were meetings in defense of

---

organized crime; guarding the government's gold and diamond reserves, from the mines to the storage vaults; guarding state secrets; and doing counterintelligence work. I knew many KGB personnel, mostly at a fairly high level, from lieutenant colonel on up, and I was often simply amazed at their honesty, decency, education, and intelligence. This may be why there have been such a large number of free thinkers and nonconformists among KGB personnel.

Zhirinovsky, with TV cameras and newspaper reporters present at many of them. The TV program *Good Evening, Moscow* broadcast numerous interviews with Zhirinovsky. The upshot was that, although Zhirinovsky lost the battle to become a candidate to the district soviet, he won a gigantic political victory over the party apparatus and became a hero to many Muscovites.

From this point on, Zhirinovsky, now a well-known personality in Moscow, attended every meeting of the democrats, protesting against the Communist Party's dominant position, Gorbachev, the Afghanistan war, and so on. A couple of times, the police informed me that he had been arrested in Pushkin Square for participating in illegal protests there. Once he arrived at work covered with bruises and with both eyes blackened, his arm in a cast—he had been severely beaten by the police. On another occasion, he was fined heavily for participation in illegal meetings, and our accountant had to deduct 20 percent from his salary for several months.

His growing popularity caused me many difficulties. Around this time, Gorbachev had promulgated a new law authorizing the formation of a council of the work collective (*soviet trudovogo kollektiva*, or STK) at each socialist enterprise. In deciding all questions relating to production, an STK would have rights equal to those of the director, who had previously held sole authority. This caused me great concern. There were unprofitable editorial groups at Mir that did not earn enough political capital to make up for their financial losses and needed to be cut back. The publishing house needed to expand its premises, repair its buildings, install computers, make changes in its editorial policies, and reassign personnel. Previously all such matters had to be cleared with the ministry, the party's Central Committee, and the district party committee, as well as with the trade union committee and the party committee at the publishing house itself. Now to all these obstacles Gorbachev had added one more.

I knew that if Zhirinovsky got onto Mir's STK, I would not be able to put through any proposals that might prove unpopular. As a result, I devoted every effort to preventing his being elected to the council. In a speech to the work collective as a whole, I argued that Zhirinovsky was a demagogue, that his promises of solving publishing problems easily (for example, by having Mir print only literature for which there was a big demand, abandoning narrowly scientific material) could not be trusted, that if he were on the STK, he would create more problems than he would solve. The vote of the work collective by secret ballot supported my position. Zhirinovsky didn't even make the list of candidates.

In March 1989, when the first free elections to the Supreme Soviet of the USSR were held, Zhirinovsky again offered his candidacy. This time, I managed to convince him not to do so, arguing that it would be more constructive not to complicate the election of another candidate—Vitaly Korotich, editor in chief of *Ogonyok* magazine, a sharp critic of the Communist Party in general and Gorbachev personally, and then a champion of democratic reform. When Korotich visited Mir to meet with the employees, who supported him almost unanimously, instead of offering himself up as an opponent, Zhirinovsky made a speech in praise of the candidate.

Not long after that I moved to New York to take up the position of director of publications at the United Nations. A competition was held to fill the position I was vacating at Mir. Anyone could apply for the position as long as he or she met certain criteria (top-level management experience in publishing, an academic degree, a knowledge of foreign languages, etc.). The competition was held in February 1990. There were six applicants: my first deputy director, Dr. Gennady Kurganov; four relatively unknown figures from both inside and outside the publishing house; and, predictably, Zhirinovsky. When it came to presenting his proposals for a publishing program, however, Zhirinovsky was at something of a disadvantage compared to the other candidates. Whatever talents he showed for making positive contributions to developing Mir's list of publications were far inferior to those he manifested when skewering the company with his penetrating criticisms. Whereas Kurganov outlined the same kind of program that he and I had been following up to then, Zhirinovsky proposed several exotic but totally impractical ideas. Of the required 321 votes (half the employees, plus one) he was able to pick up only a few dozen. The competition was won by the more experienced Kurganov, who to this day remains the director of Mir.

Here are the recollections of one of my former colleagues at Mir, now an economist:

[Zhirinovsky] changed drastically during the perestroika years. Around 1986 he took every opportunity to attack the Communists, shouting that "those bastards covered all the world with blood." He was outraged with "the crimes of the Soviet military clique in Afghanistan." I remember there was a fistfight once. . . . Later he began making these statements at our [publishing house workers'] meetings. We attended those meeting as if they were performances and joked that we had a performer better than Khasanov [a famous Soviet comic artist] himself. He had one notable feature: as soon as he appeared in an auditorium, he would switch himself on and nobody could stop him before he hit full cry—and more. It was useless to contradict him. . . . such absolute shamelessness! Still, a lot of people in the publishing house liked what he said (or screamed) because he didn't just make generic attacks against the Communist mafia; he would mention particular names—the director's, his deputies, and others. Mir's collective divided, with some of the young workers supporting Zhirinovsky. The culmination of the conflict was the election of the [new] director of the publishing house. Zhirinovsky proposed his candidacy for the post, promising "two-month paid vacations and thousand-ruble salaries" to everyone. As a result, he got a miserable percentage of the votes. . . . Why? It's easy to understand. Enjoying oneself by laughing and making some noise at a meeting is one thing, but when you are thinking about your own pocket, you want to know the price. . . . Almost everybody voted for the old leadership, which offered stability and predictability.[5]

Another of Mir's editors recalled:

When I think of Zhirinovsky during his time at Mir and compare his behavior then with what he is doing today, I see an almost perfect match, as if in a mirror. The principle is the same: the worse things get, the better. He keenly picks up on people's points of dissatisfaction, skillfully fans the flames of their discontent, and uses it for his own interests. . . . The worse the situation in contemporary Russia, the more reasons he will have to yell and to attract new voters. There are very cultured and literate people at Mir; Zhirinovsky's bluffing could not fool us. . . . But now, in 1994, the situation in the publishing house is so miserable, people would not only vote for Zhirinovsky but for a devil with horns.[6]

Starting with his first election campaign, Zhirinovsky began developing his populism, which can sometimes take on a very unattractive form. Take his alleged anti-Semitism, for example. During the course of six years working with him closely, I never noticed anything like it, yet I am not at all surprised now when some of his remarks can undoubtedly be interpreted as anti-Semitic. Zhirinovsky is a true populist: he says what his audience is starved to hear. Like a chameleon, he changes

5. Menzheritsky, "Vladimir Volfovich protiv Vladimira Volfovicha" (Vladimir Volfovich versus Vladimir Volfovich), 5.
6. Ibid.

his views, at least superficially, to suit his present audience. Consequently, Zhirinovsky's anti-Semitism could be understood as a sign of increasing anti-Semitism among the electorate.

It is very educational to read Zhirinovsky's program for replacing me as director of Mir. I quote some particularly interesting passages here:

> I am a partisan of the Western civilizations. In the Western world, with its enormous achievements, intellectual cadres are the main decisive element. Eighty percent of all posts are occupied by university graduates who studied the humanities—lawyers and economists. I have two university degrees, one of them in law.
>
> In our unfortunately still uncomputerized world the personality of the leader is extremely important. What should it look like? In the absolute majority of cases, the leader is a man of average age, with a university degree, preferably in law; a métis (this is a prerequisite in our multinational society); open to compromise; not a CPSU member; a supporter of multistructural economics and the multiparty system, not bound by the privileges of this dying regime; ingenious; familiar with international problems (economics, culture, languages); and with working experience in different organizations and systems. I think that I fit all these parameters. I am able to be the director and I want to be.

This document was clearly designed for Mir: a cultured, liberal, predominantly Jewish, Westernized audience. Addressing another audience, Zhirinovsky would have changed the text completely, leaving only its gist.

Zhirinovsky, although defeated, remained as energetic as ever and soon involved himself completely in the affairs of his newly founded party and the elections for the position of president of Russia. This was the first time in Russian history that such elections had been held. Six prominent figures were running for office, among them Boris Yeltsin and former Soviet Premier Nikolai Ryzhkov. Hardly anyone outside Moscow knew of Zhirinovsky or his Liberal Democratic Party of Russia, which had just been officially registered. Still, the fact that it was the first legal political party in the USSR other than the CPSU aroused the interest and curiosity of a good proportion—say, half—of the voters. Almost certainly contributing to their interest was his ten-point program, which was conservatively democratic in tenor. One of its notable points was the call for an end to the general bad-mouthing of the CPSU. Its penultimate point was more demagogic—a demand for cheap vodka.

ZHIRINOVSKY'S PROGRAM

If elected to the presidency of Russia, I propose:

1. To reject the policy by which Russia and the center [i.e., Moscow, then capital of the USSR] are placed in opposition to each other, and to abolish the "war of laws" [in which local authorities were passing laws conflicting with those adopted by the central government in Moscow, and vice versa].
2. To remove all limitations from all forms of economic activity and to influence such activity only through taxation.
3. To change the direction of foreign policy in order to allow all necessary material resources to enter our country and to guarantee the security of foreign investment.
4. To undertake a gradual elimination of universal military service and a systematic transition to the formation of a professional army.
5. To demand repayment of foreign debts [i.e., Russian or Soviet loans to foreign recipients] or their refinancing by third-party countries.
6. To adopt a new USSR constitution and a new system of legislation.
7. To adopt measures within the limits of the law for stopping anti-Communist hysteria and witch-hunting.
8. To adopt effective legislation to defend citizens from the criminal element.
9. To lower prices on alcohol and demand its sale in all commercial outlets.
10. To resolve national problems as they are resolved throughout the world, that is, by rejecting the division of the country on the basis of ethnic territories and switching instead to a system of division into regions and provinces.

Zhirinovsky won third place, after Ryzhkov and Yeltsin. More than six million Russian voters cast their ballots for him. It was only then that people realized they were dealing with a shrewd and truly professional politician. Each early defeat had taught him something. This became especially clear in December 1993, with the results of the elections to the lower house of the Russian parliament, the State Duma.

5

The LDPR Program: Politics and Economics

The idea of forming a party, which had ripened in Zhirinovsky's mind as early as 1987, was given final form in 1991. Around this time, a pamphlet appeared containing an address by Vladimir Zhirinovsky, chairman of the Liberal Democratic Party of Russia, to members and sympathizers of the party, as well as the LDPR program and statute. The exact date when these documents were adopted by Zhirinovsky's party is unknown; however, an analysis of Zhirinovsky's ideas and the dynamics of his thinking, as revealed in his speeches, suggests that the main tenets of his party's current program took shape during the 1991 campaign for the presidency of Russia, the elections for which took place that June.

The most important task for Zhirinovsky was to mark out the party's position on the Russian political landscape. In his opinion, there were five main political trends in Russia. First, there were the ultralefts: the United Front of Workers; the All-Union Communist Party (of Bolsheviks), led by the notorious Nina Andreyeva; and Working Russia, led by Oleg Anpilov. These forces, in Zhirinovsky's opinion, simply wanted to go back to Stalin-Brezhnev socialism. Second, there were the moderate left parties: the Civic Union and the parties led by Arkady Volsky, Aleksandr Rutskoi, and Ivan Travkin, all of whom came out of the CPSU and are ex-Communist "pinks." Third were the people in power, a mixed bag of reds, pinks, and radical reformers, with dozens of different leaders, such as Yegor Gaidar, Anatoly Sobchak, Gavriil

Popov, Grigory Yavlinsky, Gennady Burbulis, and Sergei Shakhrai, the main ideologists of this movement being Gaidar, Burbulis, and Popov; as Zhirinovsky has put it, "Just as Suslov stood behind Brezhnev, whispering in his ear, so it is with these three" in relation to Yeltsin. All the other leaders of the reform bloc tag along after them. Fourth is the LDPR, which is not tied to any other group; it is a moderate party, not of the left, a party "just to the right of center, by about twenty degrees." Fifth are the ultraright nationalist groupings—Aleksandr Sterligov's Russian National Assembly, Nikolay Lysenko's National Republican Party, and, last but not least, the Russian Christian Democratic Movement of Vladimir Aksyutchits, which calls for Russian Orthodoxy and a purely Russian state.[1]

That is how the political playing field appeared to Zhirinovsky up to mid-1993. Then came the events of October, with the shelling of the Russian parliament building—the prevailing opinion is that the number of victims of the shelling and the later armed raids by the special "antiterrorist" groups is much higher than has been declared officially—and the banning of several parties and newspapers, at least temporarily. The political vacuum created by Yeltsin's suppression of the parliamentary opposition increased Zhirinovsky's appeal dramatically, and he was the main winner in the parliamentary elections of December 1993. Although the political landscape changes literally from day to day—with new parties, blocs, and movements appearing and old ones disappearing—in principle, the scene portrayed by Zhirinovsky continues to the present. There is the radical reformist group (which has "discredited itself"), the left, "dogmatic" Communist wing, and the right-wing, extremely nationalistic, and racist group akin to the tsarist "Black Hundred." To the left of center (Zhirinovsky does not say by how many degrees) stand the parties of Rutskoi, Volsky, and Travkin, and to the right of center stands the LDPR.

This appraisal of the political forces on the Russian stage is reflected in the LDPR program, at least in one of its versions.[2] In the section called General Propositions, there are no indications of movement toward either socialism or capitalism. All the formulations in this sec-

---

1. See *Liberal'no-demokraticheskaia partiia Rossii* (Liberal Democratic Party of Russia); *Politicheskaia Rossiia segodnia: Vysshaia predstavitel'naia vlast'* (Political Russia today: The supreme representative authority); *Politicheskaia Rossiia segodnia: Ispolnitel'naia vlast'* (Political Russia today: The executive authority); and Koval', *Partii i politicheskie bloki v Rossii* (Parties and political blocs in Russia).

2. Unless otherwise noted, all the quotations in the following paragraphs are from *Obrashchenie Vladimira Zhirinovskogo* (Address by Vladimir Zhirinovsky).

tion are extremely vague, open to any interpretation. The party's goal is "to create conditions in the country for the free exercise of the creative powers of the populations inhabiting it, and the assiduous utilization of the natural resources of our country." A party for the realization of creative potential? For creative freedom? Moreover, the second part of the statement doesn't jibe very well with the first. In any case, any program could be set up under this canopy. There are no specifics here, nothing to fight over, nothing to criticize—who could find fault with a party for the people, for their free creative development, and for their "assiduous" economic activity in their own land? This blandness explains why LDPR supporters can hold such mutually exclusive viewpoints. That was precisely Zhirinovsky's intention.

What is the party's program? It is "a program for the development of our society in accordance with its own needs without any interference from the outside." The first part of this formulation seems to tip its hat slightly in the direction of the socialists (recalling the phrase of Marx and Engels, "from each according to ability, to each according to need"). Later, that impression recedes. The soft reference in the first part to the Marxist idea of self-development, or development in itself, is suddenly and abruptly sharpened in the second part with the reference to outside interference. All distinct political coordinates are absent except for the notion of *outside*, which most likely implies the West (although those who believe in an outside threat from the East—or the South, or even the North—may readily seize upon this formulation as well).

A hint of a political platform emerges from the definition of what constitutes a member of the LDPR: a person who does not separate personal interests from those of the motherland; a "creator capable of carrying out the priority tasks of the motherland aimed at preserving peace and raising the standard of living of all the population of our vast country." This section of the LDPR program contains two commonsense items—peace and a higher standard of living—hardly likely to arouse objections.

The next paragraph of the program furnishes a clear-cut definition of the LDPR's political boundaries:

> The political activity of the LDPR is directed toward the restoration by peaceful means and the preservation of the Russian state that was created over the course of centuries; the restoration and guarding of the borders of the country; the realization within the country of the peaceful coexistence of all the populations inhabiting it—both small and large—with the right of preservation of traditions and customs, and

the development of each individual's national culture and religion. Russia is a motherland for all, without any kind of discrimination.

This paragraph contains the central core, the very essence, of Zhirinovsky's politics. He puts it more colorfully in his speeches: "For me, the touchstone for every individual is his attitude toward Russia's state borders. If someone contends that Ukraine is a separate state, standing outside of Russia, he is not my traveling companion." It is this portion of the program that has provoked bitter criticism from both Russian democrats and the Western mass media. On the other hand, because of its extremely clear and radical expression of the idea of restoring the Russian state, it also has drawn a large number of supporters to Zhirinovsky's camp.

It is important to note that although this paragraph calls for the restoration of the Russian state, it specifies that this must occur *through peaceful means*. Judging from this paragraph, the LDPR is not proposing to seize any territory. Even Zhirinovsky's harshest critics—for example, Eduard Limonov, the former minister of state security in Zhirinovsky's shadow cabinet—agree that the LDPR program and the public election rally speeches of Zhirinovsky, which admittedly contain expansionist rhetoric, are two quite different things: "For many run-of-the-mill 'democrats' and 'progressives,' Zhirinovsky's name is virtually a synonym for 'fascist,' " writes Limonov. "Yet hardly one in a thousand people who can't stand Zhirinovsky has read the program of his Liberal Democratic Party."[3] Zhirinovsky himself emphasizes the principled nature of the position stated in this paragraph of the LDPR's program.

In the LDPR program's chapter on domestic policy, Russia is subdivided not into republics but into provinces (*gubernii*, reviving the term used in the tsarist era). The LDPR holds that rule on the basis of such *gubernii* would exclude national hostilities and potential ethnic conflicts. The program further states that "the creation of national states on the territory of Russia is ruled out." This view, which many critics consider racist, ultranationalist, or even fascist, nevertheless has tremendous support among the masses of the Russian population, sick and tired of the "parade of sovereignties," and the bloodshed, poverty, and misery resulting from that same parade in the majority of cases (Chechnya is a good "bad example"). Solzhenitsyn, making a presentation in the Duma, virtually supported this view in full.[4] So did "democrat" Shakray.

3. Limonov, *Limonov protiv Zhirinovskogo* (Limonov versus Zhirinovsky), 16.
4. Solzhenitsyn, "Rech' v Gosudarstvennoi Dume" (Speech in the State Duma), 14.

It is enlightening to compare Zhirinovsky's nationalistic ideas with those of his adversary Eduard Limonov, head of the National-Bolshevik Party, expressed in the June 13–19 issue of Moscow *Den'*: "We don't want your liberal-democratic international Russia. . . . We want national Russia: only the Russian language and Russian schools from Leningrad to Kamchatka. We would like to Russify the entire country through a national revolution, which could be spiritual and bloodless if you don't block us but will happen by force if you try to strangle it."[5] Even more radical views are expressed in the newspapers *Russky put'*, *Za Russkoye Delo*, *Rodnye prostory*, and Aleksander Barkashov's *Russky poryadok*. As Alexsandr Burtin reports, groups such as the Confederation of Free Trade Unions and Russian National Unity skillfully exploit the radical democrats' mistakes in their foreign and domestic policies and criticize Zhirinovsky for being "too mild" and "seeking compromises with the powers-that-be."[6]

Zhirinovsky reacts sharply to accusations that he is a fascist. Recently he won a lawsuit against Yegor Gaidar, who had labeled him a fascist in *Izvestia*; a Moscow court found both the newspaper and Gaidar guilty of libel and fined them 500,000 rubles apiece.[7] Zhirinovsky has won similar lawsuits against a newspaper in Finland. And it seems quite possible that he will also sue Penguin for its recent book about him.

This domestic policy section of the LDPR program also proclaims the primacy of law. (The word *law* appears in the LDPR emblem as well, together with the words *freedom* and *Russia*.) At the same time, rather than using the usual phrases *legislative authorities* (referring to the State Duma) and *executive authorities* (referring to the presidency), this section refers to *the legislature*—no authority is given here. Authority is attached, however, to the functions of the presidency (the *executive authority*), and I think this is deliberate. Zhirinovsky is a proponent of a strong presidential authority—in practice, a dictatorship. Without this, in his party's opinion, Russia cannot emerge from its downward spiral. "The president has the right to dissolve parliament, to call new elections, and to veto laws." A very weak counterbalance to this very strong statement appears in the following clause: "The president bears responsibility in relation to the parliament in the event of the commission by him of anticonstitutional actions." In practice, it is impossible to make effective use of this clause, as revealed by the events of Sep-

5. Cited in Lulechnik, "Liberal li gospodin Zhirinovskii"? (Is Zhirinovsky really liberal?), 5.
6. See Burtin, "Fashisty, govoriashchie pravdu" (Fascists telling the truth), 6.
7. AP, Moscow, September 15, 1994.

tember-October 1993, when the parliamentary call for Yeltsin's impeachment led to a bloody confrontation.

A section aptly entitled "The Economy" spells out the economic credo of the LDPR: "The aim of the LDPR's economic policy is to create a worthy and happy life of dignity and prosperity for every inhabitant of Russia—gradually, without 'revolutionary leaps' and convulsions" and, a few paragraphs later, "without any prompting, or granting of enslaving credit, 'from the outside.' " Privatization would begin by affecting only small enterprises and the service sector. Enterprises slated for privatization would not be sold to individuals having no direct connection with them; rather, such enterprises would become the property of the collective (i.e., the workforce) employed at them. Only later is free sale of such enterprises envisioned. In the immediate term, the land would remain under state ownership; citizens would be allowed to use plots of land free of charge for periods of twenty-five to fifty years, with the right of inheritance, on condition of the land being used for agricultural purposes.

The three whales of the LDPR economic program, which, as Zhirinovsky sees it, will bring a 100 percent improvement in Russian life, are (1) the cessation of any kind of aid to other countries; (2) an end to the conversion of military industry to civilian uses; and (3) a determined war against crime, including the elimination of all five thousand of the known gangs on the territory of Russia.

The section entitled "Social Policy" stresses the need to preserve "all the positive things achieved by the previous development of the country: [in particular,] free education and medical care (with the rights to paid education and medical care to exist for those who want them)." Also, each national group is to have the option of carrying out instruction in its native language.

The section entitled "Ecology" was obviously written with an eye to outward appearances. It does not contain anything noteworthy, unlike "Foreign Policy," the section that follows, which proclaims as main principles noninterference in the internal affairs of other countries and resistance to all attempts at dictating to Russia the terms of its existence or threatening it with the use of force "from the outside."

This section also includes Zhirinovsky's celebrated geopolitical blueprint: the transition he proposes from the existing East-West relationship to the more advantageous prospects and reduced tensions of a North-South alignment. Achieving this would require an agreement among the leading powers and a division of the world into spheres of influence reflecting economic interests, these to be established exclusively by economic and political, never military, means. The sphere of influence for the United States and Canada would be Latin America and the Caribbean; for the developed countries of Europe, it would be West Africa; for Russia, Afghanistan, Iran, and Turkey; for Japan and China, South Asia and Oceania. The same ideas are contained in Zhirinovsky's famous book *Poslednii brosok na iug* (The last dash to the south). While acknowledging that the calls for a dash to the south are completely absurd and while condemning resolutely the imperial ambitions that are evident, along with some discreet saber rattling, in Zhirinovsky's book, one must admit that Zhirinovsky, by the very act of raising the question of Russia's geopolitical role, its potential allies, and its future place in the world is one step ahead of his rivals in the Yeltsin administration and the Russian Foreign Ministry. Disregard for Russia's geopolitical interests or lack of clarity about Russia's future will inevitably produce a conflict between long- and short-term interests. This is like concealing a land mine in the path of progress in international relations. All the lords and sovereigns of the tsarist and socialist eras had their geopolitical plans for Russia and pursued them as far as they could. These plans were not secret, and they made the policies of the Russian government to a certain extent predictable.[8] Sometimes, though, Zhirinovsky's geopolitical plans are frightening. On January 29, 1994, *Le Monde* published a model of Europe designed by Zhirinovsky and showing the future borders of Eastern Europe.

> Poland is divided between Russia and Germany, with Russia including Belarus and Ukraine, now independent states. True, the shrunken Poland received the Lvov district as a compensation. Königsberg is safely returned to Germany. As it was planned, the Baltic states go to Russia. True, Zhirinovsky leaves Tallinn and Kaunas independent, granting each of them the status of a "city-state," like Luxembourg or Lichtenstein.
>
> Under Zhirinovsky's plan Austria, Czechia, and Slovenia will be annexed to Germany while Slovakia will go to Russia. By a resolute inscription Zhirinovsky drives UN troops out of former Yugoslavia. According to his plan, it will be divided in half between the Serbs and Croats.[9]

Clearly, however, the image of Russian soldiers washing their boots

8. See Moscow, *Russia Under the Czars*; Massie, *Peter the Great*; Hodgetts, *The Life of Catherine the Great*; *Nikita Sergeevich Khrushchev*; and Medvedev. *Lichnost' i epokha* (The individual and the era).

9. I. R., "Zhirinovsky Recarves the Map of Eastern Europe," 25.

in the Indian Ocean so familiar from Zhirinovsky's speeches would have no chance of realization under the terms of his party's main document. On paper, anyway, the LDPR program is not straightforwardly fascist, expansionist, or the like; in fact, it is a fairly unexceptionable, if extravagant, party program. One must always keep in mind that, as a postmodernist politician, Zhirinovsky seems not to ascribe any importance to what he says in his speeches, and only occasionally does he try to explain himself. The so-called facts asserted in any of his various speeches may not correspond to reality, may contradict statements in other speeches, and may even contradict supposed facts cited in the same speech.

Zhirinovsky is not a typical professional politician, and for the majority, he is a completely unacceptable one. He is not a professional diplomat whose words conceal hidden meanings and whose speeches reflect shadings of intent too subtle for the uninitiated to comprehend. He bears no resemblance to the party apparatchiks of the Soviet period, notably the period from Khrushchev to Gorbachev, whose speeches, bereft of new ideas, merely refashioned ancient party dogma. His are not the pronouncements of a government minister operating on the basis of specific facts. His speeches are impressive precisely because of their departure from what is standard and predictable and because of their liberal applications of emotional color. For those qualities many people are ready to forgive him his unverified facts, his tortured logic, and his preposterous claims. That's how things were during his time at Mir, and that's how things are today.

6

The Smashing Victory: The December 1993 Elections

More than any other candidate, Zhirinovsky took the election to the Duma and the speeches connected with it extremely seriously. His two-week preelection campaign was filled from morning to night with radio and television interviews and constant meetings with the people. On one day—November 30—he gave interviews to the radio station Mayak and the television studio Rossiya, and from then until December 10—the final day of the campaign—he appeared four times at the Ostankino television station, once on Leningrad television, and once on Moscow television.

On December 9 he participated in a televised roundtable debate hyped as an interparty preelection meeting among the leaders of the other parties and movements, with the exception of Yeltsin, whose absence angered a segment of the population. (Although Zhirinovsky would later play this circumstance to his advantage, there was really no reason for Yeltsin to attend. The event was intended to be a debate among the leaders of the competing political parties, and Yeltsin did not fit that description.) During this clash of opposing viewpoints and ideologies Zhirinovsky came off looking much more energetic, forceful, and telegenic than all the other party leaders. Viewers who subsequently recalled the debate said that Zhirinovsky told them exactly what they wanted to hear at that particular moment: he praised Russia, soundly castigated the foreigners who had won the cold war, promised relief to retirees, high pensions for the military, low taxes to the industrial and banking sector, free education to students, husbands to single women, and law and order to citizens fed up with violence. The other speakers at the round table, though they tried to outdo Zhirinovsky with fancy turns of economic and political phrase, did nothing to excite the television audience, which had tuned in for a real show. Only Zhirinovsky met their expectations.

The LDPR printed up a huge number of its publications—*Liberal* (The liberal), *Pravda Zhirinovskogo* (Zhirinovsky's truth), *Sokol Zhirinovskogo* (Zhirinovsky's falcon), and *Iuridicheskaya gazeta* (Judicial newspaper)—and sold them at a discounted price of a hundred rubles or simply gave them away. *Iuridicheskaia gazeta* printed the party's most bombastic slogans:

I WILL DEFEND THE RUSSIANS!
PAY BACK DEBTS TO RUSSIA!
WARMTH AND TENDERNESS TO WOMEN!
WE WILL OVERCOME CRIME AND LIVE BETTER!
PENSIONERS NEED OUR ATTENTION!
OFFICERS! I SHALL HELP YOU!

Of these promises, only one seems at first glance to be clear and concise: that calling for the USSR's debtors to repay their debts.

Zhirinovsky had taken the bull by the horns, appealing directly to those elements of society most hurt by hasty Russian reforms: Russians feeling not only the unprecedented loss of superpower status but total humiliation, women once again suffering under the double duty of work and home, all citizens caught up in the general fear of the organized crime that was spreading like cancer and paralyzing the instruments of public order, pensioners already devoid of hope and mercilessly criticized every day by the new breed of brazen journalists, and military personnel, stripped of official roles, ideals, and family life.

In his efforts to sway the different members of the humiliated Russian population, Zhirinovsky continuously reached for higher passion, more artistry, and correspondingly greater effect, playing up for each group the most attractive points of his party's program, its arguments, and even its language. Consider, for example, these selections addressed to various groups around the country (each excerpt's target should be easily inferable):

My fine citizens! How good you are! You have worked so hard. You have such emaciated hands. Your body and soul are so weary. You want so much just a little kindness from the society in which you live.

And warmth in your apartments to keep you from freezing. Just a little something in your refrigerators. You are content with a glass of kefir, kasha, lean necks, sweet tea with a bun. You would just like to read a few kind words about yourselves in the paper, to watch television without any violence or horror, or any distasteful scenes of immorality.

Our history can be likened to a history of sexual perversities, crimes, and diseases. We never had real sex. The October Revolution raped the people, the Stalin era can be compared to homosexuality, the Khrushchev years to masturbation, and Brezhnev to impotence. I promise that, if you elect the representatives of the LDPR, you will experience a real orgasm for the first time in your lives!

Our party's program wants, first and foremost, to think about you and your families. We promise you always the highest salary, regardless of the economic situation in the country. Always—and we promise this once and for all—housing. Not one single family will ever be without an apartment. Pensions must correspond to the high living standard of retired officers and generals. Education, medicine, and relaxation for the whole family must become the concern of the Ministry of Defense. Upon retirement, an officer or a general, if he wants it, must absolutely receive several hectares of good land with buildings (an abandoned village or a collapsed large collective farm).[1]

We declare that everything done in the name of the Russian Army of the Russian Empire, the Soviet Army during the USSR, and the Russian Army during the past two years of the current regime, is justified and correct, including their connection to events in the Baltics, the Caucasus, and Central Asia. No one has the right to criticize our army.

Russian people from Izmail and Pridnestrovye to Sakhalin and Kamchatka, from Murmansk to Chukotka! Throughout the entire territory of our huge motherland your settlements are and always have been. Millions of Russian people thought of you and still think of you as free people. From time immemorial your lives have basically been lived within the borders of great Russia. It was a terrible time when they tried to erase you from the memory of our people, from the history of our motherland as a class, as a part of Russian history.

1. Note that the LDPR program specifically states that land will remain under state ownership, available only to those private citizens who plan to use it for agricultural purposes.

You should live no worse off than highly qualified workers and aver-age entrepreneurs. The better you live, the more developed and healthy will be the citizens of Russia. The LDPR maintains that there will be no happy future for our country without happy teachers, doc-tors, lawyers, and artists. I promise, hand in hand with you, to think up and make law those privileges that will better your life, like free comfortable housing and communal services not only in the village but in the city as well, in addition to a significant raise in salary and health care on a high level. Your children will be entitled to special enrollment in higher institutes of learning, especially if they have chosen to follow you in your specialty.

Whose heart is not rent in two, looking at our towns and villages, which have been forcibly rendered without prospect? Pensioners and former collective farm workers will live out the rest of their lives there without doctors, without electricity, without shops. And this is happening just a few hundred kilometers from our biggest cities! The mortality rate of Russia's rural population is almost as high as that of Africa's. How much longer are we going to put up with this?

In his campaign speeches, Zhirinovsky skillfully made use of the government's mistakes: "Two years ago more than six million Russians voted for me, and I came in third in the presidential election. Today, two years later, you see the deplorable results of those whom you voted into power in nineteen ninety-one." Naturally, he understood that he had to explain exactly why the LDPR would be the better choice. His first point concerned the "purity of the party's biography": "In four years we have never once deviated from our position, nor have we run from one camp to another." Such consistency was guaranteed to appeal to the Russian population, which had long been a silent but judgmen-tal witness to the seat-of-the-pants chaos in Russian domestic and for-eign policy.

Zhirinovsky also touched on another sore spot: the status of former Communists—Communists by both conviction and calculation—of which there were sixteen million throughout the empire and ten mil-lion in Russia alone. The democrats' failures had elicited nostalgia for the wretched and rather boring but completely secure and peaceful times under the Communists: "By no means do we advocate that a spirit of anti-Communism reign in the country, and neither do we want the blame for everything bad that happened to fall only on the rank-and-file members of the Communist Party. Our party is perfectly aware that too many mistakes, at times tragic, were made by the former lead-ers of the Communist Party, but when we take into account that in the

Russian Federation alone there were ten million members, we outright reject anti-Communism in our domestic policy."

Then, in order to put the fears of democrats to rest, Zhirinovsky immediately proclaimed: "Our party is right-centrist, moderately conservative, and patriotic. We oppose extremist tendencies with a leftist or ultrarightist stance. We are for parliamentary methods and participation in elections."

Other concrete proposals slipped through in his radio and television appearances before different audiences:

Zhirinovsky was against the USSR and the CIS; he was for Russia, a Russian state undivided by the borders of republics artificially created by Stalin for peoples who previously had had no states of their own. Instead, he dreamt of a Russia with the borders from 1900, the year when it included Finland and Poland, or, in the worst case, from 1975, when its borders, encompassing all fifteen republics, were recognized by all the heads of state of Europe and the USA, signatories to the Helsinki Accords, as eternal and inviolable European borders. But he considered this to be a concern for the future and for the moment simply envisioned the coming restoration of a great Russia "by lawful means only," without revolutions and wars.

In later speeches he began defining the basic elements of the LDPR's program, which came to be known as the Zhirinovsky program: "We are against the restoration of the USSR, because within a USSR-like framework, Russia would once again contain several former national republics. We are also against the CIS [Commonwealth of Independent States], because the dismemberment of the USSR into a host of states led to Russia losing lakes, ports, enterprises, communications, territories, and land. Millions of Russians and Russian-speaking inhabitants of Russia are now beyond its borders. They have become pariahs, second-class people deprived of their blood, their means of existence, and turned into refugees, bums, and beggars.

"Each and every one of us wants to know when this tragedy will end. Seventy-five years of revolution, war, and perestroika. For ninety years—since 1904—from the first Russo-Japanese War up to the second Russo-Afghan War, the country has been drenched in blood. Parents receive 'killed in battle' notices as young Russians perish for the freedom and interests of others, giving up not only their lives but their honor, freedom, and property as well. In order to disperse more quickly this black cloud over Russia, this night of long knives, in which one group or another, carrying out large-scale provocations, pits brother against brother over and over again so that one group can sit more sturdily in the thrones that they took illegally, we need new forces to take over the helm of government."

Zhirinovsky delicately sidestepped one complex question: who was in the right in the October 1993 conflict between Parliament and Yeltsin? His position was brilliantly uncomplicated: "Our party does not support those who barricaded themselves inside the White House, nor does it defend those who ordered that shots be fired against them." Avoiding the need for any tortuous deliberation involving moral convictions, political savvy, or intellectual rigor, this stance was comprehensible to any politically unsophisticated man or woman on Russia's streets. Its very simplicity led many to greet it with loud huzzahs.

About the democratic freedoms proclaimed by the LDPR, Zhirinovsky did not specify anything in particular. Recognizing that all the promises of freedom doled out so carelessly by the other parties had already turned off the electorate, which would gladly have accepted partial freedom in exchange for better food and warmer clothes, he kept things short and sweet: "Our party will grant you all freedoms intrinsic to a civilized world. We will not allow any discrimination on social, political, ideological, religious, or other grounds."

The next part of the program dealt with economics. Money was needed for everything—state reconstruction, the border, the army, police, education, and health. The mean standard of living in Russia had fallen to unprecedented levels: the number of people living not just below the poverty line but below even the level of subsistence was measured in tens of millions. The potential was building for a gigantic social cataclysm. The people needed relief. But not from charity: "We don't need humanitarian aid. Russia is not a country that needs leftovers. We are not second-class people. We are for equal relations, for partnership. We will not strive for world domination, but at the same time we will not allow the hegemony of any other power in the world. We don't need the capital of any foreign government to dictate to us how to run our affairs." Where, then, would the money come from? Zhirinovsky's answer was again simple: to the slogan PAY BACK DEBTS TO RUSSIA!, he added "We will halt all aid to any region outside Russia's borders." The refusal of such help, he believed, coupled with a retrieval of old debts from foreign countries, would elevate Russia's living standard by approximately one-third.

Other plans for financing the government programs existed as well. "We will put a halt to the conversion of military industry to civilian purposes." In Zhirinovsky's opinion, this would raise the welfare of the people by still another one-third. Then, "We will stop strangling the state sector and destroying collective farms and state farms. We will give complete freedom to the private sector, but at first this will have to be a private sector devoted to additional new production. There will be benefits and privileges. We will not allow middlemen and speculators to flourish. This will prevent prices from being sharply inflated and each one of us from being cheated." Once again, Zhirinovsky deftly supported two opposed groups—the private sector and the many people who had grown to despise "the new Russians," businessmen who earned millions of dollars without producing anything, simply by moving papers back and forth and inflating prices.

To gain the final third, thereby doubling the standard of living, he promised to deal with "the five thousand organized criminal gangs" operating on Russian territory. This position again struck two responsive chords at once: it promised an improvement in the quality of life and the simultaneous deliverance of the populace from its constant fear of falling victim to the next run-in between criminal bands, errant bullet, or car explosion. (Incidentally, Zhirinovsky did not come up with the one-third fraction out of the blue—according to Russian businessmen who, as usual, prefer to remain anonymous, this is about what the Russian mafia demands as protection money from every legal enterprise.)

The LDPR's program acknowledged that its articulation of economic issues was superficial. Even Zhirinovsky admitted this in one of his speeches, though only in context with other political parties: "Today neither the Communists, nor the democrats, nor any other party has an economic program. We don't even have a home. How can one speak seriously about what kind of furniture to put in the apartment if we don't even have an apartment? How can we speak of order in the house when the house has no doors or locks? Therefore we first have to come to terms with our home, with our motherland. We have to begin with our state borders, the army, the constitution, the law, the national emblem and hymn, a new police force and customs."

The foreign policy of the future Russia, according to Zhirinovsky, would be an independent, traditional Russian policy, maintaining contacts with "our brothers in the Balkans," the Serbs, and other Orthodox peoples. It would promote friendship with Arab countries, especially Iraq. Good relations with India would continue, while a balanced and mutually beneficial policy with China and Japan would also be realized. Economic ties would be restored in full with Eastern Europe.

The Zhirinovsky campaign duplicated millions of copies of the preelection program to distribute throughout the country, where party activists attempted to disseminate it to every household. Its main selling point was its significant difference from the program of the government group, Russia's Choice, which was teeming with scientific phrases but out of touch with the current mood and feelings of the voters. Moreover, the simple fact that they were in power was the kiss of death for the ruling parties. Many people, like Zhirinovsky, figured that everyone belonging to this bloc was directly to blame for the nightmare happening around them, for the tragedy that could be traced not to the October 1917 revolution but to April 1985, the advent of perestroika, and especially to August 1991, when the radical democrats came into power. Many were outraged by the fact that those in power not only denied all blame but had become filthy rich, gaining for their personal use a huge amount of state and party property.

Television, radio, and some newspapers, still largely under government control, unleashed a violent attack against Zhirinovsky and his party, criticizing him as a "hawk," psycho, fascist, and clown and never recognizing that by tailoring his speeches to specific audiences Zhirinovsky had already managed to elicit sympathy from every segment of the population. Only a small segment of the media supported him directly, but it often failed to mention the LDPR program.[2] The contumely piled on Zhirinovsky by the mass media only affronted the voters, firming their resolve not only to support him individually but to bring into his camp as many other votes as they could muster. One more factor was at play—Russians love to support the underdog. Not only will they not kick a man who is down, they'll pick him up and brush him off.

Letters of support from Volgograd, Taganrog, Voronezh, Tver, Kazan—in short, the Russian hinterland—began pouring in to the party's headquarters. Zhirinovsky actively fought for votes, not allowing a single opportunity to meet with the people slip by. Not daring this time to stray too far from Moscow, he concentrated his efforts just outside the capital, trying to create the image of himself as an individual close to the electorate—a regular guy, just like them.

In the final countdown to the election, Zhirinovsky's primary focus

2. The newspaper *Podmoskovnye izvestiia*, for example, reporting on his meetings with the Moscow suburban population, referred to him as a sophisticated politician, a habitué of fine restaurants—preferably intimate and privately owned—theaters, and gallery openings, a man who loved to dance and was capable of engaging in sparkling conversation.

was directed toward television, where he appeared practically daily, acquiring in the process both adherents and enemies. (Some witnesses claim that his party paid thirty thousand dollars in bribes to appear on popular shows.) Following one interview, for example, in which he spoke out against Kazakhstan's independence and declared that that country should be incorporated into Russia as a province or territory, Kazakh television screens went blank every time his name was mentioned.

Various polling services tried to predict the results of the elections. On February 24 Vox Populi ranked the different parties and movements according to their popularity. The Democratic Party, headed by N. Travkin, topped the list, followed by the Social-Democratic Center (led by O. Rumyantsev), and the Russian Union of Industrialists and Entrepreneurs (Arkady Volsky). Zhirinovsky's LDPR trailed in twenty-fourth place, ahead of only the Front for National Salvation (Sazhi Umalatova), Nina Andreyeva's All-Union Communist Party (of Bolsheviks), Pamyat (Dmitry Vasilyev), the Democratic Union (Valeria Novodvorskaya), and, finally, bringing up the rear at number thirty, the Socialist Workers Party of Roy and Zhores Medvedev.

Two months later, the Institute of Sociology of the Russian Academy of Sciences measured voters' trust and distrust of different political parties and alliances. Zhirinovsky's party was the most distrusted, with a reading of 13.6 percent, followed by Pamyat at 10.7 percent, the All-Union Communist Party (of Bolsheviks) at 5.3 percent, and the Russian Communist Workers Party with 1.9 percent. The party voters trusted most was Travkin's Democratic Party, with a rating of 8.3 percent.

In August democrats hired the All-Russian Center for the Study of Public Opinion to carry out a survey to determine which party the population would be most likely to vote for if the elections were being held right then. More than twenty choices were offered. The results had to have been disappointing for Travkin. Rutskoi's party, the People's Party of "Free Russia," which was then in open opposition to Yeltsin, garnered first place with 7 percent, while only 3.5 percent of those surveyed said they would cast their votes for the Democratic Party. Gavriil Popov's party, the Russian Movement for Democratic Reforms, received 2.8 percent, and the remainder of the parties trailed with less then 2 percent each, with Zhirinovsky garnering a measly 1 percent. The majority of voters—70 percent—were still indecisive, and almost a third proclaimed that they were keeping clear of the elections altogether.

This situation changed radically following the storming and shelling of the Russian parliament barricaded inside the White House and the prohibition of several parties and movements—and their publications—taking part in the uprising. VTSIOM, the All-Russian Center for the Study of Public Opinion, analyzing the popularity of the parties and their leaders at the end of October 1993, found that the most popular leaders were Yegor Gaidar (12 percent), Sergei Shakrai (7 percent), Anatoly Sobchak (7 percent), Nikolai Travkin (6 percent), Arkady Volsky (4 percent), Vladimir Zhirinovsky (3 percent), Konstantin Borovoy (2 percent), Gavriil Popov (1 percent), and Yuri Skokov (1 percent). One out of every five people polled indicated that he or she would not vote in the elections at all.

The last poll of public sentiment before the elections, carried out by VTSIOM from November 13 through 22 and published in *Moskovsky Komsomolets* on December 1, promised a complete and crushing victory for Yegor Gaidar's Russia's Choice Party, predicting that it would earn 34 percent of the vote. A good chance was also indicated for the YBL ("Apple") bloc of Yavlinsky-Boldyrev-Lukin, who polled in at 18 percent. The LDPR, however, could count on only sixth place at best, behind the Russian Federation Communist Party, Travkin's Democratic Party, the Party of Russian Unity and Accord, and the Russian Movement for Democratic Reforms. Interestingly, some polls didn't even mention Zhirinovsky in the lists of possible victors. (The Federal Service of Counterintelligence [FSC], however, conducted its own secret research and predicted that Zhirinovsky would win with 23.5 percent of the vote.[3])

The results of the voting, however, turned out completely differently and struck a heavy blow against the radical democratic forces. Zhirinovsky's party garnered almost a quarter of all votes cast in this first democratic election for the Duma (the election was monitored for signs of abuse by former Pennsylvania governor, former U.S. attorney general, and my former boss at the United Nations Richard Thornburgh). All other parties lagged far behind. On election night, representatives of the Russia's Choice Party who had gathered in the Kremlin to prepare a celebration banquet in anticipation of their victory, were shocked by the results of the election. One of them, Yuri Karyakin, exclaimed, bringing his face close to the TV camera, "Russia, you are crazy!"

The victory cannot be explained simply as the result of the schism that developed among the democrats before the elections. It would also be wrong to attribute it to Zhirinovsky's clear advantage in television

3. Tsyganov, "FSK v traditsiiakh KGB" (FSC acting in KGB tradition), 40.

and radio interviews, his animated contacts with the populace, or the unpopular shells that rained down on the parliament and brought death to hundreds of defenders, men and women, children and elders. Nor was it caused only by the wrath of an impoverished people, who saw in Zhirinovsky their knight in shining armor, their champion against the democrats. Clearly, the people responded to some of the principles in Zhirinovsky's program. What, besides the demagogy and the promises and dreams of future Russian greatness, did they find in the speeches and programs of the LDPR's bombastic leader?

PART THREE

Bespredel and Zhirinovsky

7

Piratization: Privatization Russian-Style

As airplanes begin their final descent into Moscow's Sheremetyevo-2 International Airport, both local and foreign passengers inevitably press up to the windows. The beautiful landscape is difficult to resist. The bend in the Moscow River gleams like a well-polished saber. From above can be seen churches concealed at ground level by forests hundreds of years old. Some date back to the reign of Ivan the Terrible, and their cupolas, onion domes, and orthodox and crescent crosses create a dazzling scene. The steeple atop Moscow State University, a Stalinist skyscraper built in 1953, sparkles like a silver needle, while an endless expanse of snow-white multistory apartment buildings, constructed from the 1960s to the 1980s, are lit up with millions of lights. Also on display is evidence of the furious building of the 1990s—villas and luxurious stone dachas on the outskirts of the city, the likes of which have not been seen here for more than seventy years.

Moscow's center, with its fine restaurants and European stores, lives up to the promise of this aerial introduction. Services for the newly arrived include bars, cabarets, tourist agencies, thousands of chic prostitutes and gigolos (minimum price two hundred dollars, with a ballerina from the Bolshoi Theater going for a thousand), and sixty casinos. The streets are clogged with late-model automobiles—and not just middle-of-the-road mass-produced American cars, but Mercedes, BMWs, Volvos, stretch limousines, and other luxury vehicles. (During the single month of December 1993, more than thirty Mercedes and

Ferraris priced up to 125,000 dollars, as well as seven Rolls Royces costing a quarter of a million each, were sold for cash in the single city of Moscow.)[1]

What the newly arrived do not immediately notice is the now considerable numbers of people who feel that they have been brutally misled. Too many are convinced that privatization is legalized theft conducted for the benefit of criminals. No wonder they respond when Zhirinovsky declares, "What's happening right now—the looting of the nation—we will stop all this. I know that you are sick and tired of it. You are frightened, you are angry. They call me an extremist. That's OK. If that's what we need to prevent vandals from stealing our country, let us be extreme."[2] This is one of the arguments Zhirinovsky uses in his campaign for the presidency of Russia.

The nationalization, or, more accurately, the expropriation, of 1917–24 caused suffering for the educated and well-to-do, but today the majority of the population is suffering. The capitalist revolution that was supposed to benefit the general population has been a fiasco. So far, only a narrow stratum of the population—including former Communist functionaries, former directors of state enterprises, con artists, and criminals—has seen any gains. "Today an unthinkable order has taken shape in this country. It has become disadvantageous to work and absolutely safe to steal. Show me just one person who would labor honestly and live well in this country. There is no such person. In this country he who lives well either steals, works for foreigners, or is at the government's corrupt feeding trough."[3] During socialism, modesty was valued; shows of wealth were not only discouraged but could lead to unpleasant investigation. Now wealth is openly flaunted. In the streets of Moscow's poorer sections, traffic is snarled and rules of the road openly disregarded. On view are luxurious imported vehicles full of arrogant people, their dazzling companions, and their sullen bodyguards. "We live as if there is no tomorrow," one

1. Incidentally, the first buyer of a white Rolls Royce with white leather interior was twenty-three-year-old Oleg Dolganov from Yekaterinburg, who was too proud to accept the attendant bonus of a free BMW. He had made his fortune by using a bank credit of 1,200,000 rubles to buy automobiles, which he exchanged for nonferrous metals to sell through the Baltics. Among his other purchases was an emerald-processing factory.

2. Specter, "Why Russia Loves This Man," 32.

3. Govorukhin, *Velikaia kriminal'naia revoliutsiia* (The great criminal revolution), 10–11. The writer and film director Stanislav Govorukhin is a fierce critic of the past Communist regime.

of Moscow's nouveau riche said to me: "Maybe tomorrow Zhirinovsky will come to power, and then the party will be over."[4]

The transformation of a portion of the Russian public into millionaires has not brought any palpable benefits to the Russian economy, nor has it led to the creation of any new goods and services or conveniences for the mass of Russian consumers. Likewise, the wealth does the country no good sitting in European and offshore bank accounts in amounts estimated by Nikolai Petrakov, an economist and adviser to President Yeltsin, to be fifteen to twenty billion dollars per year—many times the combined annual foreign aid to Russia and foreign investments in Russia, untouched by the taxes, instability, and inflation. It appears that Russia invests in the Western economy today but that the reverse isn't true.

The democrats, free-market zealots, didn't mind into whose private hands state property was transferred or under what terms; the main thing was to create a new class of owners as quickly as possible. No one cared whether the true owner—the people—would be properly compensated when this property was transferred to private hands. The people had survived uncounted terrors, whole generations of dissidents had rotted away in the gulag, only to have yesterday's secretaries of district committees, provincial committees, and trade union and Young Communist apparatchiks, in league with the rest of the leadership and the kings of the shadow economy, make themselves into presidents of brokerages, banks, and joint ventures and the most consistent and ardent defenders of the free market. Power was exchanged for money.

Out of the hundreds of examples I am familiar with, I will cite only a couple. The former Komsomol city committee in the city of Ulan-Ude in the republic of Buryatia controls the biggest bank in the republic. Using bank funds, the committee's first secretary bought a gold mine from the government and assumed ownership of it. In a similar case, the director of a Novosibirsk tin plant, the largest in all Europe, decided to privatize it for himself and the "right people." First he illegally lowered the already low price of its stock by one billion rubles, then equivalent to five hundred thousand dollars. He then gave a sizable block of shares to a foreign firm, which tendered it practically for free. The operation was consummated in such a way that the entire tin plant—the only one in the whole country and vitally strategic—can go private. The State Prop-

4. In summer 1994 a group of "new Russians" rented a public swimming pool and hired twelve models to stage their own Olympic Games. Encouraged by the shouts of two hundred guests, the girls competed to see who would be the first to undress and traverse the length of the pool on an inflated raft.

erty Committee, which was specially created for monitoring privatization, along with the State Committee for Antimonopolistic Policy, the Federal Property Fund, the Ministry of Interior Affairs, and the Federal Counterintelligence Service, turned a blind eye to the numerous violations of the law. Only the Novosibirsk prosecutor's office is trying to save this wealth for its rightful owners—the population as a whole.[5]

I don't know why Russian reformers were so certain that reform would be easy and quickly successful. Their program of changing from what is called "mature" socialism to the completely different social form of capitalism was initially calculated to occur in five hundred days. (Grigory Yavlinsky's program was even called "Five Hundred Days.") A somewhat longer-lasting but equally unrealistic deadline was set for the transition to a market economy (Yegor Gaidar's so-called shock therapy). The democracy euphoria clouded a fundamental truth: it takes a long time—generations—to establish economic systems. The capitalist societies of Europe and America developed over hundreds of years; the building of socialism in the USSR was an ongoing process over its seventy years. The transfer of government enterprises to the private sector takes five to eight years even in developed capitalist countries such as the United States and France, which are already equipped with well-established laws and judicial systems, as well as populations familiar with the workings of private property. Russia, with its historical tendency toward turbulence and craving for immediate solutions, seems to have decided to reform its system based on the principles of Russian roulette.

With no long-range planning, the reforms attacked on all fronts, internal and external, national and international, political and economic. First to go was the entire existing, long-suffering, established order. Journalists sought out more and more flaws in the socialist society, and in the midst of the euphoria no one dared come to its defense. History repeated itself: just as in 1917, the new system had to arise from the ruins of the old. Nothing of value was found in the old Communist system; it was damned for eternity. Actions seemed to be based on the Russian wording of "The Internationale":

> We will destroy the whole world by force
> To its foundation, then
> We will build our, our new world.
> He who was nothing, will become—all.

5. Ironically, one of the plant's shareholders is Oleg Soskovets, first vice premier of Russia, and untouchable because of his proximity to Yeltsin.

In the rush to change, no prognosticators, futurists, sociologists, political and economic analysts, specialists, or professionals were widely consulted about the upcoming reform. Overseeing the entire process were Yegor Gaidar, a Russian journalist in his thirties who had never managed even a small enterprise, and Jeffrey Sachs, a Harvard economist and self-proclaimed adviser who basically just set up teams of U.S. graduate students that furnished reports to Gaidar's deputies. Gaidar stood at the helm of Russia, a gargantuan ship crammed with uncertainty and explosive potential, accepting an assignment that he was incapable of fulfilling. He attempted to steer the ship on a proper course without forecasts, without a clear vision of the future, without the guidance of more mature politicians, and without the experience, financial means, or preparation necessary to face a hostile environment. His first step was to destroy all the old mechanisms.

What could the democrats have been counting on? Was it the untapped potential of the population, disenchanted with the old order and thirsting for change? They took a shot in the dark, without envisioning the immensity of the task before them, and thereby spawned the unforeseen irresponsibility of bespredel. A more cynical explanation is that the reformers worked from a plan about whose consequences they were more or less clear, a plan only intended to serve as a cover for those intending to take advantage of the ensuing chaos. This interpretation is very widespread in Russia today.

Initially, Western Europe and America watched the events unfold in Russia with a sense of triumph, which then gave way to dismay and finally, after the reform process lost direction, to a premonition of new dangers even greater than those of the old Evil Empire days. During the Evil Empire era, at least the dangers had been well defined and emanated from a single source. Now the evil has spread and mutated; as with the hydra, for every threat dispatched, two more take its place.

Russia's transition from a socialist structure was stymied from the start by the ownerless state of property. Property belonged to everyone and no one. Privatization meant that it was simply up for grabs, ripe for looting. Quite naturally, virtually everything of value ended up with those situated the closest to the feeding trough—that is, the members of the party organs, the armed forces, the KGB, and other established ministries and departments in cities and villages throughout the country. They found themselves in advantageous positions and quickly snatched up the previously public wealth. Using bribery, cajoling, and other tactics, another group of capable people, comprising actors, directors, singers, and theater entrepreneurs, joined in seizing the country's assets. Criminals utilizing their connections, bribery, or coercion were also able to participate in the looting party. There was no one to safeguard the nation's wealth in 1992, because all the Soviet agencies responsible for law and order, including the party, legal system, army, KGB, and police were either destroyed or severely compromised.

To create the impression of fairness, the government decided to endow every former Soviet citizen with his or her share of the nation's value. Every former citizen of the USSR became the proud owner of a voucher for ten thousand rubles, supposedly worth approximately the cost of two Volgas, a midrange Soviet vehicle. Shortly after it was issued, however, a voucher could at most buy a loaf of bread. Sharpies sold their vouchers on the black market for ten to twenty dollars, and certain companies and individuals, with the permission of the government, began to purchase them. Those who purchased large quantities of the vouchers were then able to buy up businesses and stores for a tiny fraction of their real value. (I know one person who, having bought 150,000 vouchers, became one of the owners of a large automobile plant.) But many, who *could* have used their vouchers to obtain a share in the market or in the business where they worked, failed to do so; others, like me, who refused to sell their vouchers at the low prices, nevertheless did not benefit from their prudence. Effective July 1994 (but then changed to the end of December), the vouchers were declared invalid for redemption. When the population recognized the colossal cheat that had been perpetrated by the democrats, millions switched their allegiance to the opposition, primarily to Zhirinovsky.

It seems that the democrats have simply revived a Soviet tradition— the shameless plundering of the population in the name of reform. My family's three vouchers are now in our scrapbook near some large and beautiful five-hundred-ruble bills, watermarked and adorned with pictures of Peter the Great, that were issued in 1913 and canceled by the October revolutionaries. (My grandfather had wanted to use them to pay for the family home.)

A second form of plundering occurred with the so-called price liberalization instituted after Yeltsin's victory in 1991. Prices of all goods previously supported by the state, including necessities, increased a thousandfold as a result of Gaidar's reforms. Inflation of a severity never seen during the Soviet years swept through the country. All savings held at home or in savings banks became worthless. Government attempts to index deposits and raise their nominal value in relation to inflation were, as they say in Russia, like putting a poultice on a dead man: far from keeping up with inflation, their only purpose appeared to be to create the appearance of fairness.

My elderly mother, living on a pension, lost everything she had managed to save during the course of her life, including her funeral money. All my relatives lost their money. I lost all the money I had received in royalties, as did my author friends, who had also saved their royalty money in the hope of better times for the ruble. Practically everyone in the country who had not put their money into something offering a thousandfold return—the only investment that could keep pace with inflation—lost all their savings. Keep your money in the savings bank, the most frequently heard advertisement during socialism, began to sound like a sick joke.

Means of production could not grow rapidly enough to keep up with inflation and so could not produce profits. The kind of return necessary was only available through stock market speculation and transactions involving bonds and money. Only the most daring were able to make money in these conditions, thereby further escalating the inflationary spiral. Take Sergei Biryukov, for example, the richest person in the Siberian city of Krasnoyarsk. Biryukov was not afraid to borrow money in 1992 at the unthinkable rate of 40 percent interest per month, a wise decision, as it turned out—with real inflation rising at a rate of 140 percent per month, he doubled his money. Utilizing this profit, he purchased telecommunications technology from a military and outer space contractor and converted it to civilian use. Biryukov now lives luxuriously in a ten-room apartment with a swimming pool and sauna. He is not ashamed of his wealth and likes to think he lives better than a New York millionaire.

The very rich "new Russians" appeared suddenly and unexpectedly. Dollar as opposed to ruble millionaires, they owe their wealth to a unique set of conditions: the simultaneous existence of state and private systems and the lack of laws regulating their coexistence and relationship. The state socialist system had been practically a general welfare system, with its own scale and prices. Within this system everything was cheap, including materials, labor, food, energy, oil, and gasoline, and certain items were free. The pay was also very low, sufficient only to cover the costs of necessities such as basic furniture, clothing, food, and transportation. The government used the money left over after paying the workers' low wages for its own purposes, returning some to the people in the form of free housing, education, medical care, and pension provisions. By controlling the mechanism of distributing this wealth, the state was able to determine people's fates. Good behavior was rewarded, and bad behavior punished, both good and bad being determined in part by an individual's political views.

In addition to the normal monetary system in the Soviet Union there existed a cashless accounting system between government enterprises. Here the rubles existed only on paper and were transferred between enterprises in payment for raw goods, finished goods, and services. It is likely that the sum total of these cashless rubles far exceeded the cash funds of the country. Enterprises were totally dependent on the cashless system, yet according to government laws and decrees the rubles involved could not be converted into cash or transferred to the ownership of a specific person for private use. The cashless money ensured the stability of the financial system and was practically immune to inflation.[6]

An open market existed alongside the government system. Its prices were completely different, parallel but much higher. For example, a Soviet car, the Zhiguli, cost six thousand rubles in a government store, and authorization was required to purchase one. In the open market and without authorization, the same car cost twenty thousand rubles (thirty thousand in the Caucasus). Similarly, in the state store a kilogram of lamb cost two rubles; on the open market, it cost ten rubles. Many goods were rarely available at the state store but always available—and of better quality—on the open market. Government housing was free, but when apartments were legally traded, each square meter was valued at three hundred to a thousand rubles. The person who obtained the larger apartment typically paid his trading partner the difference, and this money went from person to person, bypassing the state.

When Gorbachev permitted the establishment of cooperatives, something unexpected occurred: the laws governing cooperatives engendered criminality. The endemic small-scale corruption of the socialist system assumed massive proportions during the perestroika years. Despite strict official decrees and limitations, cooperatives purchased raw goods at government prices and sold them at open market prices. For instance, the law decreed that street cooperatives selling shashlik were obligated to buy lamb on the open market, that is, at a cost of ten rubles per kilogram; however, by bribing the right person at

6. For the purposes of this discussion, it is necessary to overlook the creeping inflation that began with the monetary reform of 1961, when, even though the ruble was worth ten times as much, many goods remained at the same price. Prices did increase slightly and slowly, however, and it was thought that this was to improve models, materials, and goods.

the state store, a cooperative could buy lamb for two rubles a kilogram. The shashlik was then sold at the open market price of a hundred rubles per kilogram. In effect, such a cooperative was stealing from the rest of the labor force, since it was their artificially low salaries that had subsidized the low cost of the lamb. In addition, using bribery, the cooperatives snapped up all the more desirable items from the state stores before anyone else had a chance even to look at them. Inevitably, the cooperatives also began interacting with government enterprises, offering them services and buying their raw goods. This initiated the previously unthinkable transfer of means between the cashless and cash markets and promoted inflation. In other words, not only criminal activity but the trade deficit and inflation can be attributed to this ill-conceived law.

One of the best-known beneficiaries of the Law on Cooperative Activity is Artyom Tarasov, Russia's first legal millionaire. Tarasov started his business in 1985, following the publication of the law. Buying at the negligible government price materials needed by the West, such as gas, oil, and industrial scrap high in rare and valuable metals, he sent whole trainloads of it abroad. The money he earned on the free market numbered in the hundreds of millions of dollars while his expenses were minimal. In one instance, a computer worth 1,000 dollars at Western market prices sold for 100,000 rubles on the Soviet Union's free market. After making the sale, Tarasov purchased twenty thousand tons of raw oil at the official price but valued at 2,800,000 dollars in the West. In other words, each dollar that went to pay for that single computer had increased in value by twenty-eight hundred.

Although this scheme sounds simple, it was not such an easy thing to pull off. One must have the government's permission to sell oil and valuable metals abroad. Tarasov's talent lay in the fact that, without violating a single law—or so he claims—he was able to maneuver his way around the complicated Russian system of official licenses and laws that limit the transfer of money out of the country. As a result of some clever deals he made with foreign companies, millions flowed across the border, most of it ending up in his private accounts.

The scandal came later. Being a law-abiding Communist, Tarasov, like everyone else, paid his party membership dues, which as a rule were 3 percent of an individual's wages, which normally amounted to about ten rubles per month. The comptrollers of the Central Committee, which kept track of all the party's monetary transactions, were quick to react to large contributions—for example, the six hundred rubles I once paid based on royalties of twenty thousand for my biography of Sir Isaac Newton immediately became cause for suspicion. The furor that ensued at party headquarters when the monthly contributions recorded next to Tarasov's name began adding up to millions of rubles was so great that it even attracted the attention of Gorbachev. Apparently he had not expected capitalism to start working so quickly. Experts were immediately found to explain to the general secretary the means by which one person could end up with so much money. After sending another twenty-eight million petrodollars abroad, Tarasov came under investigation by the special services.

In spite of the fact that Tarasov was at that time a people's deputy and a member of Moscow's city government, his apartment and offices were searched, and questions were asked in parliament regarding his legal immunity. In a piece he wrote for the newspaper *The European* in July 1992, Tarasov said, "When I discovered that the Russian police had taken out a contract on my life and offered hired killers a large amount of money to exterminate me, I left the country. This was in March 1991. There was no alternative." In the same interview, Tarasov claimed that he had delivered a sixty-minute cassette to Boris Yeltsin and Ivan Silayev, then prime minister. "I expressed my opinion on how a market economy should be managed. I suggested that we should not abandon the important and positive key factors which had been passed on as an inheritance of socialism. I pointed out that with proper training it would be possible to drive the economy along the road towards a market economy smoothly and without disruption. I also suggested that prices should not be freed overnight. It would lead to the kind of hyperinflation we are witnessing today. I received no response."[7]

Tarasov resurfaced in London's chic Mayfair district, where he organized a company to aid Russian businessmen. Although he lived in luxury and went fishing in Florida, Colorado, and Hawaii, he was nonetheless in constant fear of being robbed or even murdered until December 1993, when the Russian authorities finally assured him he was in no danger. To be on the safe side, though, he bought himself citizenship in the Dominican Republic for twenty-five thousand dollars and founded a bank in Monaco. In his spare time, he wrote a book about his adventures, which he is currently shopping around to publishers.

In Russia's December 1993 elections Tarasov was elected a deputy of the Duma, which instantly brought him parliamentary immunity. He is now free to travel to Russia without fear of criminal investigation. At the present time he is developing a power base from which to

7. Tarasov, "The Russian Millionaire Who Fled," 10.

challenge Boris Yeltsin and Vladimir Zhirinovsky for the presidency in 1996.

Tarasov believes that Zhirinovsky's violent rhetoric is sowing alarm in the West. "Zhirinovsky is not a madman," he said in an interview in December 1993. "He ran a clever campaign aimed at sweeping up the popular vote. He knows he cannot do things like turn the clock back to the old Soviet borders, but he also knows that these are the words the old Communists like to hear."[8]

The huge fortunes made in Russian publishing also owe their existence to the simultaneous presence of a state system for allocating resources—in this case, paper and printing—and private channels for the sale of finished products—printed literature—without any regard for price. Under the state system, prices for books were strictly regulated, determined exclusively by genre and number of pages. A 16-page booklet, for example, had to cost eight kopecks, while the price for a 320-page book was set at one ruble sixty kopecks. This created, on the one hand, vast reserves of unsold books, generally those having to do with politics, literary criticism, or poetry, and, on the other, a shortage of belles lettres and books on the sciences, copies of which could command inflated prices. For instance, a volume of works by, say, Mikhail Bulgakov sold for two rubles sixty kopecks in a state store but for sixty rubles on the street. Private publishing cooperatives thus could print the collection at a cost of about eighty kopecks a copy using cheap state paper and low-cost state presses but sell it exclusively at the market price of sixty rubles. All the profits—made even larger because no one was paid any royalties, copyright infringement having become an everyday occurrence—would go straight into the cooperative members' pockets. Even if a publisher sold the books to distributors at a 50 percent discount, it would net a clear profit of three million rubles—around two million dollars—on an edition of a hundred thousand, with the distributors receiving a similar amount for their trouble.

Naturally, such schemes would require the assistance of government bureaucrats from Goskomizdat, a trophy only acquired through bribery. Over time the cooperatives had to share their profits with the private or semi-governmental papermakers, printing houses, and booksellers (but not with authors who, as before, received pittances), but the initial period of amassing money had already made millionaires of many entrepreneurs.

Other cases are less innocent. Perhaps an employee of a state bank secretly informs his friend that a certain government office that has bor-

8. Smith, "Mayfair MP," 17.

rowed money from the bank does not have the funds to pay off its debt and instead will give it several hundred computers at the state price. The friend immediately cobbles together a firm using all his savings of a thousand rubles, borrows money from the same bank, uses it to buy the computers from the bank at the state price, and then quickly resells them at the market price. The profits, in the millions, are divided fifty-fifty between the bank employee and his buddy. The whole operation, including registering the firm, takes two weeks. The two become millionaires, while the state—and, by extension in the socialist definition, the whole Soviet people—is ripped off, and inflation jumps up another notch.

In order to become a millionaire in Russia, one need not be terribly smart, educated, or resourceful, nor does one have to sweat over creating products, goods, and services. All one needs to participate in the plundering of Russia is an export license. I remember very well how the collapse of the state monopoly on foreign trade and the selling off of the country's resources began. Goskomizdat, knowing that Gorbachev's wife, Raissa, had a great liking for *Burda Moden*, a West German magazine of sewing and homemade fashions, assigned large amounts of foreign currency to the printing of a Russian edition of the magazine. The Russian edition was printed abroad, at the same location as the German original.

"Government resources were recklessly squandered in making presentations and in buying Mercedeses," wrote Stanislav Govorukhin. [9] The money earned did not cover the costs of the magazine, and because of the faulty economic calculations involved, the Russian edition of *Burda Moden* should have failed rather quickly. But that did not happen. The Soviet government, wishing to please Gorbachev but not wanting to waste any more government money on the project, offered the German firm that printed *Burda Moden* a license to export aluminum from the USSR in lieu of cash—perhaps the first time in Soviet history that an export license was granted to a nonprofessional agent.

"Where to get the aluminum?" Govorukhin continued. "The state-owned plants had not yet been drawn into the vicious circle. *Burda Moden* was allowed to buy food containers made of aluminum in Nizhny Novgorod. The price was six rubles apiece. First-class, ecologically pure, ready-for-use, food-safe aluminum. . . . They all found their way to the Hammer and Sickle factory in Moscow, where they were crushed

9. Govorukhin, *Velikaia kriminal'naia revoliutsiia* (The great criminal revolution), 10.

and shipped abroad as aluminum scrap. I'm sure you will agree this was a crafty stratagem. Morally debased, but very astute."[10]

For those without export licenses, there are other means, namely, bribing and deceiving customs officials. Customs in Saint Petersburg recently directed its attention to several railroad cars of unusual-looking faucets earmarked for export. The transport was halted, and the faucets closely examined. It turned out that, lacking an export license, some Russian handymen had fashioned the faucets out of pure nickel, a product that requires licensing and is in demand abroad. From titanium and platinum they made contraband shovels and axes. This is just one example among hundreds. According to Anders Aslund, the optimistic economist, adviser to the Russian government, and proponent of "Russia's success story," every fifth ton of oil produced in Russia and every third ton of metal are taken out of the country illegally. Tiny Estonia, a country without resources, was in 1992 and early 1993 one of the largest legal and illegal exporters in the world of rare and nonferrous metals.

The subornation of customs officials has reached unprecedented levels. The criminals who sell off Russia's natural resources are extremely well organized, with entire economic structures in place, from production to export branches. Corrupt heads of state enterprises such as mines or metallurgical and shipbuilding factories are an important link in this chain. In 1993 criminal cases were brought against eight thousand people accused of contraband activities, five thousand of whom were government employees. The smugglers have their own people in the factories, their own people accompanying goods during transport, and their own people safeguarding the windows of opportunity at the border. Not long ago the director of the Amur Shipbuilding Works was arrested for attempting to smuggle 15.4 tons of titanium out of the country. A casual check of a Russian ship that had run aground revealed that it was crammed with smuggled copper—and the ship had just been searched by customs. The ill-fated *Estonia* ferry, which sank in the Baltic Sea on September 28, 1994, drowning some 900 passengers, also was involved in smuggling. Investigation showed that 40 metric tons of contraband cobalt and 150 kilograms of contraband osmium were on the ferry when it sank. In 1993 the number of cases involving the illegal export of Russian raw materials was 9,477, more than twice the previous year's total. Overall, smugglers were collectively relieved of 17,800 metric tons of metals, 97,900 metric tons of oil

10. Ibid., 11.

and petroleum products, and 157,400 metric tons of lumber. Experts believe that these finds represent only a small proportion of what has been illegally taken out of Russia. Everything, from oil and lumber to plutonium, uranium, and the mythical "red mercury"—a supersecret Soviet material supposedly used in small-scale nuclear charges—is available for sale.

The army represents huge possibilities, for this is where Russia's true wealth lies. Vast sums of money were put together during the removal of Russian troops from Germany, other Warsaw Pact countries, and even the former Soviet republics. One incident from the beginning of 1994 is typical.

At the Speerenburg Airport outside Wünsdorf, headquarters of the supreme command of the Army Group West in Germany, two heavy transport planes landed under cover of night, loaded with 327 cases of an unknown product. In the morning the cases were off-loaded to a German truck that, escorted by light vehicles, set off for an unknown destination. After a few kilometers the truck and its escort were stopped by German police on orders of the military prosecutor of Wünsdorf, and all eleven persons accompanying the load were arrested. Among them was thirty-three-year-old Anatoly Golubev, chairman of the Russian army's hunting club in Wünsdorf, who insisted that the truck was carrying sporting rifles to a firm in Hamburg. A search of the cases revealed, however, that the goods had nothing to do with sport: the cases contained about ten thousand 9-mm Makarov pistols intended for illegal sale. It turned out that Golubev, who had also founded a trading firm in the Berlin region of Karlshorst, had already been fingered in an earlier attempt to sell seventeen carloads of ready-made parts to hunting lodges for wealthy Germans, at a price of thirty thousand dollars per lodge.

Gangsters, primarily from countries of the former USSR, approach the gates of military bases offering payment for military property. Not everyone agrees, but the stubborn holdouts are becoming fewer and fewer. Soldiers in the Russian army sometimes do not receive their pay for months on end; bribes become much more palatable to people worried about how to feed their families. Sometimes the buyers resort to direct blackmail and threats. The various mafia groups hanging around the bases fight among themselves. The environs of Wünsdorf have been the site of murders. Several corpses both in and out of uniform have been fished from the Brandenburg lakes.

Again, everything is for sale: from land and housing in former military camps and plants to weaponry. A group of Russian air force officers sold a Berlin company a complete set of aerial reconnaissance pho-tos of the former German Democratic Republic that they had purloined from a secret safe at headquarters. The former deputy to the com-manding officer of the Army Group West, Lieutenant General Leonid Shcherbakov, was accused of trying to take money and raw materials out of Moscow on a military airplane. Charges of illegally appropriat-ing military property and violating customs regulations were brought against the former commander in chief of the air force's Army Group West in Germany, Lieutenant General Alexey Seliverstov, who gained notoriety in 1992 for buying off senior officers in Berlin and sending a Mercedes limousine worth 90,000 dollars to the upper echelon in the Ministry of Defense in Moscow. On one occasion, journalists pretend-ing to be buyers convinced an officer from the Army Group West to sell them a rocket with nuclear warhead for 150,000 dollars. The deal did not go through only because the unit to which the seller belonged was relocated at the last minute.

The looting of state property in Germany was the object of a special investigation by the Chief State Inspector of Russia Yuri Boldyrev and his colleagues. The commission came to the conclusion that there was indeed criminal activity in Germany and military officials at the high-est level, including General Matvei Burlakov, were involved. This report was presented to President Yeltsin in November 1992, but no action was taken. The Liberal Democratic Party raised the issue in the Duma. "I am proposing to vote the issue about corruption in the Army Group West. There are widespread rumors concerning the appoint-ment of Colonel-General Matvei Burlakov to the post of general chief of infantry in the near future. Please understand: if this post is occupied by a general who is under the surveillance of the Berlin police, who is in the pocket of the criminal classes of Germany, for all practical pur-poses we will have a corrupt chief of infantry! This kind of appoint-ment cannot be approved until the facts of corruption in the Army Group West are given full consideration." The proposal was rejected, mainly because of resistance from Yegor Gaidar's Russia's Choice Party.[11] But the story doesn't end there. On October 16, 1994, Dmitry Kholodov, a reporter for *Moskovsky Komsomolets*, a pro-Yeltsin, anti-Zhirinovsky newspaper, got a call from an informant allegedly in the Counterintelligence Service, who said that he had left a parcel with some interesting documents in a safe-deposit box at the Kazansky rail-way terminal. Kholodov, it is said, had been working on the facts sur-

11. "LDPR v Gosdume" (The LDPR in the State Duma), 4.

rounding corruption in the Army Group West. The next day, Dmitry picked up the parcel at the terminal, returned to the newspaper, and opened it in the office of the political department. The ensuing huge blast demolished the office, killing Dmitry on the spot. The next morning *Moskovsky Komsomolets* emblazoned a huge headline on its front page: "The Criminal Should Sit in a Prison Cell, not in the Minister of Defense's Chair." Inside the paper were details about criminal activities in the Army Group West and the personal involvement not only of Burlakov but of Minister of Defense Pavel Grachev himself. The newspaper unequivocally demanded that Yeltsin dismiss Grachev. Yeltsin refused. Zhirinovsky supported him, stating that the death of a talented journalist was being used by certain political groups to discredit the Russian army. From that day on, practically every newspaper with a democratic orientation began to criticize Yeltsin on all fronts, sometimes very offensively, despite the fact that he had dismissed Matvei Burlakov. Informed parties in Moscow told me that the whole affair, including Kholodov's tragic death, was just a reflection of the struggle going on among different political circles for control of the army and its key figures.

Americans as a rule, like Europeans, have already learned how to distinguish businesspeople from crooks, but in Russia, where capitalist realities are still a novelty, the financial naïveté of the population brings the unscrupulous truly huge dividends. Concepts such as stocks, assets, and investments were virtually unknown until 1991. The average Soviet led the simplest financial life imaginable; what money could not be kept in a bank account or inside a sock fit in a pocket. Checkbooks, credit cards, stocks, and retirement, health, and insurance plans were nonexistent; saving money for a child's education was unnecessary. Other than the bonds the government issued from time to time, purchase of which was made mandatory in order to extract surplus money from the population and stem inflation, the Soviet people had no knowledge of financial instruments. Money management did not take up a single moment of a Soviet person's life. As for taxes, in the majority of cases, 13 percent was automatically deducted from income; Soviet citizens were completely free of tax reporting. It is therefore not surprising that in the period of perestroika, when the Soviet people were flooded with millions of proposals from various companies, many felt panicked.

Among the recent scandals that have caught up millions of Russians was that involving the most respectable and oldest (five years!) financial company in the country, MMM, in the summer of 1994. It all began with a television commercial featuring a nondescript man named Leonid Golubkov who had purchased stocks from a company named MMM and instantly become wealthy. He had bought an apartment, a summer cottage, a car, and a mink coat for his wife and traveled to the United States for the World Cup soccer match, with a stopover in Paris. The commercial so exactly played on the Russian fantasy of a fortune falling from the sky, that it moved millions of people to buy shares in MMM. The company, run by Sergei Mavrodi, a forty-year-old mathematician, and the Mavrodi family, issued one million shares for 1,000 rubles apiece. All of them, thanks to the widely shown commercial (10 billion rubles, or about 5 million dollars in one week, it is said, was spent on advertising), sold out immediately. At the same time, Mavrodi organized another company, called Invest-Consulting, that regularly announced the purported per share value of MMM stock. In the course of two years this company reported steady increases in the value of MMM's stock, and in July 1994 Invest-Consulting quoted MMM shares at 125,000 rubles apiece. Curiously, MMM was prepared to pay exactly that price for the stocks. Many people sold their shares and were thrilled to discover that their investments had grown a hundred times over. Few could resist the temptation to reinvest in MMM. The next issue of shares were sold—naturally—for a higher price, and these shares were snapped up as enthusiastically as before. After all, some holders of MMM stock had already become millionaires.

MMM's secret was incredibly simple: it depended on a pyramid scheme. The company paid out dividends to its investors using the money of the subsequent generation of investors. As financial publications in Russia state, the MMM money was not invested anywhere, did not produce anything, did not subsidize any services, and did not earn anything. Its main source was the next pool of investors. It was inevitable that one day there would not be another round of backers and the pyramid would collapse. But until then everyone could live happily and earn huge returns, and that is exactly what Mavrodi did (on the eve of the collapse the company was raking in five million dollars a day). When the new generations of investors asked to sell their shares, he simply printed another issue of coupons, known as "mavrodik," bearing his likeness and circulating on a par with rubles and dollars. Only Mavrodi himself knows how many millions of mavrodiks were issued, but the shareholders numbered between five and ten million. In a television interview broadcast on November 1, 1994, just after his release from prison, Mavrodi claimed there were thirty million.

MMM collapsed in August 1994. Many believe that Sergei Mavrodi engineered it himself. Supposedly, sensing that the end was near, this hero of modern-day Russia, a billionaire, who single-handedly had paid for the broadcast of one of the country's most popular soap operas, who was capable of paying for the entire population of Moscow to ride free on the metro for an entire day, sent a letter to the tax inspector, who immediately asked to see MMM's books. Because it was not Mavrodi but the government that forced MMM to stop selling and buying its own securities, he was clean in the eyes of his shareholders.

It is interesting that immediately following the request of the Department of Tax Police for Moscow for documentation of his company's activities, Mavrodi sent a letter to Moscow's tax services and the leaders of Moscow and Russia stating that in the four years of his company's existence three suits had been filed against it, in the course of which all his financial records had been thoroughly scrutinized. All three cases had been dropped for lack of evidence of criminal activity.[12] Mavrodi hinted that another analysis would cause a panic among shareholders, and considering that there were millions of them, Mavrodi politely warned the government that the situation could get out of control. He also warned that any checking would compel him to put a halt to Invest-Consulting and MMM's activities and shift all responsibility on the government. With this threat, Mavrodi hoped to prevent the government from disclosing the facts of his wrongdoing to his investors, whose wrath could destroy him: By law, a suit for inadequate financial documentation and nonpayment of taxes could only get him five years in prison and a fine of one thousand dollars. His property, however, would invariably be confiscated.

Meanwhile, MMM shares fell from 125,000 rubles to 1,130—or from sixty-two-and-a-half dollars per share to about fifty-seven cents. The shareholders organized a defense fund for Mavrodi, insisting that he be left alone to deal with his investors, and swore to vote for Zhirinovsky in the next election. This was not a promise to be taken lightly: according to the constitution, by which Yeltsin was elected, one million voters is enough to constitute a national referendum. MMM's millions of investors could overthrow the government.

12. This very fact leads one to speculate about deeply penetrating corruption in government. In fact, MMM had violated financial discipline: a financial accounting had never been carried out, and it was unknown how much money had been taken in and how much spent; there was no list of shareholders; the value of MMM shares was not determined by the market but by the company itself; and, finally, MMM did not pay all its taxes.

Mavrodi was called down to the Ministry of Finances to discuss the situation. His response was to close all Russian outlets for the sale and purchase of MMM shares, in order to direct the shareholders' reprisals against the government of the Russian Federation. The Ministry of Finances, acting on behalf of the government, issued a late statement clearly showing that in no way did it plan to compensate citizens for their losses and appealing to them to be wary of both MMM shares promising a super return and the promissory notes and certificates of other financial and trading companies like MMM. The warning came too late. Several such firms had already crashed, taking with them the money of millions of investors.

On August 4, 1994, about ten employees of the tax police, wearing masks and bullet-proof vests and armed with machine guns, knocked at Mavrodi's apartment door as prelude to a search sanctioned by Moscow's attorney general, Boris Ponomaryov. Through the closed door Mavrodi called the action a provocation by the Russian government and refused to let the men in. The agents, who had expected this reaction, descended by means of rope ladders and wires onto the balcony of Mavrodi's eighth-floor apartment, broke in through the balcony door, and detained him. A search of his apartment and office turned up a few hundred million rubles—worth only about two hundred thousand dollars—but many trillions of unsold MMM shares and coupons. Mavrodi declared that he had been planning to issue these on stock markets around the world, including Germany's, where the MMM coupons were printed. "In essence," he said during the November 1, 1994, interview, "we were halted on the eve of a huge breakthrough, after which Russia would have become the richest country in the world." Mavrodi, it appears, had decided to build his pyramid to its highest, disseminating MMM shares to all of humanity, with Russia reaping the rewards at the expense of the rest of the world.

Mavrodi was charged with concealing income of twenty-four billion rubles—twelve million dollars—and tax evasion. Charges were also filed against Invest-Consulting. Yet when Mavrodi was led out of his apartment under armed guard to a temporary solitary confinement, he smiled enigmatically. In a way, he was brilliant; before anyone else, he had caught the mood and desires of the masses who have money but not enough to buy anything serious with it. People, who had had their fill of inflation and were touched by the living example of Golubkov [the hero of MMM's television commercials], believed him.

The directorate of the MMM called Mavrodi's arrest "legal bespredel" and an "attempt by the government to revive a totalitarian style of lead-

ership, by which the principle that everything is permissible for government bureaucrats is the norm." The company called on its shareholders
to "unite to defend its interests," for in the worst case they, too, could be
arrested and the "whole country turned into a gulag." "We don't consider stones and bottles filled with gasoline to be the best arguments for
solving economic disputes. But if the government will not take into consideration our interests," the shareholders of MMM warned, "we will
have our say at a referendum and in the upcoming elections. You can not
irresponsibly play with the fates of millions of people."

The MMM affair is by no means the only instance of investment
fraud in Russia. Nor have all investors responded as peacefully to
being fleeced. Enormous tension has been provoked by the unprecedented and dangerous freedom from obligations and laws on the free
market. Writing in the newspaper *Vestnik*, Valery Lebedev observes,
"The authorities who set out to build capitalism and circulate stocks,
promissory notes, and certificates in a country that had never seen such
things suspiciously did not spell out in the law what a security is and
what it is not. Thus it turned out that MMM had not violated a single
law! Every piece of paper with the word 'stock' written on it is considered legal, and it is up to the individual to believe it or not."[13]

Zhirinovsky interpreted the MMM problem in his own way:

> I told voters in May 1991: if you vote for Boris Nikolayevich [Yeltsin]
> you will get brigandage and destitution. And that's just what you
> got—all of you, shareholders of MMM, Tibet, and Russian Home
> Selenga. The real swindler is the government, unable to collect taxes
> and pay salaries. The government is designed to obtain the money
> necessary to pay the workers who form the life support system of the
> country. If they go on strike, the country will freeze, and the trains
> will stop. If the average robber stops the average citizen on the street
> and robs him, we say, "That's against article 146—go to jail." But
> when the government robs us, we call it reform.
>
> Why does it feel entitled to steal from you? Because you were
> silent when in January 1992 your money in the banks was taken from
> you and your deposits diminished by a factor of one thousand. We
> were silent because those little Gaidars explained to us, "This is the
> beginning of the market economy. Please wait for two or three years."
> We waited. Three years passed. Millions of people gave their money

13. Lebedev, "Moguchee Moskovskoe Moshennichestvo" (Huge Moscow swindle), 7. The title of the article is a play on the name MMM. An even larger swindle
occurred at the end of 1994 with the crash of Vlastelina, a company also based on a
pyramid scheme.

to new commercial and financial structures. That was exactly what the government wanted. It was time for a new harvest. And they started to exert pressure on organizations like MMM, Russian Home Selenga, and others. Naturally, those companies began to go bankrupt, and the government explained it by saying they did not have licenses for financial activity. But, wait a minute? Was the government blind, deaf, drunk before? Couldn't it have seen earlier that they were acting without licenses? If the government needs three years to see that there are criminal commercial ventures around, it means that the government is either foolish or criminal itself. . . .

Why was the first blow reserved for MMM? Because they didn't throw the government any crumbs. Those who did not share their profits were the first to be attacked. First the government will destroy all honest commercial structures, then it will finish off all the others. It has no pride, it has no conscience, it does not recognize law and order.[14]

The populist Zhirinovsky supported Mavrodi and millions of his shareholders, hoping that they would eventually support him in return. In November 1994, however, when Mavrodi was elected to the Duma (replacing a deputy killed by the Russian mafia) and became immune from prosecution, he immediately reneged on his campaign promises and refused to compensate those who had lost their money. He did, however, promise to support Zhirinovsky financially if Zhirinovsky asked for it. Mavrodi is thinking about starting a party of his own and does not deny rumors about his intentions to become president of Russia.

MMM's logo—three butterflies with the meaningful inscription "From shadow into light"—is now the symbol of one more theft from the Russian population. But again the government must assume the blame: how could it have allowed this to happen? Strangely enough, the answer is to be found in Russia's recently approved budget. The amount of the budget set aside for government employees is one and one-half times greater (in comparable prices) than it was for the vastly bloated bureaucracy of the former USSR—which was 2.2 times larger than Russia. In effect, a government employee's salary is 3.3 times more than it used to be, a huge difference in income. The difference is obtained at the expense of various firms, joint-stock companies, commercial banks, and other businesses.

The chaotic situation in Russian financial institutions is perfectly

14. Zhirinovsky, "Seichas eshche mozhno ostanovit' razval strany" (It is still possible to stop the disintegration of the country), 1.

illustrated by Operation Avizo, carried out by certain citizens of Chechnya, undoubtedly with the help of Russian bank employees. This suddenly well-known small and fiercely independent-minded republic, which unilaterally announced its break from Russia, has today become the mafia capital of the country.[15] Several dummy companies and individuals presented to Russian banks counterfeit letters of advice—*avizo* in Russian. These documents, drawn up at other banks, testified to the presence of significant hard currency balances in the companies' accounts, of which each company asked that a certain amount be transferred to a different bank. The payment instructions used special numbers and secret code words. Lacking a general system for checking letters of advice and even the most basic order in banking institutions, auditing centers confirmed the authenticity of the letters and greenlighted the issuance of credit to the various firms. The subsequent loss to the Russian treasury as a result of Operation Avizo was calculated at several billion dollars, truly a financial disaster for the whole country.

Without losses like these, Russia might not be in the position today of having to extend its hand for donations. However, the government and its present leaders have no one to blame but themselves for such disasters. The slapdash system of privatization created nine hundred thousand "new Russians"—an owner class that is arguably half criminal—while impoverishing almost half the population. The policy has sharply undermined the peoples' trust in the democrats and their reforms. It is precisely on this issue that all the opposition parties agree, just as it is generally conceded that Zhirinovsky has been the harshest and most consistent critic of today's democrats on this score.

It would be interesting to know what Zhirinovsky would have done had he been in Gorbachev's place in 1985 and in Gaidar's and Yeltsin's in 1991. One can conjecture from a speech entitled "Politics and Economics" that he gave at a theoretical conference of the LDPR held on June 7, 1993. This speech exhibits Zhirinovsky's idiosyncratic style of only slightly organized stream of consciousness, in which he improvises dissonant conclusions to the same theme, each of which, in principle, can almost be found acceptable. In this respect, he is similar to Lenin, who in one speech could call for the destruction of the Soviets and in

15. Before the Chechen war there were more than six hundred dummy companies in this small republic alone, and crime in general abounds. For example, on December 16, 1994, ITAR-TASS, quoting President Yeltsin's press representative, reported that, during 1993, 559 trains—a total of 4,000 cars—had been robbed; 120 trains—1,156 cars—were robbed during the first eight months of 1994. As a result, all trains are now being routed around Chechnya.

the next for their support or in one article curse war and in the next glorify it. The speech contains everything from original thinking to outright contradiction, from subtle psychology to straight demagoguery. Zhirinovsky's "truth" has many faces. This is the key to the huge influence he exerts on different audiences or on an audience composed of individuals with different views. If people cannot agree with him on one point, they can find reassurance in another. The memory of what is loathsome disappears as soon as the next apparent truth is uttered. Excerpts from the speech follow:

> Communism did not collapse because the idea was bad. It was the one-party system that collapsed. And with a multiparty system, if one party is too long in power, the people get tired. It's not so much ideology as it is the fact that people grow tired of one party, its actions, and the impossibility of change.
>
> The Russian empire was destroyed, and now Communist Russia is being destroyed. Right down to its roots. All of downtown in the capital has been destroyed. Crumbling buildings have been standing there for eight years, and no one gives a hoot because they're government buildings. Private property is more effective. . . . Therefore, the capitalists have overtaken us economically and politically. . . .
>
> In Russian, what does it mean to be a Communist? A Communist is a communal man, a defender of the community . . . It is better to do some things collectively. . . . Take a huge field, for example. Of course, we'll plow it together. . . . If this communism had been built three hundred years ago, before there were tractors, we would have won. Now, when there is individual technology, I don't need anything. Why do I need a collective? I've figured everything out by myself, done everything on my own. But we were a little too late. Or, on the contrary, too early. In general, we did not hit the phase at the right time. That is why we lost. . . .
>
> The same thing with Gaidar's reform. It wasn't a bad idea. It's okay to liberalize prices and privatize, but it has to be carried out radically. But what did they do? They struck a blow at the Communists, but all of industry remained in the hands of the Communists. They removed the party as the ideological center but forgot about economics. They should have immediately replaced the entire body of directors. And shut down all unprofitable plants and restructured them. . . .
>
> In any case, the reforms that they began should have been carried out intelligently. Hermetically seal the country but seal it without breaking the monopoly of foreign trade. Close it up, like in Stalin's time. Stalin closed the country's economy in order to build socialism.

In order to build capitalism it should have been closed again, at least for ten years, and they should have tried to turn the governmental sector inside out. They should have kept State Supply [Gossnab]: it provided. But they even got rid of this. In other words, they destroyed the whole system without introducing a new one.

The idea itself is good. It can be done, but the people who did it unfortunately screwed things up more. They were thinking more about politics than about economics. Nothing should have been destroyed. This is the style of Bolshevism. The pity is that a real perestroika, a change in thinking, did not take place. The same people. Because they can't do anything any differently. They should have been completely removed. Gorbachev's mistake is that he should have replaced the KGB chairman with a new person, the minister of defense with a new person, the minister of internal affairs with a new person. He should have stopped convening party plenums and congresses, shut down *Pravda*, taken out the ideology and just left the economics. . . . In the regional committee the number of apparatchiks has been cut in half. In ten years they would have disappeared. Halt entry into the party. Don't assign positions on the basis of membership in the party, remove the clause on party membership, take out the clause on nationality and social origin. In so doing they would have gradually reformed everything. Then a new kind of economics would have started to work, and prices would have come down gradually over ten years. More rights would have been given to the provinces. In ten years we would have received fifty percent of the private sector, fifty percent of the state sector. Nothing would have been destroyed. And then finally, at the end of the century we would have gradually shifted to a multiparty system, where a middle class of entrepreneurs, shopkeepers, and merchants would have appeared. But history cannot be turned back. People make it. If they don't have the smarts, we get what we got. Practice makes perfect. They ruined half the country, ruined the economy, and people died in the process. Now they understand that it didn't work.[16]

The vast majority of authors—Russian and foreign—recognize now that Gaidar's economic reforms and the voucher privatization à la Chubais created more problems than they solved.[17] Therefore I was

---

16. Zhirinovsky, *S moei tochki zreniia . . .* (As I see it . . .), 38–42.

17. See, for example, Zbigniew Brzezinski's pessimistic view in Hobart Rowen, "Russian Reform: The Reality," *Washington Post* (National Weekly Edition), October 24–30, 1994, 5.

startled to read Anders Aslund's article "Russia's Success Story" in the November 1994 issue of *Foreign Affairs*, in which the author highly praises the success of privatization in Russia. Aslund's views can be explained, however: he was an adviser to the Russian government in the course of reforms and understandably seeks to defend his own ideas and actions. Other authors are much more skeptical about the reforms and their apologists. Dr. Grigory Yavlinsky, the leader of the "Apple" (YBL) Party and a famous economist and proponent of the transition to a market economy, wrote:

> I have always felt uneasy when I think about the reasons behind such irresponsible behavior by some of my colleagues among Western experts and advisers. I reached a very sad conclusion—*they just didn't care*. In February 1992, at the outset of yet another ill-designed reform attempt, I remember talking to one such contented adviser in Moscow. I told him at the time that he was making a fatal mistake, as Russia is not a whore you can sleep with, get your satisfaction and then pass on to someone else. In the old days in Russia, the engineers who built a railway bridge had to stand underneath it when the first train crossed. You either stake your life in this transformation, or you should go and do something else. I want to advise all those advisers, who care so little about the countries they purport to help that they cannot even theorise properly, to stay at home.[18]

The fact remains, however, that advisers should not be the scapegoats for the failure of voucher privatization. "Young reformers (like Gaidar, who probably has never seen a real-life worker before he became de facto prime minister) made an awful lot of mistakes pursuing abstract schemes and following the advice of self-proclaimed specialists like Jeffrey Sachs, who was completely unknown before his escapade in Russia and who I hope nobody has heard from since. . . . But this was their own foolishness—nobody forced them to use Sachs and his ilk. American pressure is irrelevant here."[19]

18. Yavlinsky, *Laissez-Faire Versus Policy-Led Transformation*, 73.
19. Trofimenko, "Rossiiskaia politika v teni Zhirinovskogo" (Russian politics in Zhirinovsky's shadow), 7.

8
The Rise of the Rafia

The headstrong growth of the Russian mafia, or *rafia*, which has entangled all of Russian life in an ever-expanding spider's web with frightening speed has become one of the central issues in the LDPR's domestic program.

In March 1994 I met the owner of a flourishing private business in Saint Petersburg that makes pistons for motors used in the Hungarian Ikarus buses that are used throughout Russia. To say they make them, however, is an overstatement. Only a huge, well-equipped factory, possessing modern foundries, metal-working shops, an advanced level of manufacturing experience, and contemporary technology would be capable of producing such pistons. At a small plant with only thirty employees and a few machines, it would be impossible.

When I expressed my surprise at the owner's claim, he confessed, "Well, of course, we don't make any pistons ourselves. We buy obsolete tractor motors from collective farms. It just so happens that the dimensions of the pistons and rings on an Ikarus bus and a Kirovets tractor are approximately the same. All we do is alter the tractor rings slightly so that they exactly fit the diameter of the Ikarus cylinders."

The prices, naturally, are lower than for new motors and pistons, and the small plant even had a waiting list for its products. Because its main customer was the mayor's office of the city of Saint Petersburg, under whose jurisdiction is a huge lot filled with old and new Ikaruses, the firm does not raise its prices. As a sign of gratitude, the mayor's office sells to the firm at a low price products intended for the general population by the overseas humanitarian aid programs that send them. The firm maintains several kiosks on the streets of Saint Petersburg, through which it resells these goods at higher prices, and it is this operation, and not the production of pistons, that is the main source of the firm's prosperity. A portion of the profits is kicked back to the mayor's office, for "support," and another portion goes to the rafia, for "protection." The rafia's share is larger.

This troika of private firm, official institution, and rafia, so characteristic of Russia today, warranted investigation. "How do you handle relations with your 'protectors'?" I asked the firm's owner. "As far as I know, not a single kiosk has managed to avoid having racketeers demand a portion of its revenues. You couldn't possibly be an exception?" The owner hesitated, and only after I promised not to mention his name did he agree to give me some background information.

Racketeering as such was practically unknown in Russia until about the middle of the 1980s, when several criminals demanded onetime protection money from several executives caught embezzling from warehouses and stores. One such case involved the personal chauffeur of Irakli Chkhikvishvili, first deputy chairman of Goskomizdat, and Chkhikvishvili's black Volga with license plate number MOTS 0001.[1] This black automobile had the habit of showing up in front of carpet shops during the lunch hour, when they were closed for business. While outside the shops honest customers would form queues stretching several blocks long waiting to get inside, a stream of people would file through the back doors and emerge with rugs, bought at twice the state price, tucked under their arms. Irakli Chkhikvishvili's driver and an accomplice would approach a lucky customer and the attending salesperson at exactly the moment of the deal's consummation. Identifying themselves as undercover agents for the government department charged with combating the theft of socialist property, they would twist the suspects' arms behind their backs, push them into the car, and drive off, ostensibly to the police. Along the way, the detainees usually managed to persuade the bogus agents to let them go. In compensation, and as a sign of gratitude, they would offer the driver and his buddy a rug or two and some cash for

1. A plate beginning with MOTS was a dead giveaway that a vehicle belonged to someone from among the highest echelons of the Soviet nomenklatura in Moscow, and the number one preceded by three zeros signified, as every Muscovite knows, great power and influence (even militiamen on the street froze at the sight of such a vehicle and saluted).

good measure. This simple scam took no more than a lunch hour each time and lasted for several years.

Until 1987 such incidents were relatively rare, but after Gorbachev allowed the establishment of cooperatives, they became inevitable. Nevertheless, racketeering did not become more widespread for a number of probable reasons. For one thing, the population as a whole was law abiding. For another, the police force had not yet become completely demoralized, and the KGB was still generally above corruptibility. And even the presence of the party, with its pious, impracticable, naive, but at times romantically noble ideals, tended to discourage criminal activity. But with the development of privatization, characterized by unfair distribution of the nation's booty among those who stood closest to the shelves on which the riches were placed; with the appearance of unemployment, both concealed and open; with the fall of communist morality and the resulting moral vacuum; with overt examples of embezzlement by officials; and with the rise of a cult of money and power pitted against an obviously weak central authority reluctant to enforce elementary order in a society because that would have immediately revealed its own abuses—with all this, the pressure of the criminal world on business drastically increased. It is today axiomatic among Russian citizens that all stores and more than three-fourths of all business organizations pay protection money to rafia groups.

Consider a hypothetical retailer. First he needs space, so he goes to his prefecture. After repeated visits, during which he offers bribes and gifts, he is finally assigned some space in a ramshackle building on the city's outskirts—an unpromising site for his clothing store. Goods ordered for his business are stolen at the ports, from the warehouses, and during deliveries. He is harangued for bribes at every step, and the demand for his goods noticeably suffers because of his location.

Eventually a couple of athletic-looking young men, probably clad in black leather jackets with diagonal zippers across the front, approach him, politely inquiring how things are going. After all he's been through, the new businessman is delighted to talk about his problems. Soon numbers are discussed. The young men volunteer to take on the responsibility of safeguarding the entrepreneur in return for 25 to 30 percent of the company's profits or up to 50 percent if he wants them to get directly involved in the firm's day-to-day affairs. If he accepts the arrangement, the entrepreneur's life will be transformed. Suddenly the prefecture will turn up a vacant space suitable for a major business and located nearer to the center of town, on a busy street, and near a metro

station. If members of a different group begin bothering him, the entrepreneur simply gives them the telephone number of his patrons and
lets them work things out on their own. Racketeers who do not play by
the rules of the game have a rough time of it and are fortunate to survive. Usually, the negotiations end peacefully and the status quo
remains unchanged, but if, for some reason, the new group gets the
upper hand, the entrepreneur simply cozies up to his new protectors.

This symbiosis of entrepreneur and rafia is subject to ebbs and flows.
Sometimes a protector puts on a small show, complete with stunt
props—bullet-proof vests, bags with imitation blood, and so on—and
stages a fake assault on a shop. A shoot-out ensues, blood flows, people fall, corpses are carted away—all this in full view of the horrified
shopkeeper. Later the entrepreneur is visited by one of the leaders of
the organization, who informs him that murder is more than he had
bargained for. The usual result is that the protection fee is raised.

Or sometimes an entrepreneur tries to conceal a portion of his earnings. When the discrepancy is discovered, as long as it's no more than
about 10 percent, the entrepreneur pays the difference with apologies
and even gives a little something extra for "moral damages," and that's
the end of it. For more egregious violations of the agreement, however,
the entrepreneur may be punished. He may, for example, be driven to
a secluded woods for a "conversation." He may undergo "physical
therapy" from electrical shock or a red-hot iron. It may be hinted that a
favorite child could accidentally disappear. Or he may simply, and
without ceremony, be threatened with death. Conversations of this sort
are usually terse and to the point.

Entrepreneurs are often killed when they are obstinate enough not
to heed the advice of their protectors. In July 1994 an acquaintance of
mine, the director of a polygraphic firm in the city of Chekhov, was
murdered. It was said by his friends that he had resisted protection.
Other contract killings (ranging from one thousand to fifty thousand
dollars per hit) for 1993–94 claimed the lives of the director of
Kuzbassprombank on January 10, 1993, the director of musical programs at the Ostankino television station on January 27, the owner of a
chain of computer stores on February 10, the producer of the Kombi-
natsiia group on March 5, the head of Inkombank on June 24, the general director of a joint venture on July 9, the director of the firm
Videonas on July 21, the president of Agroeksport-7 on July 29, the
director of the Valeri casino on August 4, the chief financial officer of
the Russian Municipal Bank on August 13, the chairman of Pragma-
bank on September 17, the director of the Saint Petersburg Commercial

House on September 30, the director of Rosselkhozbank on December 2, and the president of the publishing house Novoye Vremya on February 1, 1994. Since then, resistance to the rafia has been weakening, and the number of contract murders has dropped. Society is becoming more peaceful. The end has justified the means. The rafia got what it wanted most: 25 to 30 percent of all profits earned by private companies and banks. With money came power. Connivance at the official level and the long chain of compromises allowed by the government in distributing the nation's wealth and in trying captured racketeers have nurtured Russia's special form of secret patronage.

Who belongs to the rafia? Its members are often retired athletes, army reservists, former employees of the police, security forces, and KGB, and even young people who have abandoned their studies. For this reason, the Moscow criminal investigation department uses the term *organized athletics* instead of *organized crime*.

Not long ago Vagankovskoye cemetery in Moscow hosted a burial unprecedented for the quantity of its mourners. Hundreds of Mercedes, Volvos, and BMWs fought for parking spaces on the streets near the cemetery. Thousands of athletic and nonathletic people decked out in designer mourning joined the funeral procession of Otari Kvantrishvili, former USSR wrestling champion and chairman of the Aleksandr Yashin Foundation for Aid to Needy Athletes (named for a well-known soccer goalie). His brother, a notorious Moscow gangster, had been murdered a few months before in a gang shoot-out.

It would be difficult to name a person in Moscow who enjoyed such widespread respect and influence as Otari Kvantrishvili did. As one of his best friends, the well-known singer Iosif Kobzon, said of him,

> He would go to a bank and say, "Do you want our country to have a healthy society? Don't think just about how to rip off Russia, but how to build it up. Think about the physical health of the nation. Give money for sports." And they gave. From time to time it is reported that people would come to him and complain, "Some mafia guys are leaning on us." Otari would say, "Okay, I'll speak to these mafiosi. But with one condition: you will give money for sports." They would answer, "Of course. We'd rather give money to sports than to the mafia."[2]

Such successful linking of racketeering to concern for the needs of athletes (or children, or culture, or pensioners) has persuaded many that

2. Grant, "Mir spasaet Krasota" (The world will be saved by aesthetics) (May 5), 7.

people like Otari Kvantrishvili are contemporary Robin Hoods, rob-
bing the rich to help the poor. The very existence of such a view testifies to the adolescent state of social consciousness among Russian citizens; only gradually are they becoming aware of the realities of Russia's version of capitalism.

Just as disingenuous is the attempt to present Russian gangsters as
"market attendants" who simply organize the disposition of goods on
the market in accordance with its laws. For example, the rafia often
claims to help set fair prices or guarantee the observance of contractu-
al obligations otherwise impossible to achieve through the courts, arbi-
trage, or government watchdog agencies. With its connections to local
seats of government, the rafia is able to help when an entrepreneur
loses heart and is ready to call it quits. It can supply the best lawyers
and accountants. It has links to the state, which grants those most
important of documents, export licenses, and with customs, which will
look the other way as the nation's wealth leaks away.[3] For the entrepreneur willing to pay, this is truly a dream regime. That is why the
concept of protection is so universally popular.

In any case, there is no alternative. My Saint Petersburg acquaintance stated that he would gladly make use of official protection and
services if the government were capable of providing them. But the
truth is that the government can only guarantee one-time protection,
not constant attention.

The profession of mafioso is becoming prestigious for young men,
just as the profession of hard-currency prostitute is for young women.
The borders between the normal and criminal world are disappearing.
"Are the mafia really those who endanger citizens?" philosophized
Otari Kvantrishvili. "The real mafia are those who distribute quotas in
their own interest for the sale of raw resources: oil, diamonds, gold,
metals, woods. . . . That's the mafia."[4] Proposals for legalizing the rafia,
or for giving it at least semi-legal status as the contact between official-
dom and the criminal powers, are not dismissed out of hand. As Iosif
Kobzon has observed,

> When criminal activity in the country increases, the authorities, tak-
> ing the circumstances into account, find themselves making compro-
> mises with the "authorities" of the criminal world. This is done for

3. Some experts believe that for every ten tons of oil legally crossing the border,
not less than one illegal ton ships out as well (tankers usually leave port laden with
10 percent more than their officially allowed tonnage).

4. Grant, "Mir spasaet Krasota" (The world will be saved by aesthetics)
(May 5), 8.

the sake of keeping peace in society. For the "authorities" do not rob or kill pedestrians on the street. In the argot of the criminal world, this is done by "locusts"—drug addicts, hooligans, and prostitutes. The government makes compromises with the "authorities" for the sake of helping people escape the danger of street crime. Do you think that if you get rid of the leaders of the criminal world, you will bring order to the city, because it's easier to deal with the locusts? You won't. They are many, and there is not enough manpower to fight them.[5]

The rafia has already acquired such power in Russian society that it would be difficult to name an arena in which it does not, or could not, exercise influence. Contact between the official and criminal worlds is widespread. The rafia actively promotes its own people to executive positions in joint ventures, banks, privatized institutions, the mayor's office, and the government of Russia. Figures like Otari Kvantrishvili serve as links between the world of official power and the openly criminal underworld. The rafia has its own list of people whom they support in elections and whose campaigns they help to finance. "The money spent promoting a deputy pays for itself in just a few months," one of the criminal world's leaders said to a friend of mine. "Recently we supported somebody for elections to the Duma. He won." This coalition of a strong criminal sector and a weakened central authority will culminate in one of two scenarios: either the two will conclusively unite, or the rafia, recognizing the powerlessness of the government, will become first a parallel ruling power (as has already happened in many places) and later the sole legal entity.

Some Russian businessmen, despite the obvious risks, are trying to fight the rafia's influence. Police in Saint Petersburg recently stopped a Zhiguli (a popular Russian car) towing a Mercedes. When they examined the Mercedes, the police discovered three corpses in the back seat and four more in the trunk. An investigation determined that the passengers in the Zhiguli were employees of a private firm, whom the rafia had tried to coerce into cooperating. The employees had decided to resist the pressure, but having no faith in the police, they decided to solve the problem themselves—using automatic rifles.

Some people are inclined to interpret the murder of Otari Kvantrishvili as a similar protest against the encroaching rafia, although the possibility cannot be excluded that he was bumped off by a competing

5. Grant, "Mir spasaet Krasota" (The world will be saved by aesthetics) (May 5), 8.

rafia group, and one major Russian banker, the chairman of a well-known fund, thinks the government was responsible: "Think about it. Kvantrishvili was getting out of hand. Speaking on television, he addressed the head of the Moscow criminal investigation and told him he'd better feel sorry for his children. The next month Kvantrishvili was dead."[6] Just before he was killed, Kvantrishvili had been interrogated by the police and spent much of the time moaning about the erosion of the criminal cartels of the past. He also proclaimed that "the Moscow city authorities are the most corrupt government that has ever existed."[7]

A figure prominent in the world of Russian finance told me that he had cast his vote for Zhirinovsky and would support him in the future. When I asked him why, he answered, "He is the only one crazy enough to take on the mafia and defeat it. Practically all their leaders and lieutenants are known. The only thing lacking is the political will. Someone in the government fears that trials of the mafia will leak embarrassing information and names. It is more advantageous for them to remove the mafia leaders quietly, without trial or investigation. By not participating in the privatization and allocation of national riches to the 'right' people, Zhirinovsky has been able to give the impression of honesty, in spite of all his buffoonery. I think he can overcome the mafia."

The fatal question of who is ruling Russia today resonates for the Russian people. Zhirinovsky's publicized resolve to wipe out the rafia has earned him the sympathy of many voters, notwithstanding the fact that his plan for keeping his promise is a far cry from the generally accepted methods used in the civilized world. It calls for destroying all five thousand of the known criminal bands in Russia with merciless terror: if caught red-handed, gangsters will be executed on the spot; if tried, their fates will be decided by a single judge and two people's assessors, as was formerly the practice in the USSR. President Yeltsin's May 1994 decree on fighting crime is, to a large extent, an attempt to

6. The murder was completely professional: The perpetrator hid in the attic of a building not far from the Krasnopresnensky baths on Stolyarny Lane, where Kvantrishvili liked to relax with his cronies and bodyguards. The shot was fired from a German 5.6-mm industrial rifle with a telescopic sight. The first bullet struck Kvantrishvili in the head, and there was nothing his bodyguards could do. Except for the rifle and three bricks that served as a brace, nothing was discovered at the scene of the crime. The rifle's stock, which could have carried fingerprints or traces of hair, sweat, or saliva, had been splintered, another practice common among professional hitmen.

7. "Russian Mafia," 19–22.

use Zhirinovsky's popular slogans to restore his own dwindling support among the population. It would not be the first time Yeltsin has borrowed from Zhirinovsky.[8]

Nevertheless, the crime bill was supported by the vast majority of the Russian population. Almost everybody in Russia has stories to tell about crime, not taken from the press but based on personal experience. I have plenty of my own tales. In my apartment house in Moscow, for example, four people have been killed during recent years. Professor Kazovsky, mentioned earlier, was murdered during the armed robbery of his art collection. A millionaire friend of mine, the president of a media company, is abroad hiding from the rafia. I don't know his telephone number—he calls me when he feels lonely. And a charming person who wants to buy my dacha has threatened me in various ways, the most mild being "Your dacha is made of wood, and wood burns easily." A former colleague of mine was killed for resisting rafia demands. And my daughter was robbed and raped in an alley twenty yards from the entrance to our building.

The focus of a three-day U.N. conference of member-states' interior ministers on international crime, held in Naples, Italy, at the end of November 1994 was a new global strategy to combat rising international crime syndicates. "Traditionally insular and clannish, the world criminal powers like Hong Kong's Triads, Colombia's Cali drug cartel, the Italian mafia, Japanese Jakuza, and Russia's Vory v Zakone have changed tactics and begun to make deals among themselves."[9] The rafia had finally gained international status. The 1990s imperatives of privatization, deregulation, and competition for investments, markets, and hard currency opened the doors wide for organized crime.

Before 1985 there were only four banks in Russia, all closely regulated by the USSR Central Bank. The *Diplomatic World Bulletin* states,

---

8. Two provisions of Yeltsin's decree provoked bitter criticism in the parliament and the media: the first would permit the detention of suspects for up to a month without the sanctions of a prosecutor or formal criminal charges; the second would allow investigators to check the bank accounts not only of suspects but of all those with whom the suspects had lived for the previous five years. The only oppositional faction that unconditionally supported Yeltsin's crime decree in the Duma was the LDPR. Yeltsin's views on NATO, the former Yugoslavia, and other important topics have undergone drastic changes and more and more resemble those of Zhirinovsky. Zhirinovsky's party was the first to support Yeltsin's policy of armed involvement in Chechnya. Later, though, a majority of the Duma supported the war in Chechnya.

9. "Another Evil Empire Is on the Rise," 3–4.

Today, there are at least 2,000, and until recently bank charters could be purchased for the price of a luxury car. Many if not most of these banks are reportedly fronts for criminal organizations.

Russian crime groups . . . acting on behalf of international syndicates "buy privatization vouchers or directly purchase businesses and thereby exercise control over a vast range of enterprises," according to a report to an international conference on money laundering.

Rubles as well as smuggled arms and valuable metals worth billions of dollars leave the country in an unregulated fashion every month. . . .

"There are all sorts of conspiracy theories floating around as to how the ruble is being manipulated for speculative advantage," said Guy Dunne of Control Risks Group, a London-based consulting firm. "But we can safely say that the monetary system is so immature, and the amount of illegal money flowing in and out of the country so huge, that the Russian financial system is held hostage by the mafia." During the October 1994 currency crisis, the central bank halted a one-day 30 percent drop in the value of the ruble with an $150-million intervention, and "if you can temporarily stabilize currency for that much, you can destabilize it for the same amount."

Another expert, Louise Shelley, foresaw the imminent possibility that "state ownership of the economy will be exchanged for control of the economy by organized crime groups which have a monopoly on existing capital."[10]

Some analysts in Russia think that criminals control 81 percent of the voting shares in privatized enterprises and warn that "Russia could become the biggest criminal state ever to exist."[11] TASS–Krym Press reports that the rafia has "privatized 50 to 80 percent of all Moscow stores, warehouses, travel agencies, hotels, and other services."[12] One of the outstanding "new Russians" and a deputy of the Duma, millionaire Mark Goryachev, makes the same point: "We are an amazing country. Such a criminal past! Barrels of blood on our conscience! People abroad were very happy at the beginning: the atomic war would never happen, because the threat of atomic war had emanated from Russia. It is too early to be happy. Our all-embracing black market splashes out to the world. They have already set up house, but it is just the beginning. The Russian mafia is justly labeled the wildest, cruelest mafia in the world."[13]

10. Ibid., 3.
11. "Russian Mafia," 19.
12. Sinel'nikov, "Russkaia Mafiia: Vy ee eshche uznaete" (Russian mafia: You are going to know it much better), 24.
13. Chernov, "Volk v ovech'ei shkure" (Wolf in sheep's clothing), 6.

The crimes of the rafia in the USA, Germany, Greece, Cyprus, Israel, Turkey, and Poland are widely known. (The German press called recent slayings of Russian prostitutes the "cruelest crime in the history of Frankfurt"; murders in London, Paris, and New York have also been laid at the rafia's door.) One of the leaders of the Russian criminal world, Vyacheslav Ivankov, also known as Yaponchik, or "Little Japanese," lives in New York City, along with one hundred and fifty of his men. According to the *New York Times*, FBI agent Jim Moody thinks that as many as two thousand Russian emigrants in New York City may be hardcore criminals; of some five thousand gangs that sprang up after the collapse of the Soviet empire, members of twenty-nine gangs have been seen in the United States, Mr. Moody noted.[14] What's next?

14. Selwyn Raab, "Top Echelon of Mobsters Is a Threat: Rise of Russian Gangs Troubles FBI," *New York Times*, August 23, 1994, A1, B2; Nila Banerjee, "Russia's Organized Crime Became Global," *Wall Street Journal*, December 22, 1994, 6.

9

Bespredel

The Russian slang word *bespredel* (bess-pruh-dell') first entered the general vocabulary during perestroika and has been increasingly used ever since. It often pops up in Zhirinovsky's speeches, a popular sound bite that has direct and unambiguous appeal for whatever group he happens to be addressing. By constantly promising that as soon as he ascends to power, he will immediately "put an end to bespredel," Zhirinovsky gains more and more new "falcons" (young converts) to his cause.

Morphologically speaking, *bespredel* is a back formation from *bez predela*, which means the absence of limits or borders; in mathematics it is expressed by the symbol for infinity. Originating in Russian labor camps and jails, the word was widespread in the criminal world, where the real power to judge, punish, and pardon belonged to the Vory v Zakone, a special criminal category endowed with and observing its own authority, morality, rules of conduct, and etiquette. This criminal authority openly coexisted with the official state authority in places of incarceration. Gradually its influence spread throughout the entire Russian nation.

Bespredel, too, has outgrown its original usage. Today in Russia the word has a clear moral significance, representing the highest degree of unconditional condemnation. In essence, *bespredel* connotes the removal of any and all moral prohibitions—nothing in moderation, everything to excess. But the condition of bespredel is not anarchy, for even anarchy derives from a theoretical basis that distinguishes it from other beliefs, whereas bespredel springs only from a void.

In June 1994, a Russian military pilot took off from a military airport. Instead of guiding his late-model fighter plane on its designated course, he began circling the airport and adjacent areas, now hurtling toward the ground, now swooping away again, all the while in full view of everyone in the airport. Attempts to make radio contact with him were futile. A background check revealed that the pilot was experiencing tremendous problems at home. It soon became apparent that he had decided to commit suicide and had chosen a new bespredel method for carrying it out. He continued his circular flight pattern until the plane ran out of fuel and crashed into a populated area. That only the pilot was killed was mere luck. The multimillion-dollar craft burned with its pilot.

Nothing like this would have happened in the former USSR, where pilots did anything to avoid crashing their airplanes in populated areas. Nor were sacrifices reserved for the saving of human life—test pilots often disobeyed orders and refused to eject themselves, choosing to risk their lives in attempts to save their expensive experimental machines. The behavior of the suicidal pilot was the antithesis of everything not merely promised but fulfilled in the Soviet Union. Bespredel is socialist morality in reverse, the flip side of all that was positive within the late Soviet empire, its society, and its morality. The current, extremely dangerous Russian experiment is proof that even a bad ideology is preferable to no ideology at all.

Russia is fervently searching for a new morality, a new ideology. Thousands of churches have opened throughout the country, although the flow of converts is still sparse. On Orthodox holidays President Yeltsin visits the Kazan Cathedral to pray. As a man of the people, well versed in their daily cares and concerns, he understands that the lack of ideology and morality is more frightening than even the destitution that has befallen most of the Russian population. It is difficult to believe that a party apparatchik, one of the pillars of the nomenklatura and a devout atheist, could make such a rapid conversion to Orthodox Christianity: he doesn't even cross himself in the Russian manner; the action seems artificial and unnatural. Still, religion is commonly viewed by decent people as an effective—even the only—counterbalance to bespredel, so the gesture must be made.

Statistics point to the growth of various religions, including Hare Krishna, in contemporary Russia, but I am skeptical of their continued success in this field long rendered barren by Communist ideology. I myself tried to turn to the church after the collapse of Communism. I visited houses of worship of every denomination, beginning with Orthodox. Nothing came of it. Orthodox belief (despite my love for the

Russian cathedral in Vladimir, built nearly a thousand years ago), its icons, and its music seemed shamefully outdated. On the other hand, the more refined Catholics struck me as insidious tempters, while the Protestants were sanctimonious. As for the exotic Eastern religions, to me, they seemed like vignettes from "A Thousand and One Nights." I felt closest to Rajneesh, but this was probably because I first learned of his teachings from lovely red-saried women at the 1984 Frankfurt Book Fair. Still, bowing to the golden calf of capitalism, without any other ideology, seemed to me—and I would venture to say to many in my position—to be pure paganism, and though in Western languages *pagan* impassively conveys the meaning of "nonbeliever," in Russian the word suggests something loathsome, physically disgusting, and intolerable.

It is not surprising that in this moral vacuum many former Communists, and even non-Communists, have returned to the old doctrines, unexpectedly finding there much that was worthwhile. Today around Moscow and Saint Petersburg so-called red belts have formed, provinces ruled by duly elected former Communist Party district committee and regional committee first secretaries. The seventy years of the Soviet Union may someday even be lionized as a tragic, noble, if flawed social experiment. Perhaps Marx's busts will be reinstated on their pedestals, and Lenin's body will be removed from its grave in the Volkov cemetery in the former city of Leningrad, where Mayor Sobchak now wants to place it, and returned to the mausoleum on Red Square for the respect and contemplation of all. For now, however, bespredel is running the show in Russia and other former Soviet republics.

What was once considered the strongest taboo under socialism is out in the open today. Hundreds of books previously judged to be subversive poured onto bookstore counters from 1990 to 1994. To the total amazement of some, however, such literature did not become popular. It turned out that all the criticisms of Communism and all the anti-Communist arguments had been presented during the cold war. Both leftist intellectuals and members of the party elite were already familiar with anti-Soviet literature, having discovered Orwell, Solzhenitsyn, Andrei Amalrik, and Svetlana Alliluyeva during Brezhnev's time. I published Orwell's *1984* and *Animal Farm* at Mir in 1989 in an edition of a hundred thousand copies, but the publishing house Progress had already issued *1984* in a limited edition of a thousand copies for the party elite in 1983. "Ideologically subversive" books, including Alexander Orlov's *A History of Stalin's Crimes*, Arkady Shevchenko's *Breaking with Moscow*, and even John Naisbitt's *Megatrends* were all published by a top-secret printing house located on the grounds of Mir, to which even I was denied access. (Naisbitt was dumbfounded when I told him in 1987 that the entire leadership of Russia had already read his book; he simply did not believe me.) The extremely clandestine books produced by this press, printed in editions of only a few hundred, were distributed through hush-hush channels, and virtually the entire intellectual community of Moscow copied and read them. Other books, published abroad by "reactionary" Western presses such as Ardis and Grani and distributed one way or another, were easy to borrow from friends. We all had small anti-Soviet libraries segregated from the rest of the tomes on our bookshelves.

With the advent of developed socialism in 1980, such literature became less of a worry for the KGB, and the need for discretion diminished apace. Around this same time, the American and other Western embassies began making these books available in cultural centers such as Moscow and Leningrad. Diplomats and tourists started bringing them in by the tens and hundreds, and American publishers, encouraged by the United States Information Agency, distributed them at the annual Moscow book fair.[1] Any slightly interested and motivated Muscovite had access to anti-Soviet literature without risking a jail term. When the KGB noticed anyone displaying curiosity about such books, they would record the fact in the person's dossier, but by the mid-1980s such record keeping instilled little fear.

Some wildly popular works exploiting the theme of perestroika, such as Viktor Yerofeyev's *Russian Beauty* and Aleksandr Kabakov's *The Defector*, appeared in this period, but works like these could have been produced in principle under Gorbachev or even, for that matter, during Brezhnev's final years. As early as the 1970s, Kabakov did not need to write in secret; on the contrary, as he admitted to me once, everything he wrote at the time was published almost immediately. As for *Russian Beauty*, aside from criticisms that it was pornographic, there were no obstacles to its publication in Russia. And even when all criticism of the Communist Party, socialism, the Soviet state, and Soviet social order was clearly forbidden, Anatoly Rybakov's *Children of the Arbat*, Yuri Nagibin's *Live and Remember*, Lev Razgon's gulag reminiscences, and Yakov Rabinovich's *The Doctors' Plot* were all published.

Similarly, after the well-known decisions in the 1980s regarding the creation of a painting section in the Moscow Union of Graphic Artists

---

1. Lengthy negotiations held several weeks before the book fair between representatives of the USIA and Goskomizdat determined which books the Americans would be allowed to exhibit and in what quantity, as well as how many could be given away without charge.

and the denouncement of the postwar Zhdanov Resolution of the Central Committee of the Communist Party condemning Vano Muradeli's opera *Great Friendship* and the journals *Zvezda* and *Leningrad*, Soviet artists, writers, and actors—let's be honest—had little reason to complain about limitations imposed by the authorities on creative expression. As for music, the ultramodernists Alfred Shnitke and Rosa Gubaidullina were extremely popular—and not just among Moscow's intelligentsia—and their compositions were performed often.

The unknown geniuses, their spirits hitherto crushed by the Soviet system, who were expected to offer new ideals and moral support to a people lost in dreary reality have yet to surface. Instead, Russia today is filled with all sorts of ordinary rubbish: astrology, palmistry, vampires, visions, sex-crime novels, masochism, sadism—in short, everything that the ideological department of the party's Central Committee and state censor prevented from being published as "banality" unworthy of print. The publishing house Raduga, which had previously introduced the best American literature—Steinbeck, Faulkner, Capote, Fitzgerald, Oates, and Wilder—has switched over to romantic novels. Soviet ideological purism has been replaced by an orgy of unbridled pornography, presented with the professed intention of emancipating previously forbidden vocabulary. Books are written in the "bright, liberated language of sexual permissiveness." An American television viewer with the standard number of cable channels would be shocked by what is shown on Russia's central channels, still under government control.

The bespredel pendulum, which keeps swinging further away from Communism, demands a new ideology more anti-Soviet than anything expressed before. The problem is that there *is* nothing more anti-Soviet. Journalists are now going to excruciating lengths to uncover anything new that blemishes socialism, and to say anything kind about the old Soviet Union is the biggest sin of all. Yet as the old guideposts are rejected, the new ones set up in their stead do not seem so unconditionally attractive and readily acceptable.[2]

2. Many Russians would never agree with those who called the Soviet Union the Evil Empire. Not everything in the system was bad. For instance, the holy grail of the Clinton presidency—universal health coverage—existed in the USSR almost from the inception of Soviet rule. The educational system, up to doctorate, was accessible to anyone from any stratum of society, and again it was free. Everybody knows about Soviet achievements in the arts, science, space exploration. But most important, nobody had to worry about the future. Full employment was guaranteed, life expectancies had risen; prices were low; and the society, though not very rich by American standards, was virtually crimeless. Moreover, the typical Soviet citizen, or *sovok*, an object of derision for the entire anti-Soviet camp—and for him-

Now Russia is saying its final good-bye to its past. In December 1993 Sotheby's held an auction in New York featuring Soviet space program memorabilia. Konstantin Tsiolkovsky's and Yuri Gagarin's autographs were auctioned, as was a slide rule belonging to Sergei Korolev, the "Columbus of space." Also on the block were fragments of lunar soil, belonging to Korolev's daughter, and Gagarin's and Aleksei Leonov's spacesuits. With several million dollars raised, the auction had to be considered a success. Gagarin's widow was in attendance, and she received her share of a million dollars, as did Korolev's daughter, who immediately transferred her cut—the lunar soil had sold for three hundred thousand dollars—to her twenty-year-old son Sergei—named for his grandfather. The cosmonauts got less, raking in only several thousand dollars apiece. Some objects had not been sold, however, and because of my long-standing friendship with cosmonauts (we had compiled the book *Home Planet* together), General Vladimir A. Khokhlov, of Glavkosmos (the national space administration) asked me to take care of forwarding these to Moscow by Aeroflot.

Aeroflot, with its three thousand airplanes and six hundred thousand employees, once the largest airline in the world, had splintered into dozens of smaller carriers belonging to republics, cities, organizations, and even individuals. Some of these companies are so financially strapped that they cannot pay for their long distance calls, not to mention the maintenance of their airplanes, crew training, and first aid services. Embezzlement is common. And bespredel was in evidence as soon as I came in contact with the airline's agents in the United States— United Transport Associates. All the items—among them, Sergei Korolev's hat and neckties, his diamond cuff links, clothing belonging to other cosmonauts, medical equipment, diaries, training books, and wristwatches worn by the cosmonauts during their flights—vanished after they reached the warehouse for Aeroflot freight at Kennedy Airport. To make matters worse, General Khokhlov, experienced in such matters, had told me that it was pointless to insure anything, since insurance companies working with Aeroflot always torture one with endless forms and inquisitions before paying a penny.

Tragic as it may be, this loss, even valued at several hundred thou-

---

or herself—was not so bad. The Russian Revolution gave rise to a new, perhaps naive, but sometimes noble nonmercantile relationship among people. The majority of authors who recklessly, passionately, and uncompromisingly criticize all Soviet people as *sovoks* are either politically limited or not particularly inquisitive.

sand dollars, is insignificant when compared to the loss of human life that has become normal for Aeroflot under bespredel conditions. Here are just a few of the larger air catastrophes during recent months:

December 1993: A cargo plane exploded in Armenia. Thirty-five people perished. The catastrophe could have been avoided if the pilots had adhered to elementary rules of aviation safety. Instead, they ignored the report of a malfunctioning engine and continued the flight rather than returning to the airport. The airplane was carrying two automobiles poorly secured in the same area as the passengers' luggage. These were packed with canisters full of gasoline. During the flight, they broke loose, spilling the gasoline. When the engine shorted out, the cargo hold was a tinderbox.

March 23, 1994: An Airbus A-310-300 owned by Russian International Airlines crashed into the north slope of the Kuznetsk Alatau Mountains near Mezdhurechensk in the Kemerovo region on its flight back to Moscow from Hong Kong, resulting in the deaths of 63 passengers and 12 crew members. An analysis of the airplane's black box revealed something extraordinary: the last sounds on the flight recorder are children's voices—during the final seconds the aircraft had been piloted by the pilot's fifteen-year-old son. Apparently, the boy and his sister had been at the controls throughout the flight. During their lesson, the plane's autopilot had been switched off. The airplane went into free fall, and the pilot was unable to right the plane. The position of the control panel and fuselage on the ground indicated that the plane's descent could have been corrected had it been at a higher altitude.

August 5: An AN-12 crashed in Zabaikalye, killing 47 people. The accident was caused by an unrepaired engine built almost forty years before.

The chaos in the airline industry has also led to transport violations. Planes are consistently overloaded. For a bribe of twenty thousand rubles, an additional passenger or cargo will be taken aboard, regardless of the circumstances. Lack of discipline and training result in technical errors. Irresponsibility prevails. There are reports of pilots flying under the influence of alcohol. It is no wonder that the 110,000-strong International Airline Passengers' Association warns its members not to fly to, in, or over Russia. It's simply too dangerous.

The American Embassy in Moscow also advises its citizens to use alternate forms of transportation in Russia, but for different—though equally valid—reasons. Many foreign visitors remember the luxurious night trains between Moscow and Leningrad (the Red Arrow), Moscow and Tallin (the Blue Arrow), and Moscow and Kiev (Dnipro). Ticket prices were cheap, the trains ran exactly according to schedule, the conductors and guides in their elegant uniforms were pleasant, the dining cars were wonderful, and there were comfortable sleepers. Those days, sadly, are long gone. Under the new lawlessness, coupled with a weak government and international and interregional opposition (these trains cross into other nations, including some that were once part of the Soviet Union), railroad robbery has become routine. For example, bandits usually board the train from Moscow to Orel in Belgorod at 3 A.M. Choosing an entire car to plunder, they open the outer door, either by using powerful magnets or the keys to the car (such keys are sold openly at all train stations for fifteen hundred rubles). The bandits then rob the passengers as they sleep (or pretend to sleep). Passengers who resist are risking their lives. Conductors who object are coerced into submission. The railroads have been forced to take self-defense measures that include rerouting or shortening routes. A third of all trains now travel with armed guards.

Trains heading in a southerly direction—for instance, from Moscow to Adler on the Black Sea—with their luxury compartments favored by the elite, are especially vulnerable. Yevgeny Mashkov, a member of President Yeltsin's inner circle, relates the following incident: "I went to visit my parents in Rostov-on-the-Don. There were no economy tickets, so I had to purchase a luxury seat. I immediately noticed some strange-looking hooks fixed to the door of the compartment. The conductor explained that the hooks were necessary to ward off bandits. Hooking a shelf across the door created an effective barricade and prevented entry. In response to my wide-eyed stare, the conductor told me, 'It's a good idea.' After further consideration, she said, 'Generally speaking, so far they've been necessary.' "[3]

Travel by bus would seem to be a safer choice, but buses, including city buses and those carrying passengers from the Sheremetyevo-2 International Airport, are also held up on a regular basis. Nor does taking a taxi from the airport to the center of Moscow guarantee safe passage. Recently a gang of thieves that preyed on airline passengers was arrested, but this did not stem the problem. Bespredel established a foothold in this area long ago. Customs workers furnish thieves with lists of people entering the country. These lists identify the amount of hard currency and luggage carried by each passenger. It does no good

3. Cited in *Novoye Russkoye Slovo*, March 11, 1994, 11.

for passengers to bribe customs workers, because the taxi dispatcher has already been bought off and will ensure that targets are placed in the proper taxi, leaving them at the mercy of the thieves.

Intercity bus travel is beset by looting and robbery. The incidence of buses being seized and their passengers held hostage is on the rise. Near the city of Mineralnye Vody in Stavropol, Mikhail Gorbachev's native region, for example, a bus was hijacked by Chechens three times over the course of a year. On each occasion the bandits had been quickly disarmed, the hostages freed, and the money at least partially recovered. Then, despite the previous failures, the crooks tried again, demanding fourteen million dollars, arms, bullet-proof vests, and helicopters. The hijackers, landing near a village in Chechnya, in the Caucasian mountains, in their newly acquired helicopter, attempted to vanish with the money, but they were captured, with the help of local residents in cooperation with Russian officials. Later (according to *Argumenty i Fakty*), under direct orders from General Dzokhar Dudayev, president of the self-proclaimed Republic of Chechnya, all the Chechens who had aided in the capture of the bandits were executed for working with the Russians, their severed heads displayed in the town square for the edification of the populace (An assistant to Russia's minister of internal affairs told me that the heads, which were shown on television, actually belonged to members of Dudayev's political opposition.)

Judging by what takes place in civil aviation, one can only imagine what goes on in military aviation. According to persistent rumors, during military operations between Georgia and Abkhazia, a Russian military plane stationed in the Caucasus was somehow put into general service, and a hired pilot took off in the unfamiliar machine. According to the pilot, the airplane did not seem to maneuver properly, so he decided to jettison what he thought were two supplementary fuel tanks housed under the airplane's wings. These were actually rockets armed with nuclear warheads, which fortunately, thanks to a multitude of safety devices and codes, did not explode. Instead, they fell harmlessly into a narrow gorge formed by a mountain stream, where efforts to find them have been unsuccessful. The bombs are probably there to this day—that is, of course, if they are not already somewhere in the Middle East, Chechnya, Moscow, Jerusalem, or New York.

It is possible to buy anything at the giant Russian garage sale. The collapsed economy has forced more than just pensioners selling old boots out into the streets. Everything is for sale—bombs, satellites, space stations, and arms—and at very reasonable prices. In a deal that is now under criminal investigation, two huge battleships belonging to the Baltic fleet were sold for ninety-six dollars apiece. The nonferrous metal found on just one of them was worth thousands of dollars. Pistols of various makes, automatic Kalashnikovs, anti-infantry mines, grenades, submachine guns, cannons, armored tank carriers, airplanes, tanks, and missiles are all up for sale. In just a few months of 1994 alone, "brokers" removed from military sites 1,946 automatics, 140 submachine guns, 33 grenade launchers, and 6 cannons. The Internal Affairs Ministry estimates that more than 150,000 illegally purchased and traded arms are in the hands of the general population.

The system for calculating the amount of nuclear material throughout the territories of the former USSR has been severely compromised by the country's disintegration. The world community may not be ready to handle the news, but it is a near-certainty that nuclear-grade material from Russia, suitable for the building of an atomic bomb, has already been sold. Stockpiles of radioactive material for atomic and hydrogen bombs stored in Russia and the "near abroad" could easily be stolen and sold to nations dreaming of joining the nuclear club or to wealthy villains of the type found in Ian Fleming novels. These stockpiles could also be sold to the Russian mafia, which is capable of implementing a massive operation to blackmail Europe with the threat of a nuclear bomb or the release of radioactive material.

Members of counterintelligence and internal affairs in the city of Srezhinsk who were tracking thieves for stealing government plutonium and selling it for ten thousand dollars a gram came upon an unexpected cache in July 1994.[4] It contained five-and-a-half kilograms of uranium-238, which had been stolen from the Russian Federal Nuclear Center. This is only one example. On July 21, 1994, a press conference was held in Wiesbaden, Germany. The leaders in the fight against organized crime, from the FBI (USA), the Royal Mounted Police (Canada), the Investigating Commission Battling the Mafia (Italy), the Federal Criminal Police (Germany), and the Russian Internal Affairs Ministry were present. The Germans stated that on May 10, during a search of one Adolf Eichl's garage in Tengen, near the Swiss border, for counterfeit money, they had discovered a lead container. According to experts from the European Institute of Radioactive Materials in Karlsruhe, the container held nearly six grams of plutonium purified to 99.97 percent and fully suitable for the preparation of a nuclear charge. The same

---

4. Black market prices for radioactive material are very steep. A kilogram of chromium-50 sells for twenty thousand dollars, cesium-137 goes for one million dollars, and lithium-6 for ten million dollars.

experts determined that the plutonium had probably been produced in Russia, most likely in one of the previously closed cities of Chelyabinsk-65, Tomsk-7, or Krasnoyarsk-26.[5] Leopold Schuster, head of the battle against organized crime for the German Federal Police, also announced that, according to data from his investigation, there are currently at least 264 pounds (120 kilograms) of plutonium for sale on the black market—enough for at least 15 atomic bombs.[6]

FBI head Louis Freeh, speaking before Congress in May 1994, expressed his serious concern that members of the Russian criminal world have the ability to steal nuclear weapons.[7] Claire Sterling, an American journalist, asserts in her recently published book *The Thieves' World* that the Russian mafia controls not only nuclear material but atomic weapons, which could end up in the hands of terrorist organizations. Such fears were confirmed by a meeting of the Bonn cabinet on June 8, 1994, which discussed a report presented by German intelligence stating that the Russian mafia groups have, as of several weeks ago, gained control of the most important components for the production of atomic bombs. The coordinator of intelligence operations, Berndt Shmidbauer, announced that criminal organizations are capable of blackmail using highly radioactive, toxic material. Germany's Foreign Intelligence Service is aware of at least 300 to 350 deals involving the sale of nuclear material previously belonging to member nations of the Warsaw Pact. Of these, only 18 have been prevented. Some of this material is suitable for the preparation of atomic bombs, and some is highly radioactive (enriched uranium-238 and cesium-137). Part of it was stolen from the Geophysics Institute in Tbilisi, and part from the army-navy depot in Murmansk, on the Bering Sea, the location of a Russian atomic submarine base. The contraband was illegally redirected from Murmansk through Lithuania and the Baltic Sea into Germany.

American officials say that Russia lacks vital experience and know-how in keeping track of its estimated thousand tons of bomb-grade

5. German intelligence posited that high-level ministry personnel, industrial concerns, and research facilities were involved with the contraband plutonium. This was disputed by Russian officials, who maintained that there has not been a single incident involving either the theft or loss of plutonium from their country— unfortunately, not a very credible statement in view of Russian bespredel. The Germans stand by their assertions.

6. Broad, "Making Nuclear Arms Is Easier Than It Looks," 1. During a tour of Chernobyl in 1989, Thomas B. Cochran, a senior scientist at the Natural Resources Defense Council, told me that in fact skilled scientists and engineers can build a bomb using far less plutonium. The same is true for uranium.

7. Broadcast on C-SPAN, May 11, 1994.

plutonium, rendering it incapable of providing reliable assurances that none of its materials is missing from storage.[8] Radioactive nuclear materials from the nuclear warheads of Soviet rockets destroyed in accordance with agreements with the USA were transported to the Siberian chemical processing plant—Tomsk-7—by regular rail; the local authorities of the towns through which the train passed were not asked for their consent. Twenty thousand containers holding a total of twenty metric tons of enriched uranium and plutonium were placed in a regular warehouse guarded by only one soldier. The warehouse walls were so thin that a heavy hammer blow could have punctured them, much less a grenade blast. Mishandling of these materials could lead to an ecological catastrophe the equal of Chernobyl.[9]

Former Soviet scientists earning less than a hundred dollars a month are capable of not only selling their knowledge and technology but pointing out the location of nuclear material. As one friend told me after visiting one of the former USSR's nuclear centers, he had met a lot of desperate scientists there who were ready for anything. Espionage activities in 1994 once again resemble the heyday from 1970 to 1980. Sergei Stepashin, director of the Federal Counterintelligence Service, which to a certain extent has replaced the KGB, announced that Russian atomic specialists were prime candidates for recruitment by foreign special services, which "had begun to work impudently against Russia."[10] Stepashin did not name any particular country, but the implication was clear: it would be difficult for foreign recruiters to pass up the opportunities offered by full-blown Russian bespredel. Countries seeking to become nuclear powers are probably similarly tempted.

Intranational conflicts amid the ruins of the former USSR also threaten to add to the venomous stew of bespredel. For various reasons, including fierce national intolerance, Russian atomic power plant specialists are abandoning their work stations in other countries. Russian nuclear specialists also have been denied access to installations where their help is indispensable. Atomic plants in Ukraine and Lithuania are turning into potential Chernobyls. Last year, at the Ignalina Nuclear Power Plant, a reactor appeared to be overheating, threatening a major catastrophe. Further investigation determined that it was a false alarm brought on by a computer virus. No one seemed worried that such a

8. "A New Call to Tighten Atom Curbs," *New York Times* (International Edition), August 21, 1994, 1, 24.

9. Zhuravlev, "Zima v etom godu budet osobenno iadernoi" (This winter is going to be especially nuclear), 1.

10. Tsyganov, "FSK v traditsiiakhh KGB" (FSC acting in KGB tradition), 40.

virus had infected the system controlling the entire plant. In November 1994, protesting against the death sentence of his son, who had murdered a Lithuanian journalist who had written about the rafia, one Georgy Dekanidze threatened to explode the plant, and the entire station was switched off for several days.

The security of the atomic power plants is also suffering because of bespredel. In the past these installations were guarded with several rows of barriers with electronic sensors, barbed wire, and watchtowers. Specially selected KGB agents guarded facilities around the clock. Within the stations themselves, a network of technical informers worked for the KGB. Subversive activity was practically impossible. After the August 1991 putsch, however, this system was destroyed along with the rest of the KGB. Penetrating an atomic power station, especially using weapons, is not particularly difficult. The reactors are unreliable and pose grave dangers to nearby inhabitants. The major plants are located near large cities such as Saint Petersburg and Kiev, as well as near the borders of European countries. Atomic blackmail is clearly possible.

The formerly powerful Soviet system, a system with its faults and its merits, whose military doctrine—contrary to the United States'—did not allow a preventive nuclear strike, has fallen. In its place now rules bespredel, a force probably more dangerous to the United States and the rest of the world than the mighty Soviet Union ever was. Meanwhile, life in Russia continues. The statues of Communist leaders have been removed, and streets have reassumed their prerevolutionary names, but no belief or ideology has replaced the Communist dogma on which the country had depended. The country's moral standards are moribund, and without law, order, and morality everything else has collapsed. In 1994 ITAR-TASS reported the following incidents (among others):

> In the city of Artem, Mikhail A., in a fit of anger, killed his wife's lover. Mikhail's wife helped him dismember and burn the corpse in the fireplace. Before they incinerated the remains, though, she cut out the victim's loins and treated her friends to cutlets made from them for several days.

> In Moscow, an excellent student, wanting some extra money, stole some polygraphic foil from a local business. Using his knowledge of chemistry, the student and several twelve- to fifteen-year-old assistants concocted homemade bombs in an apartment building. The client purchasing these bombs wanted to frighten his business competitors.

On receiving his machine gun as he began guard duty, a soldier stationed at a strategic missile base near Barnaul began shooting at the missile launching pad, next to the fuel tanks and nuclear missiles. Because of his proximity to the tanks and missiles, it was impossible to shoot at him. After killing the officer in charge of guard duty, as well as several other soldiers, he hijacked an armed troop carrier. Several hours later, the hungry soldier surrendered to authorities.

To paraphrase the famous Russian writer Fazil Iskander, the cosmic cold of bespredel howls in the black hole created by the absence of ideology. To avoid getting sucked into this hole, people will cling to any ideological support. Always happy to oblige, Zhirinovsky readily contradicts his previous assertions about Communism when the moment seems opportune. As he once said to me, "In its essence there was nothing wrong with Communism. There were mistakes. There were even crimes, but committed by individuals. Communist ideology itself is not to blame."

PART FOUR

Zhirinovsky Today (and Tomorrow?)

10
Zhirinovsky and Madonna

Zhirinovsky was probably the very first Russian politician to take seriously one of show business's vital principles: what you say doesn't matter as long as they talk about you; when they stop talking about you, you're dead. His former press secretary and the minister of information of his shadow cabinet Andrei Arkhipov calls the LDPR's media campaign for Zhirinovsky "mystified truth." "Yes, we lied, but we did it in such a way as not to be caught red-handed."[1] Arkhipov states that at the beginning of 1992 he sent false information to everyone in the media, telling them that Zhirinovsky had a big bald eagle tattooed on his chest. (This type of eagle is the trademark of the "Vory v Zakone"— the highest-level criminals in Russia.) Later he sent out a press release announcing that Zhirinovsky had asked the mayor of Saint Petersburg to give to the LDPR the cruiser *Aurora*, an important symbol of the Bolshevik revolution that is normally anchored close to the Winter Palace on the Neva River in Petersburg. Supposedly the cruiser was to be anchored in the Moscow River outside the Kremlin, presumably waiting to precipitate another uprising. Zhirinovsky's publicists have reported several attempts to assassinate their boss. Once they reported that Zhirinovsky had saved a drowning boy. But their most imaginative publicity stunt was the famous story of the Zhirinovsky falcons going into battle on the side of Saddam Hussein. This canard was happily reported by almost every important magazine and newspaper in Russia, the USA, and Western Europe, accompanied by a striking pho-

1. Khinstein, "Zvezda Vladimira Zhirinovskogo" (Vladimir Zhirinovsky's star), 4–5.

tograph of Zhirinovsky in uniform replete with pistol belt and shoulder holster making a valedictory speech to his falcons before sending them off to war. The whole thing was a carefully orchestrated fraud, designed both to ridicule and to entertain.[2]

A prominent Russian journalist recently said that if Zhirinovsky had maintained a moderate, diplomatic profile when dealing with the Western mass media, he could have won some degree of tolerance, if not support, from the West. But Zhirinovsky seems indifferent to such practical advice. Many of his statements and interviews (including the one in the March 1995 issue of *Playboy*) are so obnoxious that they drive potential supporters away. The irritants are all well known; there has been nothing new since 1991. All the rhetoric, so familiar to everyone by now, can be reduced to a few classic statements. Some of the more notorious follow.

"American Zionists offered me $100 million if I left politics. But any attempt to eliminate me is doomed to failure."[3] This statement recurs in a slightly different form: "An American offered me $10 million to leave politics. I told him: 'Never.' I steer the boat here. I know the course. No one else knows."[4] He has also made similar claims to me.

On another theme, Zhirinovsky proclaims, "All we want is three countries: Afghanistan, Iran, and Turkey."[5] I have not been able to locate any statement this definite in *Poslednii brosok na iug* (The last dash to the south) or elsewhere. Usually Zhirinovsky phrases this ambition less aggressively. During an interview with David Frost, for example, when Frost asked him bluntly, "So you have to move into Afghanistan, Iran and Turkey?" Zhirinovsky[6] replied, "We don't want capture anything, anywhere. Only one day I suppose the people who is living there

2. Zhebrovsky, "Byli dobrovol'tsy, ne bylo dobrovol'tsev" (There were volunteers and there weren't), 16–17.

3. Quoted in Fedarko, "Rising Czar?" 41. Fedarko provides no further information about the source.

4. Quoted in Frazer and Lancelle, *Absolute Zhirinovsky*, 135. The authors cite the February 4, 1994, issue of *Die Zeit* as their source, but it is not clear if Zhirinovsky said this in an interview with *Die Zeit* or if *Die Zeit* was quoting some other source.

5. Quoted in Fedarko, "Rising Czar?" 41.

6. Transcript of interview no. 34, David Frost, CNN, March 25, 1994, 2. Zhirinovsky's imperfect English is obviously unsuitable for diplomacy; that kind of thing is beyond him. His English is so poor, in fact, that it can be edited to say almost anything, which is what some journalists have done in order to achieve the greatest possible shock value. Zhirinovsky would be better served if he always spoke in Russian. Even that, however, would not guarantee pearls of oratory: as his former classmate, Vladimir Kozlovsky, has observed, "There's no need to level unjust accu-

ask us to help them because if we are not to the south—no peace in this region in the world."

Zhirinovsky has made many allusions to a mysterious superweapon that he will use to quell his enemies: "This weapon is stronger than nuclear weapons. . . . There is no way of defending against it. It is the same with sonic weapon. We also have this."[7]

There are the references to the Indian Ocean: "The last 'dash' to the south. I dream of Russian soldiers washing their boots in the warm waters of the Indian Ocean and switching to summer uniform forever. Lightweight boots, lightweight trousers . . . and a small modern assault rifle produced by the Izhevsk plant. These assault rifles are much better than UZI."[8] Morrison claims that these quotations are taken from Zhirinovsky's book *Poslednii brosok na iug*, yet I find no such passage in either my Russian-language copy of the book or the English translation. One of the pirated editions of the book, which have flooded Russia, does contain the passage, but it is suspiciously printed in italic in different typeface and has no logical connection to what precedes and follows it. Zhirinovsky himself has publicly protested the inclusion of the passage in pirated editions of his book, but his protests go unnoticed by the press.

And then there are the things he has said about America and President Clinton:

Everywhere there are hotbeds of war, you find Americans. Everywhere you find diseases, they are diseases from America. AIDS is from America. . . . [Clinton] is afraid. He's a weak president. But what can I do? I'm strong. I'm brave. I can but he couldn't. In sexual life that means impotence. Impotence! . . . I am ready, but he is scared—and so much the worse for him. Shame on such a president, let him go on playing his saxophone at home and not come here at all. . . . However, the chance of Clinton and me meeting has not been lost. . . . We will play golf and go to a ranch. We will have a rest and get to know each other better.[9]

You know what I want? I want to take him to the Russian baths and beat him with birch branches—and he can beat me. And then into a

---

sations against Zhirinovsky. Especially when there are more than enough things he can be 'justly' charged with" (Kozlovsky, "Lev Navrozov: Sverkh Zhirinovsky?" [Lev Navrozov: Super Zhirinovsky?], 13).

7. Morrison, "Vladimir Zhirinovsky," 106.

8. Ibid., 111–12. Morrison cites *Moscow Izvestia,* January 21, 1994, 1–2, in FBISS-SOV-94-105, January 24, 1994, 31–33.

9. Ibid., 113–14.

snow bank in the Russian winter. And then to Siberia, where he'd stay in one hut and I'd stay in the other. And in the morning, we'd see each other. That would end his relationship with Hillary.[10]

There's too much of your [American] culture on our television. . . . Too much violence and too much advertising. Useless advertising for cat and dog food. . . . Our people are dying of starvation and you're singing about how to feed your pets. . . . Aid is promised but not delivered, that's what we find humiliating. The best thing you can do is do nothing. Leave us alone. That's the best aid. Leave us alone.[11]

The extravagances range widely:

World War III is a possibility. I do not wish it but if the wars in the Balkans, the Caucasus, and Central Asia continue; if something happens between Iran and Iraq; if the Kurdish problem in Turkey expands, then World War III might occur. . . . I do not want it but we are slowly approaching that eventuality.[12]

Your current president [Zhirinovsky was addressing a Bulgarian audience], Zhelyu Zhelev, is a figure of the transitional period. . . . I would like to see Mr. Svetoslav Stoilov as your president.[13]

When asked how he would cope with a famine in Russia, he replied:

I'll move the troops: about 1.5 million strong, into the former East Germany, rattling my nuclear sabers, and they'll give me everything. . . . What price Paris? How about London? Washington? Los Angeles? How much are you willing to pay so I don't wipe them from the face of the Earth with my SS-18s? You doubt me? Want to take a chance? Let's get started.[14]

This last quotation appears to be based on statements in an article by Alexander Yanov, a well-known political scientist. Yanov translates a quotation attributed to Zhirinovsky in an article by Vladimir Nazarov: "I'll move the troops, some 1.5 million strong, into the former GDR; rattle my sabers—including nuclear sabers—and they'll give me everything." Yanov then continues, speaking in his own voice:

10. *World News with Peter Jennings*, January 12, 1994, ABC News, transcript no. 4008, EST edition, 5.

11. Ibid., 4.

12. Morrison, "Vladimir Zhirinovsky," 124.

13. *Otechestven Vestnik* (Sofia), December 27, 1993.

14. *Washington Times*, December 14, 1993, A14.

Let the presidents of the Western countries, exhilarated by their apparent victory in the cold war, talk about a "new world order." Much like their predecessors after the First World War [who] didn't take into consideration the Hitler phenomenon, they forget today the phenomenon of the nuclear Robin Hood. . . . Meanwhile, Zhirinovsky is certain that by the very fact of their hopeless conventionalism they dealt him all the trump cards. That's why he is able to bluff all he wants, to dare them and to blow up the conventions of civilization. He shall speak with them in his own language—the one they have never heard before. "What price would you put on Paris?" he would ask. How about London? Washington and Los Angeles? How much are you willing to pay so I don't wipe them from the face of the earth with my missiles? You doubt me? Want to take a risk? Where do we start?[15]

Apparently, some reporters quoting Yanov quoting Nazarov supposedly quoting Zhirinovsky mistook Yanov's provocative imitation of Zhirinovsky for Zhirinovsky's own words. Thus is born a classic Zhirinovsky quotation.

The genesis of Zhirinovsky's remarks about "nuking the Japs" appears to be similarly murky. As Yanov wrote, "It appears that the Western press first registered [this alleged statement] in the interview that Zhirinovsky gave to the English journalist Peter Konradi. If we are to believe the account of this interview published in *Novoye Russkoye Slovo* (June 29, 1992) Konradi was so shocked that he didn't even clearly understand what was the subject."[16] Zhirinovsky's ungrammatical, undiplomatic English strikes again.

But it is Zhirinovsky's supposed plans for Alaska that have provided Western journalists with the richest source of speculation. Claims run wild: Zhirinovsky wants Alaska back from the United States! Or rather, he wants to take it by force! Using nuclear weapons at that! Even the emblem of the LDPR shows Russia sticking out rather far on its upper right-hand side, undoubtedly signifying the reincorporation of Alaska within its borders! The revanchist, irredentist Zhirinovsky, rattling his nuclear sabers, is demanding the return of Alaska!

Let me again play the devil's advocate. Do the elements depicted in a state or party symbol always testify to that party's militaristic intentions? A central feature in the official coat of arms of Armenia is a representation of Mount Ararat, but no one accuses Armenia of expansionist designs on Turkey. In the same way, the presence of Alaska on

15. Yanov, "The Phenomenon of Zhirinovsky," 62.
16. Ibid., 74.

the party symbol of the LDPR does not necessarily mean that that party has a militaristic appetite for Alaska. More likely, Alaska is included as a symbol of Russia at the time of its greatest territorial expansion. To be sure, it is rather uncouth to depict the map of Russia this way, but then the entire LDPR coat of arms is uncouth to Western eyes. And why should it be otherwise? It is not addressed to the West but to the domestic voting public, with the intention of lifting their spirits by reminding them of past glories.

Zhirinovsky's position on Alaska—he proposes eventually buying it back from the United States—though absurd, is actually much more moderate than the official Soviet position was under Stalin. I remember learning in school (in 1950, when Stalin was still alive) that Alaska had been rented to the United States for ninety-nine years and that in 1966 we would get it back. The official documents, which from the time of Stalin until the era of glasnost received little publicity, show that this just isn't so: in 1867 Russia *sold* Alaska to the United States, with no expiration date or other temporal restrictions.[17]

It is always worth remembering that what Zhirinovsky writes or signs—his official, authorized position, so to speak—is usually much milder than what he says, especially when he is speaking to potential voters or in a foreign language. His speeches are not meant to state the precise positions of his party; rather, in and around the actual positions of his party—as recorded in the program and statute of the LDPR and in his programmatic presentations at his party's congresses, conferences, and the like—he weaves his own rhetorical fantasies, sometimes very strange ones, indeed—"sewage spewings" (*polivy*), as they have been dubbed by his former ally, the Russian emigré writer Eduard Limonov, who today stands on the extreme right.

When Zhirinovsky speaks at an election rally, he is working on potential voters; he wants to say what they want to hear. Here is what Zhirinovsky has to say about his own media interviews:

> Now, I'm not trying to boast, but Nixon has just told me that in the West they give me a very high rating for the way I conducted the election campaign. They all think I had a huge apparatus working for me and must have spent billions of rubles. Sure, the party helped by working among the masses, but no one writes speeches for me. I go

17. A recent book by Nikolai N. Bolkhovitinov gives the full text, in Russian, of the Russian-American treaty of March 30 (March 18, Old Style), 1867, which was signed in Washington and later, on May 3 of that year, confirmed by Tsar Alexander II, "emperor of All the Russians" (*Russko-amerikanskie otnosheniia* [Russian-American relations], 331–41).

right in to these TV debates, right out on the air, and they're amazed
. . . . Well, what I do is, I agree with them: "Yes, about forty of the best
political scientists in Russia, and several billion rubles spent on the
campaign. . . ." I am saying this specifically so they will understand
that this is a rich and powerful party. . . . "Entire institutes are working for me, entire institutes . . . and several physicians, several
masseurs, a special diet. . . ." "How do you keep in shape?" "Several
trainers of Olympic champions," I say, "and they train me several
hours a day. . . ." I say what they want to hear.[18]

Is he aware that most of his election speeches are pure demagogy?
Undoubtedly he is. Politics is 70 percent demagogy, he has admitted in
countless interviews, although that proportion varies—sometimes it's
50, 60, 75, 90, or even 99 percent Does it upset him that the mass media
seem to love reviling him? Hardly:

An enormous amount of attention is being paid to us in the world
today. Even if sometimes there is distortion, that too is a plus. Negative publicity can also have a positive effect. Just think: What would
happen if it was the other way around?! If they began to praise us?
That would be a disaster! Some of you go astray here; you think it's
bad that they criticize us. Maybe psychologically it's not always
pleasant, because the criticism can be pretty dirty, so to speak, and it
doesn't have a very nice ring to it. But the most terrible thing would
be if they began to praise us! That would be the end of our party, the
end of our fraction! If they start praising us, we will lose any upcoming election! Therefore, God forbid they should start to praise us. It's
a very good thing that they treat us the way they do, although granted it's pretty much on the negative side. But against the background
of the overall negative situation in our country, a minus on top of that
minus comes out a plus![19]

In an interview with Lee Hockstader of the *Washington Post* I compared Zhirinovsky to Madonna:

Zhirinovsky lives and breathes by the mass media. They have a love-
hate relationship. They can't go for a day without one another. He,
because he needs the mass media to become as well known as possible, in whatever way he can—anything, as long as they write about
him. He needs publicity and name recognition in order to win in the

18. From the stenographic record of a session of the LDPR parliamentary group,
quoted in Kozlovsky, "Zhirinoviana: V Dumskoi fraktsii LDPR" (Zhirinoviana: At
the meeting of the Duma fraction of the LDPR), 6.
19. Ibid.

presidential elections. No matter how the press beats him up, he will never refuse an interview. Even the journalists who distort him, who rearrange the facts, even those who are obviously his enemies, get interviews. They say he gives interviews for money only. That may be. But if you didn't pay him, he would still give the interview— because he needs it.

In fact he himself courts the press, just like Madonna. She's willing to strip naked and produce an album with photos of herself in that state—in order to rouse the flagging interest of the mass media. The same with Zhirinovsky. He's not only willing to undress in public to attract attention. All the photographs of him in the bathhouses, in the Russian *banya*, and under the shower are just so many tributes to his machismo. It's a way of attracting attention.

He is willing to talk about the sexual inadequacies of his youth, but today, he says, he can go all night without tiring, and he challenges Yeltsin and Luzhkov to compete with him. He makes all sorts of truly horrendous political statements; they make your blood run cold. But go up to him afterward, as some of his buddies have done— they too are stunned by what he has said. They ask him, 'You don't really think that, do you?' And he laughs, 'That's just for public consumption, for the press.'

On the other hand, it is precisely him that the journalists seek out, though they often insult him at the same time. And this is not only because he's always up to something, will always toss off some colorful or scandalous remark, make somebody's ears burn, or make a blunder himself. In other words, there is always something sensational they can write about, to increase the sales of their newspapers or magazines. They love scandals and sensations and they love to personalize politics. But there is another reason, and that is: No matter what you think, this is a man who tomorrow could become the president of a country with thousands of ballistic missiles and tens of thousands of nuclear warheads.

Professor Yasen Zasursky, dean of the school of journalism at Moscow State University, agrees with me on this point: "He [Zhirinovsky] is deliberately making those wild statements and actions to attract attention."[20]

One question remains, however, and it is the most important: Do Zhirinovsky's wild statements correspond to his actual plans? For my part, I think that all his public pronouncements need not be taken too seriously. Let's not forget that he is a politician from a postmodern

20. Quoted in Tanner, "Media Divided," 3.

bespredel era, where "anything goes." The U.S. ambassador to Russia has called on journalists to take this attitude, commenting, "One wonders in fact what the press is doing merely reporting his latest sort of screaming rather than analysing what it is he has been saying and doing. . . . I am not sure I would call that responsible journalism."[21] Experience has shown that the truth is better sought in the written documents of the LDPR. There the thought and words are weighed more carefully, and while some of the assertions in those documents are disputable and others altogether unacceptable, they are at least subject to discussion rather than being beyond the bounds of credibility.

The more mistakes the government makes and the more frenzied the attacks on Zhirinovsky by such radical democrats as Valeria Novodvorskaya, the more support he gains among his constituents. The newspaper *Nezavisimaya Gazeta* had this to say on the subject:

> Vladimir Zhirinovsky's political mother is, without doubt, the eccentric leader of the Democratic Union, Valeria Novodvorskaya. Zhirinovsky's collective political father, on the other hand, is not to be found among some mythical fascist elements, but in the ranks of the populist and radical democratic forces headed by Boris Yeltsin and Yegor Gaidar.
>
> The electorate that supports the LDPR is in its very essence highly changeable, and its quantitative parameters are determined fundamentally not by this party's program and not even by the oratorical talents of Zhirinovsky himself, but by external factors having to do with the dynamics of economic, political, and moral degradation affecting Russian society. If things reach the point where a wall of mutual estrangement finally divides the government and the people of Russia into two hostile and opposing camps, Zhirinovsky will have obtained very favorable odds for becoming the new master of the Kremlin.[22]

21. Ibid.
22. "President '96," 3.

11

The New Russian Roulette

Zhirinovsky's unexpected appearance on the world political scene as the head of the most influential political party in post-totalitarian Russia, along with the appearance of other even more truculent and radical Russian politicians with ultranationalistic and ultrapatriotic platforms, reveals a new and hitherto undetected danger in the condition of the Russian people and Russian society. Zhirinovsky's Liberal Democratic Party, despite its seemingly farcical nature, is profoundly thought out, and its leader's psychologically effective rhetoric is not only a real force in itself that sooner or later will have to be reckoned with, it is also symptomatic of the unbridled chaos of bespredel—nothing in moderation, everything in excess, and "anything goes"—that truly can and should be feared. Russian bespredel is the source, the medium, the means of existence, and the model for Zhirinovsky and his ilk.

The danger is not in the threat of Russian soldiers cooling their feet in the Indian Ocean, or radioactive waste from Russia being wafted over the Baltics, or the demand for the return of Alaska, or any of the other outrageous statements Zhirinovsky tosses off to the consternation and irritation of both the West and the Russian intelligentsia. All that nonsense is calculated to attract the attention of the media and the electorate, while simultaneously evoking a figure much beloved in Russia: the *yurodivy*, the holy fool or jester in whose torrents of disconnected speech can be discerned sober-minded wisdom and a penetratingly clear vision of the future. As such a figure, Zhirinovsky can afford to make preposterous claims, to rant and rave, to throw his weight around, and to pose for pictures in the nude. For such a prophet, anything is permissible. Let's not fool ourselves—Zhirinovsky is loved and trusted by millions of Russians, not just by society's outcasts, as some of his critics, confusing their wishes with reality, would have us believe. Among his followers are intelligent, educated, and cultivated people who in another time would have gone miles out of their way to avoid the likes of the Liberal Democratic Party and its leader. But not in the current state of bespredel.

Nothing would be more dangerous in Russia's current climate than to forget Zhirinovsky, his party, and his followers, to ignore him, consider him "scum" (Gorbachev), a nobody "unworthy of serious discussion" (Rutskoi), to brand him a "fascist" and "scoundrel" (Gaidar), a mental case, a clown, a "cur"(vyblyadok), a "caricature of a Russian patriot" (Solzhenitsyn), an idiot, a demagogue, a Nazi pig, an opportunist, or a dirty swine. Such responses are not only unconstructive but essentially unfair. Zhirinovsky's success in the elections was no accident; it cannot be explained away by Russia's temporary "stupefaction" (Ogonyok) or "insanity" (Limonov). Nor has his popularity faded away, as was predicted after his triumph in December 1993: far from being forgotten, he is inclining toward the presidency.

Russia can be dangerous again, much more so than the USSR ever was. And Zhirinovsky is a symbol and reflection of this potential threat, by no means its primary cause. Some of his opponents are said to be planning his assassination—there are even volunteers for the job—but by concentrating on Zhirinovsky, they are overlooking the real menace. The Zhirinovsky phenomenon merely reflects the disturbing realities of current Russian life.

What, according to Zhirinovsky's voters, has happened to Russia over the past ten years? From a world superpower, heir to a centuries-old history and as recently as 1985 the head of a vast socialist camp with influence all over the planet, the USSR has degenerated into a stump of territory, a poor developing country that now goes by the name of the Russian Federation, whose insides are seething with a bloody "parade of sovereignties" (Chechnya is the perfect example) that threatens further disintegration. In demonizing Communism, the people and its leaders have simultaneously demonized the components of its essence—a multinational USSR, countries of popular democracy, countries with regimes of socialist orientation, a Communist Party in almost every country in the world, the Warsaw Pact.

"Like beaten hounds, Russian troops withdrew from Berlin, where fifty years ago their grandfathers proudly entered as victors and the saviors of Europe."[1] *Time* magazine captioned the photograph of Dwight D. Eisenhower on the cover of its June 6, 1994, issue "The man who beat Hitler"; the landing of troops at Normandy is now counted as the definitive event of the war. President Yeltsin was not even invited to the memorial services held there in 1994. Meanwhile Estonian leaders have forbidden their citizens to celebrate the golden anniversary of Tallinn's liberation from the fascists, and few in the West now recall the twenty million Soviet dead—soldiers and civilians—whose sacrifices turned the tide toward victory. Russian minorities in the Baltic states are subjected to unprecedented discrimination, but United Nations commissions can only turn up "insignificant violations" of human rights there.[2]

In international affairs a double standard has begun to take hold, a tacit agreement to recognize only those accords and contracts—or even, within a single agreement, only those clauses—that place the Russians in an unfavorable position. The disgraceful Ribbentrop-Molotov pact is set aside as invalid from start to finish, with the exception of the section defining Lithuania's generous borders. No one now seems to remember the Helsinki Accords of 1975, which definitively confirmed Europe's existing borders as eternal and unchangeable. In light of all this, is there any reason to be surprised by the emergence of numerous groups (in Russia and elsewhere in the world) expressing a desire to examine anew the whole issue of borders? Now that the genie has been let out of the bottle, it will be very difficult to get it back inside.

Russians, who once helped turn the lands of Central Asia into modern countries, are now fleeing from the unorganized internecine feuding among khanates and tribes from Kazakhstan, Uzbekistan, Turkmenia, Tadzhikistan, and Kyrgyzia. Neither England nor France retired from its overseas colonies in the disgrace that faced Russia when it was forced to quit the territories that had long ago become part of it, flesh of its flesh. Many Russians today consider that this rending of the union was not only shortsighted and unjustified historically but an intolerable humiliation.

An especially bitter pill for Russians to swallow is the recognition that NATO—the system diametrically opposed to the Warsaw Pact—has remained stable and, moreover, has been strengthened and

1. Maverick general Alexander Lebed, an increasingly influential figure in Russian public life, quoted in "President '96," 3.

2. Cf. Keiser, "Latvia Strongly Denies Russia's Accusations of Ethnic Cleansing," 3; and Korneev, "Russkie, ubiraites' domoi!" (Russians, go home!), 7.

enriched as a result of its unexpectedly complete and decisive victory in the cold war. One gets the impression that Gorbachev's more experienced American colleagues simply put one over on him. The word *parity*, which had dominated summit talks at first, disappeared completely.[3] The dismantling of the Warsaw Pact did not result in a symmetrical dissolution of NATO. It did not even serve as a first step toward the gradual elimination of the Western alliance. To the contrary, NATO is ready to extend membership to Poland, Hungary, Slovakia, and the Czech Republic. I myself have heard Madeleine K. Albright, the permanent representative of the United States to the United Nations, while acknowledging that Russia no longer constitutes a military threat, officially confirm that the expansion of NATO is something that has already been decided. The only question is when and how it will happen.

It is easy to imagine the unhealthy reaction among Russians to their deepening isolation from Europe, contrary to the dreams and assurances of those who inspired the new thinking and present reforms. Most of the Russian population disapproves of the expansion of NATO. The following was broadcast on ABC on January 6, 1994:

DAVID ENSOR: [*voice-over*] . . . President Boris Yeltsin said through a spokesman that the expansion of NATO to include Poland, Hungary or the Czech republic could lead to a strong pressure from the Russian military to return military spending back to cold war levels. It could also lead more Russians to support Zhirinovsky's party. "If NATO is expanding," Yeltsin's spokesman said, "the Russian population would be bitter and feel that its national dignity has been offended. This could promote very negative, nationalist tendencies."

ALEXANDER PUSHKOV, Editor, Moscow News: It will certainly play into the hands of Zhirinovsky, of the Communists, of the conservatives and the military; of all those who would like Russia to go to a certain kind—to go back to a certain kind of isolation.

DAVID ENSOR: The Russian government's blunt language is not just a reaction to Zhirinovsky's nationalist diatribes. It is difficult to find anyone in this country who views the idea of East European nations becoming associated with a Western military alliance as anything but a threat to Russia.[4]

3. See Mandelbaum and Talbott, *Reagan and Gorbachev.*
4. *World News Tonight with Peter Jennings,* January 6, 1994, ABC News, transcript no. 4004, EST edition, 1.

Dispassionately—or, at times, with malicious glee—the West watches as Russia convulses. This was not what Gorbachev had in mind when he introduced the concept of perestroika at the April 1985 plenum of the Communist Party's Central Committee. This is not what Andrey Sakharov, soviet dissidents, and millions of Communists dreamed about while opposing Communist orthodoxy and supporting Gorbachev in 1988–89 against party reactionaries like Yegor Ligachev. This is not what the people yearned for when they attended rallies in 1990–91 in support of Yeltsin, democracy, a market economy, and complete freedom. It seems to the Russian people that their leaders, well intentioned but inexperienced in diplomacy, have been used by the West. Many Russians today feel cruelly and cynically betrayed. Says Zhirinovsky,

> It was a well-prepared, well-thought-out provocation on a worldwide scale. Americans learned from the mistakes of Napoleon, Hitler, and other conquerors who entered Russia with their swords raised and who later were destroyed by the same swords. It is much better to come to Russia with nylon tights, chewing gum, and McDonald's, with pornography and horror movies—the foolish will be only too happy to greet one. The word *dollar* will be imprinted from now on in children's minds. . . . This war is the most monstrous one. It is difficult to identify the enemy. With whom is one supposed to struggle? The slogans coming from the West—they're all very good. Everything is very nice: democracy, pluralism, new economics. Everything is very nice . . . in theory. In reality, our country is destroyed and tormented, but nobody cares. It appears now that it is to be our problem alone. Again, our evil wishers have come from the West to teach us how to change our lives. At the beginning of the century, they stealthily put to us the idea of building communism. The idea was good. [In the same way, not knowing what strings are attached,] who could possibly reject the idea of the fair society?[5]

Democracy and freedom of speech are indisputable facts of Russian life nowadays. Yet the right to read the most subversive, most sexually explicit and formerly banned books and magazines, watch the latest American films, buy any goods as long as one has the money, have one's fill of hamburgers and sneakers—in effect, to do whatever one wants, including traveling abroad and even founding an oppositionist party like Zhirinovsky's—has not brought people the happiness they expected. Hasty economic reforms, which created several thousand

5. Zhirinovsky, "My khotim zhit' po zakonu" (We want to live by the law), 3.

hard-currency millionaires and so-called new Russians, have also led to the general impoverishment of the masses. Not only has their standard of living declined, but they have lost much of what they had under the Brezhnev regime. Almost thirty million Russians now live below the poverty line as it is officially defined in Russia—at the level of bare subsistence. It is not easy for a people that lived seventy years under universal equality (though some would term it relative equality) and universal welfare to accept such sharp contrasts. Life expectancy has dropped, for the first time the death rate has overtaken the birth rate, the number of suicides, especially among youth, has risen, and once forgotten diseases such as cholera have reappeared. Smoking, habitual drunkenness, drug use, and prostitution are continually spreading and to ever-younger victims. As *Time* magazine reported on June 21, 1993 (41–43), Eastern Europe, and Russia in particular, "have emerged as a new market in the sexual exploitation of children. The case of children sold for prostitution in Russia was well covered by the international press." A UN report described the sale of Russian children—a practice existing on a massive scale up to 1992—to buyers in Western countries at prices ranging from $10,000 to $50,000 apiece.[6] Suspicion that organs from the bodies of Russian children were being used in transplant operations resulted in the recent passage of a law forbidding such practices. The UN report expressed special concern that more and more children in Russia were being used as accessories in criminal activity: during the previous year alone, the number of recorded crimes committed by minors had increased by 15.5 percent.

Material impoverishment has been accompanied by a spiritual decline. As in the first years of the revolution and the years spent debunking the cult of personality after the death of Stalin, Russia is again rejecting its past. For the third or fourth time, streets and cities have been renamed, monuments taken down, and history rewritten. Even the most thick-skinned cannot tolerate such profanation of their ancestors and their history, science, culture, architecture, music, and art, all of which suddenly turn out to have been senseless, unnecessary, artificial, or even stolen. The lives of several generations have been deprived of any meaning and inner content. In the past such sacrifices had been justified by a higher goal. Now they are just losses.

The collapse of communist ideology has not been replaced by a new faith and spiritual values. To the ideological vacuum has been added a vacuum in law, order, and morality, stemming from the dissolution of

6. United Nations General Assembly Report, 49th session, October 5, 1994, A/49/478.

the state and the social institutions once charged with maintaining its precepts. Amid legal disorder, a weak government, and an absence of moral guideposts, Russian-style capitalism is a game without rules, life without law, a system of corrupted power and criminal structures that cynically turns a profit on the national possessions of the former USSR and has quickly spread throughout the whole world in the guise of the Russian mafia.

This is how Zhirinovsky, the members of his party, his voters, and many other Russians view the situation in Russia. It is bespredel in a massively frustrated country that is gradually falling under the sway of the rafia; a country with bloody national conflicts, unparalleled crime, profaneness, and a disgraced army that has been banished from every country where it once maintained troops, its soldiers living in barracks and even tanks because adequate civilian housing is lacking back home; a country of intercontinental missiles, nuclear warheads, nuclear submarines, atomic power plants, and chemical factories maintained by a workforce that often does not get paid for months; a country of deceived, robbed, humiliated, profoundly disillusioned, and frightened people. The current splintered Russia—fleeced, anxious, seething with revenge, and driven into a corner—is much more terrible and dangerous to the world than even the Evil Empire of ten years ago in all its power.

Try for a moment to step into the shoes of your Russian counterparts. Imagine what it would be like if, because of inflation, prices increased by a factor of three thousand over a five-year period, with gasoline prices going up by a factor of twenty thousand, so that the monthly salary of a university professor would not be enough to fill the tank of a car even once. Imagine that production is being halved every year. General Motors and General Electric have been bought and taken over by local sheriffs. Lockheed is producing pots and pans. The Sixth Fleet has been sold for scrap. The stores carry only imports, and the resulting trade deficit has eaten up the gold reserves in Fort Knox: the United States is now paying for foreign goods by frantically exporting timber, petroleum, and rare metals. The borders are wide open, and all sorts of contraband, especially narcotics, are crossing them freely.

Imagine also that the average American's life span has shrunk by ten years, the birth rate has fallen off, and infant mortality has risen, so that for the first time in history the American population has begun to decline. Texas is engaged in a bloody war with Arkansas. Hawaii, New Mexico, and Alaska have declared their independence, triumphantly burning the hated American flag, proclaimed Washington, D.C., their main enemy, and called for a jihad against the U.S. government. Guam has thrown off American rule and closed its bases to U.S. warships; any Americans still living there are denied all civil rights. NATO has been abolished, but the Warsaw Pact has expanded by bringing Germany, France, and Britain into membership.

Crime has increased catastrophically, especially kidnapping and murder for hire. Nobody goes out after dark, and everyone who can afford it has heavily bolted, armor-plated doors. In the big cities, garbage is no longer collected, laundries and dry cleaners have disappeared, and drivers ignore the traffic lights. All you can see on television are old Russian films and ads for Stolichnaya vodka. The whole world condemns America for the ideology of the previous century's slave owners, for its seizure of the Louisiana territory and parts of Mexico, and for its armed interventions in such countries as Guatemala, Panama, Haiti, and Cuba. Revisionist American historians have discovered—and journalists have trumpeted to the world—that America was responsible for starting both world wars and merely looked on while the glorious armies of its allies fought the battle of Stalingrad and decided the outcome of the war.

All this takes places against a backdrop of complete helplessness on the part of government —which, in any case, UN analysts insist is on its way to becoming completely interwoven with the mafia, if it is not already. And it's all the fault of the American people, because five years earlier they had become totally fed up with their political parties, which had been in power too long, and their Russian friends had advised them to follow this course. Under such extraordinary circumstances, it is highly unlikely that Americans would seek a solution by voting for Republicans or Democrats. Even Ross Perot might not seem radical enough to them.

This is approximately how things look—adjusting, of course, for Russian realities—to millions of inhabitants of Russia. That is why Zhirinovsky, with his coarse manners and bizarre ideas, is able to win the votes of millions. I am reminded of the Weimar Republic and the sequence of events that led to the rise of Hitler as a national hero. And there are a lot of candidates besides Zhirinovsky vying for the post of Russia's Hitler.

Under these conditions Zhirinovsky is beside the point, or almost beside the point. Like a sensitive dial reading the mood of the masses, and as the outcome, reflection, and symbol of bespredel, he alerts us to the more serious danger. Strange as it sounds, it is in our mutual interest to do what Zhirinovsky pledges in his campaign speeches: to raise Russia up from its knees. A humbled Russia in a state of bespredel sets the stage for the most dangerous form of Russian roulette imaginable. The trigger is being squeezed more and more tightly, and no one knows which chamber contains the lethal nuclear bullet.

We are all playing the new Russian roulette.

Bibliography

Afanasiev, Yuri, ed. *Inogo ne dano* (Fate leaves no other way). Moscow: Progress, 1988.

Agafonov, V. and V. Rokitianskii. *Rossiia v poiskakh budushchego* (Russia in search of the future). Moscow: Progress, 1993.

Alliluyeva, Svetlana. *Only One Year*. New York: Harper & Row, 1969.

Amalrik, Andrey. *Will the Soviet Union Survive Until 1984?* New York: Harper & Row, 1976.

America Through American Eyes: An Exhibit of Recent Books That Reflect Life in the United States. Compiled for the Moscow International Book Fair. New York: Association of American Publishers, 1985.

Andrew, Christopher and Oleg Gordievsky. *KGB: The Inside Story*. New York: HarperCollins, 1990.

"Another Evil Empire Is on the Rise." *Diplomatic World Bulletin* (November 21–28, 1994): 3–4.

Aslund, Anders. "Russia's Success Story." *Foreign Affairs*, November 1994.

Babaev, Bronislav. *Rasstrel "Belogo doma"* (The shelling of the "White House"). Ivanovo: RIO of the Industrialists and Entrepreneurs of the Ivanovo Region, 1994.

Bolkhovitinov, Nikolai N. *Russko-amerikanskie otnosheniia i prodazha Aliaski, 1834–1867* (Russian-American relations and the sale of Alaska, 1834–1867). Moscow: Nauka, 1990.

Brezhnev, Leonid I. *50 let velikikh pobed sotsializma* (Fifty years of great victories for socialism). Moscow: Politizdat, 1967.

Broad, William J. "Making Nuclear Arms Is Easier Than It Looks." *New York Times*, August 21, 1994, 1, 24.

Bunich, Igor. *Bespredel*. St. Petersburg: Shans, 1994.

——. *Zoloto partii* (The party's gold). St. Petersburg: Shans, 1991.

Burtin, Aleksandr. "Fashisty, govoriashchie pravdu" (Fascists telling the truth). *Novoye Russkoye Slovo*, September 30, 1994, 6.

Buzgalin, Alexander and Andrei Kolganov. *Bloody October*. New York: Monthly Review, 1994.

———. *Krovavyi Oktiabr' v Moskve: Khronika, svidetel'stva, analiz sobytii* (Bloody October [1993] in Moscow: A chronology, testimony by witnesses, and analysis of the events). Moscow: Erebus, 1994.

Chelminski, Rudolf. "The Man Who Would Rule Russia." *Reader's Digest*, December 1994, 139–44.

Cherniak, E. B. *Piat' stoletii tainoi voiny* (Five centuries of secret warfare). Moscow: Mezhdunarodnye otnosheniia, 1991.

Chernov, Vladimir. "Volk v ovech'ei shkure" (Wolf in sheep's clothing). *Novoye Russkoye Slovo*, November 18, 1994, 6.

Cohen, David. *Aftershock: The Psychological and Political Consequences of Disaster*. London: Collins, Paladin, 1991.

Davis, Nuell Phar. *Lawrence and Oppenheimer*. New York: Simon & Schuster, 1968.

Djilas, Milovan. *Conversations with Stalin*. New York: Harcourt, Brace, & World, 1962.

———. *The New Class: An Analysis of the Communist System*. New York: Praeger, 1957.

Dolgopolova, Z., ed. *Russia Dies Laughing: Jokes from Soviet Russia*. London: Unwin Paperback, 1983.

Dunlop, John B. *The Rise of Russia and the Fall of the Soviet Empire*. Princeton: Princeton University Press, 1993.

Ebon, Martin. *The Incredible Story of Stalin's Daughter*. New York: New American Library, Signet, 1967.

Ekonomicheskii manifest Liberal'no-democraticheskoi partii Rossii (Economic manifesto of the Liberal-Democratic party of Russia). Moscow: Publisher unknown, 1994.

Fedarko, Kevin. "Rising Czar?" *Time*, July 11, 1994, 38–44.

Felshman, Neil. *Gorbachev, Yeltsin, and the Last Days of the Soviet Empire*. New York: St. Martin's, 1992.

Fenomen Zhirinovskogo (The Zhirinovsky phenomenon). Moscow: Kontrolling, 1992; 2d. ed., 1994.

Fischer, Ruth. *Stalin and German Communism*. Cambridge: Harvard University Press, 1948.

Fish, Carl Russell. *The Path of Empire*. New Haven: Yale University Press, 1921.

Frazer, Graham and George Lancelle (pen names). *Absolute Zhirinovsky*. New York: Penguin, 1994.

Frost, David. Transcript of interview no. 34, Cable News Network, date of broadcast, March 25, 1994.

Fund for Free Expression. *Through American Eyes: An Exhibit of Recent Books That Reflect What Americans Are Reading About Themselves and About the Soviet Union*. Compiled for the Moscow International Book Fair. New York: Association of American Publishers, 1989.

Ganichev, Valery and Larisa Ganichev. *Kremlin Delicacies and the Elements of Kremlin Etiquette*. New York: Fort Ross, 1995.

Golovkina, E. I. and N. V. Panina. *"Sotsial'noe bezumie": Istoriia, teoriia, i sovremennaia praktika* ("Societal insanity": History, theory, and contemporary practice). Kiev: Abris, 1994.

Gorbachev, Mikhail. *Otvety amerikansmomu zhurnalu "Taim," 28 avgusta 1985 goda* (Answers to the American magazine *Time*, August 28, 1985). Moscow: Politizdat, 1985.

——. *Perestroika: New Thinking for Our Country and the World*. New York: Harper & Row, 1987.

Gould, Jennifer. "Vladimir Zhirinovsky." Interview in *Playboy* (March 1995): 47–62, 150–55.

Govorukhin, Stanislav. *Velikaia kriminal'naia revoliutsiia* (The great criminal revolution). Moscow: Andreyevskii Flag, 1993.

Grant, Aleksandr. "Mir spasaet Krasota, a Rossiyu sportsmeny" (The world will be saved by aesthetics; Russia, by athletics). *Novoye Russkoye Slovo*, May 4, 1994, 6–7; May 5, 1994, 6–7; May 6, 1994, 12–13.

Gromov, B. V. *Ogranichennyi kontingent* (Limited contingent). Moscow: Progress, 1994.

Gross, Feliks. *European Ideologies*. New York: Philosophical Library, 1948.

Gumilev, L. N. *Ritmy Evrazii: Epokhi i tsivilizatsii* (Rhythms of Eurasia: Epochs and civilizations). Moscow: Progress, 1993.

Heiden, Konrad. *Der Fuehrer. Hitler's Rise to Power*. Boston: Houghton Mifflin, 1944.

Hockstader, Lee. "How Russia's Zhirinovsky Rose." *Washington Post*, March 6, 1994, A1, A26.

Hodgetts, E. A. Brayley. *The Life of Catherine the Great of Russia*. New York: Brentano's, 1914.

Huss, Pierre J. and George Carpozi, Jr. *Red Spies in the UN*. New York: Pocket Books, 1967.

I. R. "Zhirinovsky Recarves the Map of Eastern Europe." *New Times International* 7, no. 94 (1994): 25.

Kartsev, Vladimir. *Newton*. Moscow: "MG," 1987.

——. "Profitable Publishing at the East River." *Logos* 3, no. 16 (1993): 33–39.

——. *Regotmas*. New York: Fort Ross, 1993.

——. *Traktat o prityazhenii* (Treatise on attraction). With a preface by Andrei Sakharov. Moscow: Sovetskaya Rossiya, 1968.

Keiser, Jennifer. "Latvia Strongly Denies Russia's Accusations of Ethnic Cleansing." *Baltic Observer*, February 17–23, 1994, 3.

Kelley, Kevin/ASE (Association of Space Explorers). *Home Planet*. Foreword by Jacques-Ives Cousteau. Reading, Mass.: Addison-Wesley; Moscow: Mir, 1988.

Khinstein, Aleksandr. "Zvezda Vladimira Zhirinovskogo" (Vladimir Zhirinovsky's star), *Kurier*, November 24, 1994, 4–5.

Khokhov, Nikolay. *In the Name of Conscience: The Testament of a Soviet Secret Agent*. London: Frederick Muller, 1960.

Khrushchev, Nikita S. *Zakliuchitel'noe slovo na XXII s'ezde KPSS, 23 oktiabria 1961 goda* (Concluding remarks at the Twenty-Second Congress of the CPSU, October 23, 1961). Moscow: Gospolitizdat, 1961.

Kissinger, Henry and Vladimir Lukin. *Rethinking Russia's National Interests.* Washington, D.C.: Center for Strategic and International Studies, 1994.

Kontsevaia, Marina. "Borot'sa s fashizmom v Rossii" (To struggle against fascism in Russia). *Vesti* 43, no. 87 (January 21, 1994): 1.

Korneev, Vladimir. "Russkie, ubiraites' domoi!" (Russians, go home!). *Novoye Russkoye Slovo*, February 26–27, 1994, 7.

Korotich, Vitaly. *Zal ozhidaniia* (Waiting room). New York: Liberty, 1991.

Koval', B. I, ed. *Partii i politicheskie bloki v Rossii* (Parties and political blocs in Russia). Moscow: Marko Media, 1993.

Kozlovsky, Vladimir. "Lev Navrozov: Sverkh Zhirinovsky?" (Lev Navrozov: Super Zhirinovsky?). *Novoye Russkoye Slovo*, April 26, 1994, 13–14.

——. "Utrenniaia beseda s Zhirinovskim" (Morning conversation with Zhirinovsky). *Novoye Russkoye Slovo*, November 19–20, 1994, 7.

——. "Zhirinoviana: Genealogicheskoe drevo" (Zhirinovsky's family tree). *Novoye Russkoye Slovo*, April 7, 1994, 9.

——. "Zhirinoviana: V Dumskoi fraktsii LDPR" (Zhirinoviana: At the Duma fraction of the LDPR meeting). *Novoye Russkoye Slovo*, April 20, 1994, 6.

Kramer, Joel and Diana Alstad. *The Guru Papers: Masks of Authoritarian Power.* Berkeley, Calif.: North Atlantic Books/Frog, 1994.

Krasnovskii, A. A. *Ot vziatiia Parizha do pokoreniia Srednei Azii, 1814–1881 gg* (From the occupation of Paris to the subjugation of Central Asia, 1814–1881). Vol. 2 of *Istoriia russkoi armii v dvukh tomakh* (History of the Russian army in two volumes). Moscow: Golos, 1993.

Kurginian, S. E., B. R. Autenshluss, P. S. Goncharov, Yu. V. Gromyko, I. Yu. Sundiev, V. S. Ovchinskii. *Postperestroika: Kontseptsual'naia model' razvitiia nashego obshchestva, politicheskikh partii, i obshchestvennykh organizatsii* (Postperestroika: A conceptual model of the development of our society, political parties, and social organizations). Moscow: Politizdat, 1990.

"LDPR v Gosdume" (The LDPR in the State Duma). *Pravda Zhirinovskogo* 13, no. 36 (1994): 4.

Lebedev, Valery. "Moguchee Moskovskoe Moshennichestvo" (Huge Moscow swindle). *Vestnik*, September 6, 1994.

Liberal Democratic Party of Russia. *Politika i ekonomika* (Politics and economics). Bibliotechka LDPR. Moscow: Rait, 1994.

——. *V. Zhirinovskii—politicheskii lider* (V. Zhirinovsky—political leader). Bibliotechka LDPR. Moscow: Rait, 1994.

"Liberal'no-demokraticheskaia partiia poshla na dopolnitel'nye raskhody" (Liberal democrats decide on additional spending). *Vechernyaya Moskva*, May 30, 1994, 1.

Liberal'no-demokraticheskaia partiia Rossii: Materialy V s'ezda Liberal'no-demokraticheskoi partii Rossii, 2 aprelia 1994 goda (Liberal Democratic Party of Russia: Materials of the fifth congress of the LDPR, April 2, 1994). Moscow: N.p., 1994.

Limonov, Eduard. *Eto ya—Edichka* (It's me—little Eddie). New York: Index, 1982.

——. *Limonov protiv Zhirinovskogo* (Limonov versus Zhirinovsky). Moscow: Konets veka, 1994.

Loewenheim, Francis L., Harold D. Langley, and Jonas Manfred, eds. *Roosevelt and Churchill: Their Secret Wartime Correspondence*. New York: Dutton, 1975.

Lulechnik, V. "Liberal li gospodin Zhirinovskii?" (Is Zhirinovsky really liberal?). *Novoye Russkoye Slovo*, February 3, 1994, 5.

McClellan, Woodford. *Russia: A History of the Soviet Period*. Englewood Cliffs, N.J.: Prentice-Hall, 1990.

Malia, Martin. *The Soviet Tragedy: A History of Socialism in Russia, 1917–1991*. New York: Free Press, 1994.

Mandelbaum, Michael and Strobe Talbott. *Reagan and Gorbachev*. New York: Vintage, 1987.

Maslin, M. A., ed. *Russkaia ideia* (The Russian idea). Moscow: Respublika, 1992.

Massie, Robert K. *Peter the Great: His Life and World*. New York: Ballantine, 1980.

Materialy Plenuma Tsentral'nogo Komiteta KPSS, 23 aprelia 1985 goda (Materials from the plenary session of the Central Committee of the CPSU, April 23, 1985). Moscow: Politizdat, 1985.

Medvedev, Roy. *Lichnost' i epokha: Politicheskii portret L. I. Brezhneva* (The individual and the era: A political portrait of L. I. Brezhnev). Moscow: Novosti, 1991.

——. *On Soviet Dissent*. New York: Columbia University Press, 1985.

Menzheritskii, Sergei. "Vladimir Volfovich protiv Vladimira Volfovicha" (Vladimir Volfovich versus Vladimir Volfovich). *Vecherniaia Moskva*, May 30, 1994, 5.

Morrison, James V. "Vladimir Zhirinovsky." McNair Paper 30. National Defense University, Washington, D.C., April 1994.

Moscow, Henry. *Russia Under the Czars*. New York: Harper & Row, Perennial Library, 1962.

Mukhin, Yuri. *Puteshestvie iz demokratii k der'mokratiiu i doroga obratno* (Journey from democracy to dung-muck-racy and the road back). Moscow: GART, 1993.

Myers, Gustavus. *History of the Great American Fortunes*. New York: Modern Library, 1936.

Nazarov, Vladimir. "Chelovek, nad kotorym smeiutsa: Zria" (The man everyone is laughing at—they shouldn't). *Novoye Russkoye Slovo*, June 19, 1992, 6.

Nechiporenko, Oleg Maximovich. *Passport to Assassination*. New York: Carol Publishing Group, Birch Lane Press, 1993.

Nekrasov, V. F., ed. *Beriia: Konets kar'ery* (Beria: The end of a career). Moscow: Politizdat, 1991.

The Night After: On Ecological and Social Consequences of Nuclear War. Moscow: Mir, 1985.

Nikita Sergeevich Khrushchev: Materialy k biografii (Nikita Khrushchev: Materials for a biography). Moscow: Politizdat, 1989.

O shirokom rasprostranenii novykh metodov khoziaistvovaniia i usilenii ikh vozdeistviia na uskorenie nauchno-tekhnicheskogo progressa: Postanovlenie TsK KPSS ot, 12 iiulia 1985 goda (On widely circulating the new methods of economic management and strengthening their effect on the acceleration of scientific and technical progress: Resolution of the CPSU Central Committee, July 12, 1985). Moscow: Politizdat, 1985.

Obrashchenie Vladimira Zhirinovskogo, Predsedatelia Liberal'no-Demokraticheskoi partii Rossii k chlenam LDPR i sochustvuyushchim. Programma Liberal'no-Demokraticheskoi partii Rossii. Ustav LDPR (Address by Vladimir Zhirinovsky, chairman of the LDPR, to members and sympathizers of the LDPR. Program of the LDPR. Party statute). N.p., n.d. (probably 1991).

Orlov, Alexander. *Tainaia istoriia stalinskikh prestuplenii* (Secret history of Stalin's crimes). New York: Vremya i my, 1983.

Orth, Maureen. "Nightmare on Red Square." *Vanity Fair* (September 1994): 79–100.

Orwell, George. *1984*. Afterword by Erich Fromm. A Signet Classic. New York: New American Library, 1961.

——. *1984; Skotnyi dvor* (1984; Animal farm). Moscow: Mir, 1989.

Ovchinskii, V. S. *Strategiia bor'by s mafiei* (The strategy of the struggle with the mafia). Moscow: "SYMS," 1993.

Ovchinskii, V. S. and S. S. Ovchinskii. *Bor'ba s mafiei v Rossii* (The struggle with the mafia in Russia). Moscow: ORMVD Rossii, 1993.

Piel, Gerard. *Only One World: Our Own to Make and to Keep.* New York: Freeman–UN Publications, 1992.

Pipes, Richard. *The Russian Revolution.* New York: Knopf, 1990.

Pocheptsov, Georgii. *Totalitarnyi chelovek* (The totalitarian person). Kiev: Globus, 1994.

Politicheskaia Rossiia segodnia: Vysshaia predstavitel'naia vlast' (Political Russia today: The supreme representative authority). Moscow: Moskovskii rabochii, 1993.

Politicheskaia Rossiia segodnia: Ispolnitel'naia vlast,' Konstitutsionnyi sud, Lidery partii i dvizhenii (Political Russia today: The executive authority, constitutional court, leaders of parties and movements). Moscow: Moskovskii rabochii, 1993.

Popovsky, Mark. "OON: Vzgliad iznutri (interview s Vladimirom Kartsevym)" (UN: The view from within—interview with Vladimir Kartsev). *Novoye Russkoye Slovo*, May 20, 1994, 29–30.

"Prezident–96: Figury, litsa, obrazy" (President '96: Figures, Faces, Images). *Nezavisimaya Gazeta*, November 20, 1994, 3.

Reddaway, Peter, ed. *Uncensored Russia: Protest and Dissent in the Soviet Union—The Unofficial Moscow Journal, a Chronicle of Current Events.* New York: American Heritage, 1972.

Reddaway, Peter and Sidney Bloch. *Soviet Psychiatric Abuse: The Shadow Over World Psychiatry.* London: Gollancz, 1984.

Reznik, Semyon. *Krasnoe i korichnevoe: Kniga o sovetskom natsizme* (Red and brown: A book about Soviet Nazism). Washington, D.C.: Vyzov, 1990.

——. *Krovavaia karusel'* (Bloody carousel). Washington, D.C.: Vyzov, 1988.

"Russian Mafia." *The Economist* (July 9, 1994): 19–22.

Sakharov, Andrei. *Memoirs.* New York: Knopf, 1990.

Shebarshin, L. V. *Ruka Moskvy: Zapiski nachal'nika sovetskoi razvedki* (The hand of

Moscow: Memoirs of a Soviet intelligence official). Moscow: Tsentr-100, 1992.

Shenin, Oleg. *Rodinu ne predaval i menia obvinili v izmene* (I never betrayed my country, yet I was accused of treason). Moscow: Paleya, 1994.

Shirer, William L. *The Rise and Fall of the Third Reich: A History of Nazi Germany.* New York: Simon & Schuster, 1960.

Sidorsky, David, ed. *The Liberal Tradition in European Thought.* New York: Putnam's, 1970.

Silant'ev, Andrei. *Chetvertaia vlast': Sredstva massovoi informatsii i sovremennoe gosudarstvo* (The fourth estate: The mass media and the modern state). Moscow, 1991. Rotoprint ed.

Sinel'nikov, Boris. "Russkaia Mafiia: Vy ee eshche uznaete" (Russian mafia: You are going to know it much better). *Novoye Russkoye Slovo*, November 18, 1994, 24.

Smith, Anthony. "Mayfair MP for Moocow Ceilial." *London Sunday Express*, December 17, 1993, 17.

Solovyov, Vladimir and Elena Klepikova. *Bor'ba v Kremle: Ot Andropova do Gorbacheva* (Struggle in the Kremlin: From Andropov to Gorbachev). New York: Vremya i my, 1986.

Solzhcnitsyn, Aleksandr. *The Gulag Archipelago, 1918–1956.* 3 vols. New York: Harper & Row, 1974–78.

——. "Rech' v Gosudarstvennoi Dume" (Speech in the State Duma). *Novoye Russkoye Slovo*, November 12–13, 1994, 14.

Specter, Michael. "Why Russia Loves This Man." *New York Times Magazine*, June 19, 1994, 26–56.

Stepankov, V. and F. Lisov. *Kremlevskii zagovor: Versiia sledstviia* (Kremlin conspiracy: A version of the investigation). Moscow: Ogonyok, 1992.

Sterling, Claire. *The Thieves' World.* New York: Simon & Schuster, 1994.

Sukhanov, Lev. *Tri goda s El'tsinym* (Three years with Yeltsin). Riga: Vaga, 1992.

Tanner, Adam. "Media Divided on How to Handle Zhirinovsky." *Moscow Times*, January 20, 1994, 4.

Tarasov, Artyom. "The Russian Millionaire Who Fled with a Price on His Head." *The European*, July 23–26, 1992, 10.

Time Capsule/1923: A History of the Year Condensed from the Pages of Time. New York: Time, 1967.

Trofimenko, Genrikh. "Rossiiskaia politika v teni Zhirinovskogo" (Russian politics in Zhirinovsky's shadow). *Novoye Russkoye Slovo*, February 25, 1994, 7.

Tsyganov, Aleksandr. "FSK v traditsiiakh KGB" (FSC acting in KGB tradition). *Novoye Russkoye Slovo*, November 11, 1994, 40.

Vasil'eva, Larisa. *Kremlevskie zheny* (Kremlin wives). Moscow-Kishinev: Kantor-Tonkar, 1993.

Voslensky, Michael. *Nomenklatura: The Soviet Ruling Class.* Garden City, N.Y.: Doubleday, 1984.

Weaponry in Space. Moscow: Mir, 1986.

Wells, H. G. *The Outline of History: Being a Plain History of Life and Mankind.* New York: Macmillan, 1924.

Werth, Alexander. *Russia at War, 1941–1945*. New York: Dutton, 1964.

Yanov, Alexander. "Phenomenon of Zhirinovsky." *Slovo-Word*, no. 14, 1993, 59–77.

Yavlinsky, Grigory. *Laissez-Faire Versus Policy-Led Transformation: Lessons of the Economic Reforms in Russia*. Moscow: EPI Center, 1994.

Yeltsin, Boris. *Ispoved' na zadannuiu temu* (Confession on an assigned topic). Moscow: Tsentralnyi Dom Literatorov and PIK Independent Publishers, 1990.

——. *Zapiski Prezidenta* (Memoirs of a president). Moscow: Belka, 1994.

Zhebrovsky, S. M. "Byli dobrovol'tsy, ne bylo dobrovol'tsev—Chto iz etogo sleduet?" (There were volunteers and there weren't—what of it?). *Liberal* 2, no. 12 (1993): 16–17.

Zhirinovsky, Vladimir. "My khotim zhit' po zakonu" (We want to live by the law). *Iuridicheskaia gazeta* (special issue), July 7, 1994, 3.

——. *Poslednii brosok na iug* (The last dash to the south). *O sud'bakh Rossii: Chast' 2* (On the destinies of Russia: Part 2). Moscow: Rait, 1993.

——. *S moei tochki zreniia . . .* (As I see it . . .). *O sud'bakh Rossii: Chast' 3*. (On the destinies of Russia: Part 3). Moscow: Rait, 1993.

——. "Seichas eshche mozhno ostanovit' razval strany" (It is still possible to stop the disintegration of the country). *Pravda Zhirinovskogo* 18, no. 41 (1994): 1.

——. *Uroki istorii* (Lessons of history). *O sud'bakh Rossii: Chast' 1* (On the destinies of Russia: Part 1). Moscow: Rait, 1993.

Zhuravlev, Igor. "Zima v etom godu budet osobenno iadernoi" (This winter is going to be especially nuclear). *Moskovskii Komsomolets*, no. 214, November 3, 1994, 1.

Zyuganov, Gennady. *Derzhava* (The State). Moscow: Informpechat, 1994.

Index